THE FINE
AND THE WICKED

The Life and Times of Ouida

by
MONICA STIRLING

COWARD-McCANN, Inc.
New York

928.2
D339S

© 1958 BY MONICA STIRLING

Library of Congress Catalog
Card Number: 58-6285

To
ODETTE

Manufactured in the United States of America

CONTENTS

LIST OF ILLUSTRATIONS

ACKNOWLEDGEMENTS

FOR GENEROUS HELP, I want to thank:

Sir Shane Leslie, for the loan of letters written by Ouida to his grand-mother, Lady Constance Leslie; the Marchese della Stufa, for infor-mation about Ouida and his great uncle, and for allowing me to visit Castagnuolo; Madame Paul Sellier, for information about her grand-mother Adeline Bonaparte-Wyse, and great aunt, Marie Studholmine-Laetitia Bonaparte-Wyse; the Vicomte Fleuriot de Langle; Mrs. Mc-Master, wife of the British Consul at Florence; Mr. Francis Toye; Mrs. St. George Saunders of "Writers and Speakers Research"; Monsieur André Jeancourt Galignani, the late Monsieur Henri Gerson, and Mon-sieur Labeuge, of Galignani's Library; Miss Yvonne ffrench; Mr. Heywood Hill; and Lord Rodd.

I also wish to thank the following authors and publishers:

Chatto and Windus for permission to quote from Ouida's novels; the editors of the Atlantic Monthly for use of the article on Ouida published in that magazine in 1886; Harcourt, Brace and Company for extracts from Mabel Dodge Luhan's "European Experiences"; Rupert Hart-Davis for one of "Henry James' Selected Letters"; Secker & Warburg and Stephen Spender for permission to quote Luigi Barzini's article "Italy and its Aristocracy", published in the January 1956 issue of "Encounter"; Sir Harold Nicolson and Constable & Company, for permission to quote from "Small Talk" and "Cur-zon"; Constable & Company for the use of Henry G. Huntingdon's "Memories"; the "News Chronicle" for permission to quote from Vernon Lee's article on Ouida in what was then the "Westminster Gazette"; John Murray Ltd. for permission to quote from Walpurga, Lady Paget's "Scenes and Memories" and Gordon Waterfield's "Lucie Duff Gordon"; George Allen & Unwin for use of the edition of Augus-tus Hare's journals re-edited by Malcolm Barnes under the titles "My Solitary Life" and "My Life with Mother"; John Lane the Bodley Head Ltd., for permission to quote Sir Max Beerbohm's essays "Diminuendo" and "Ouida", both taken from "Works and More"; Sir Sydney Cockerell and Jonathan Cape for letters from Ouida to Sir Sydney; Miss Aileen Smiles and Robert Hale for an extract from "Samuel Smiles and His Surroundings"; Chapman & Hall for an extract from W. H. Mallock's "Memoirs of Life and Literature"; Jarrolds for an extract from Evangeline B. Whipple's "A Famous Corner of Tuscany"; Hutchinson and Company for extracts from Walpurga, Lady Paget's "Embassies of Other Days" and "In My Tower"; Curtis Brown for a quotation from H. A. L. Fisher's "History of Europe"; Carl van Vechten and Boni and Liveright, Incorporated, for permission to make use of the introduction to the 1923 American edition of Ouida's "In a Winter City"; the executors of Norman Douglas and Chatto and Windus for extracts from his works; Secker and Warburg for permission to quote from Wilfrid Scawen Blunt's "My Diary" and "L. J. M. Daguerre" by H. and A. Gernsheim; and Ernest Benn for permission to use "Ouida, A Memoir", by Elizabeth Lee.

In the quotations from the diary Ouida wrote as a child the original spelling and punctuation are given.

"... 'What I admire in Ouida is that Vice is Vice and Virtue is Virtue.'"

Lady Horner, repeating a saying of her mother,
to Sir Edward   Burne Jones. 1896

"... that unique, flamboyant lady, one of the miracles of modern literature."

Sir Max Beerbohm on Ouida. 1899

"... a woman of wide horizons who fought for generous issues and despised all shams; the last, almost the last, of lady authors."

Norman Douglas on Ouida. 1921

"... Ouida was not an artist, but just as surely she was a genius."

Carl van Vechten. 1923

"Oh yes," said the kindly Anglo-Italian I was questioning about Ouida, "my parents knew her. Not well, of course, but they used to meet her in various houses . . . that was after she cracked up, as you might say—so sad. Not but what she was supposed to be rather eccentric even then. But my mother always said there must be a lot of good in anyone so devoted to dumb animals. Not that Ouida kept hers dumb. . . . Her novels? Well, when I was quite a little girl I did manage to get hold of a copy of *Friendship*—that was the one that had caused such a scandal here in Florence back in the eighties, you know. It was all about prominent local people, hardly disguised at all. So feeling ran quite high, everyone took sides—though what about I never discovered, because when mother found me reading it she took it away and spanked me. I remember the occasion well"—the crumpled elderly face suddenly looked childish, aggrieved—"because it was the first time mother treated me unfairly. After having been spanked for reading the book I ought at least to have been allowed to finish it, don't you think? But of course we were brought up very differently then, before the other war . . . oh dear!"

Explosive noises drew us to the window. Looking down, we saw two boys on Vespas racing each other along the medieval street that ran, narrow as a country stream, between the cliff-like façades of milk-and-coffee-coloured palaces.

"They really *like* noise," said my companion, sighing. "You should hear the loudspeakers at election time. So very out of keeping with the spirit of Botticelli." She shook her head. "Ouida certainly wouldn't have liked *that*. She felt very strongly about the preservation of old Florence."

"She felt very strongly about everything, didn't she?"

"Well, yes," misunderstanding the question, "I suppose her books *were* rather . . . well, *far-fetched* and not *quite* . . ." The words merged into a self-conscious laugh.

Later, walking along narrow escutcheoned streets where more Vespas were rocking and rolling around horse-drawn cabs and candy-coloured American cars, I realised that the notion Ouida was someone *far-fetched and not quite* is the one most commonly entertained now by those who have heard of her books but not read them. Yet this is no more justified by facts than is the notion that Queen Victoria—a contemporary whom Ouida greatly disliked, yet resembled in the vehemence of her character—was merely a plump and censorious old lady who spent an inordinate amount of time being unamused.

There are several reasons for this. Like Queen Victoria, Ouida felt too strongly to fear ridicule and, in consequence, was often ridiculous. When she was a girl, and not in the public eye, her lively temper constituted an attraction; but later, when she was a world-famous figure, unhappiness transformed her liveliness into irascibility, her independence into eccentricity. In addition, her extravagance was legendary at a period when thrift was particularly esteemed. Most important of all, she remained a spinster, though not from choice, when a spinster was considered as much a figure of fun as a bachelor one of romance. Nevertheless her personal history was as exotic and tragic as that of any of the heroines of her best-selling novels.

Copies of these novels are rare now. This is a pity since—apart from their gorgeously illustrated covers, and advertising end-papers which include an Eno's Fruit Salts advertisement ("What is ten thousand times more horrible than Revolution or War? Outraged Nature") printed on the back of a coloured picture of Marie Antoinette preparing for the guillotine—these exuberant books can still give pleasure to readers and instruction to writers.

Who was this oddly named person whose talents are supposed to have been closely connected with the daring and disreputable?

PART I

1839—1857

"... the dome of St. Peter's is as real as the gasometer of East London; and I presume that the fact can hardly be disputed if I even assert that the passion flower is as real as the potato! ... I do not object to realism in fiction; what I object to is the limitation of realism in fiction to what is commonplace, tedious, and bald. ... I cannot suppose that my own experiences can be wholly exceptional ones, yet I have known very handsome people, I have known very fine characters, I have also known some very wicked ones, and I have also known circumstances so romantic that were they described in fiction they would be ridiculed as exaggerated and impossible. ...

Ouida: *"Romance and Realism"*

I

MARIA LOUISE RAMÉ—generally known as Ouida because this was how, as an infant, she pronounced Louise—was born at a quarter-past three on the afternoon of January 1st, 1839, in her widowed English grandmother's small stucco-fronted semi-detached house in Union Terrace (now 14, Hospital Road and a home for the resident nurses of the West Suffolk General Hospital), Bury St. Edmunds, Suffolk. This was then a small country town where Mr. Pickwick had become embroiled with a ladies' school, and which Ouida later described as "that slowest and dreariest of boroughs, where the streets are as full of grass as an acre of pasture land, and the inhabitants are driven to ring their own doorbells lest they should rust from disuse". The child's mother, born Susan Sutton, was the second of a Suffolk wine merchant's three daughters; her absent father, Louis Ramé, was French and his marriage certificate states that his father was a tailor— but this may not be true, as the same certificate inaccurately gives Louis Ramé's own profession as merely *gentleman*. What is certain about this elusive man is that both then and later he displayed an unusual capacity for provoking rumours about himself as poly-chromatic as any of his daughter's novels.

Young and pretty, Madame Ramé had what were then called, and are still thought of, as expectations, and was thoroughly at home in Bury St. Edmunds; but Monsieur Ramé's expectations, if any, were chimerical and he never, it seems, stayed long enough in one place to discover if he was capable of feeling at home anywhere. A plain but seductive man, who intermittently taught French to the young ladies of Bury St. Edmunds, he moved in a mysterious way through his English relatives' lives. His frequent absences were later ascribed by them to his having been a secret agent for the exiled Louis Napoleon, nephew of the great Napoleon and pretender to the French throne since the death, in 1832, of Napoleon's son, the unfortunate young Duke of Reichstadt. Bury St. Edmunds seems an incongruous place in which to find a Bonapartist agent—so incongruous that Louis Ramé probably was just this. Not only was Europe full then, as now, of secret agents, but Louis Napoleon had lately taken refuge in England,

and both Louis Napoleon and Louis Ramé were Carbonarists—that is, members of an important nineteenth-century secret society determined to free Italy from foreign rule and obtain constitutional liberties.

So, although Bury St. Edmunds reminded young Ouida of an "old maid dressed for a party", the English world this half-French child entered was not the rankly placid, purely domestic Victorian one created by the nostalgic imaginings of later generations. Despite freedom from income tax, English society was far from stable. The nineteen-year-old Queen Victoria who had succeeded her uncle William IV, the somewhat crazy sailor king, only two years earlier, was not the sacred figure she later became. An attempt on her life was made later, and the Lady Flora Hastings scandal—in which a woman dying of an internal complaint was accused of being pregnant merely because she had travelled in the company of a man to whom she was not married—made Victoria so unpopular that Greville wrote in his memoirs: "Nobody cares for the Queen, her popularity has sunk to zero, and loyalty is a dead letter." Prudery was not yet generally admired.

But manners were changing fast. Talleyrand had died in 1838, the last English duel was fought in 1843, and although that seductive eighteenth-century Whig, Lord Melbourne, was still the young Queen's favourite advisor, he no longer had much time in office ahead of him, and Macaulay was hailing young Mr. Gladstone, destined to be one of the Queen's bugbears, as the "rising hope of the stern and unbending Tories". It was nine years earlier, incidentally, that the stern and unbending Tories began calling themselves Conservatives, as the result of an article by Wilson Croker in the "Quarterly Review". The word Socialism, which had been popularised the year before Ouida was born, by George Sand's friend, Pierre Leroux, supplied another useful label at a time when, all over England, Chartists—opposed, sometimes, by redcoats who had fought at Waterloo—were agitating for universal suffrage, payment of members of parliament, the ballot vote, abolition of property qualifications, annual parliaments, and equal electoral districts.

Nor did stability obtain in those neighbouring countries with which Ouida's adult life was to be bound up. In France Louis-Philippe, eldest son of Philippe-Egalité, the regicide Duke of Orleans, sat uneasily upon the throne, his partiality for umbrellas doing much to make him seem ridiculous to the upper classes, and Italy, which then consisted of fourteen disunited states, was in a revolutionary condition, particularly in Lombardy and Venetia, which the Congress of Vienna had arbitrarily given to the Austro-Hungarian Empire.

Thanks to her father's passion for history, Ouida was early made aware of the size of the world in which she lived, and of the significance of such novelties as Rowland Hill's Penny Post Act, Bradshaw's first Railway Guide, and Daguerre's discovery of a method of taking photographs—a discovery which was made the month Ouida was born and caused the *Leipziger Stadtenzeiger* to ask: "Is it possible that God should have abandoned His eternal principles and allowed a Frenchman, in Paris, to give the world an invention of the Devil?" Nevertheless Ouida's childhood was also strongly coloured by the past. Where she lived the last of the eighteenth-century coaches could still be seen, as well as the first of the nineteenth-century locomotives. Policemen still wore tall hats, and footmen powdered hair; chimney-sweeps employed small boys to do their dirty work; and, in London, Covent Garden and Drury Lane still had a monopoly of drama by Royal Patent, other theatres being obliged to add music to their programmes in order to escape being harassed by the authorities—which may explain why old actors still speak of legitimate as opposed to musical plays.

In this early Victorian world, Ouida's childhood was exceptionally happy and, despite her father's distinguished unreliability, comfortable. Thanks to her mother, the family atmosphere, and her own temperament, she was untouched by the deformed sense of religion that made the lives of many socially and materially better-equipped children hell in order that heaven might be their destination—as shown by Augustus Hare's appalling true story of his Aunt Esther's taking his beloved cat, Selma, and hanging it merely in order to detach the little boy's affections from earthly things. Juvenile fiction of the period abounds in sobs, prayers, edifying death-bed scenes, and descriptions of ways of life that justified Elisée Reclus' remark: "L'ennui n'a pas cessé d'être en Angleterre une institution religieuse." Nor was the lot of poor children superior. According to Disraeli there was nothing unusual about scenes like this: ". . . naked to the waist, an iron chain fastened to a belt of leather runs between their legs clad in canvas trousers, while on hands and feet an English girl for twelve, sometimes for sixteen hours a day, hauls and hurries tubs of coal up subterranean roads, dark, precipitous, and plashy; circumstances that seem to have escaped the attention of the Society for the Abolition of Negro Slavery."

Preserved from the rigours of both upper- and lower-class childhood, Ouida found herself in a home where there was plenty of love, fun, and comfort, where religion was not allowed to get out of hand, where no attempt was made to keep her intellectual curiosity within the limits conventionally laid down for "the young person" so

efficiently satirized by Dickens in "Our Mutual Friend", and where rods
were spared—as they were not in the world of Augustus Hare who,
when under six, was regularly beaten with a riding-crop by his pious
uncle Julius, whom he later described, in a remarkable understatement,
as "never captivating to children". As a result, Ouida is one of the few
popular English writers of that period in whose books religion seldom
appears and, when it does, is not flattered. In what remains of the
diary she kept as a child the few references to religion are strikingly
uncharacteristic of their period:

> Mr. Drane proposed to go to Bickenham so into the carriage we
> got . . . it was a very pretty drive and at last we arrived at a pretty
> church with fir trees before it. . . . When we entered the church with
> the full intention of being very sedate and proper there was a most
> dreadful twanging through the nose clerk, which it was utterly
> impossible to help, to say the very least, to smile at, well this clerk
> was most dreadful during the whole of the service but still we
> managed to behave pretty well save and except some smiles and
> sundry looks . . . but when the clergyman began to preach and his
> voice went up and down in various tones joined to the sonorous
> voice of the clerk and the roguish looks of Mr. Drane we one and all
> laughed we could not help it and all the way home we laughed from
> one thing and another. I must say I enjoyed that afternoon very much.

All of which sounds delightfully unlike the atmosphere in which
Augustus Hare's Aunt Esther said of some children laid low by
measles, "I am *very glad* they are so ill; it is a well-deserved punishment
because their mother would not let them go to church for fear they
should catch it".

Although she was an only child, Ouida was neither a lonely nor a
spoilt one. Her mother and grandmother adored her—her mother
described her as "the one dear bright being" who, twelve months
after her marriage, had "brightened my eyes and heart"—but not more
intensely than she adored them; and she got plenty of young companionship from her cousins, with whom she shared games, picnics,
and excursions into the park and grounds of neighbouring Hardwick
House, a place that encouraged the visual appetite for grandeur that
already differentiated her from her cousins.

Four of these cousins—Maria, Henrietta, Fanny, and William—were
the children of Madame Ramé's elder sister Maria, who had married
a Mr. William Brown Lockwood in the twenties and died in 1831.

After this Mr. Lockwood, an enterprising man who had intended going into the church before Maria Sutton provided him with the money with which to buy a wine-merchant's business, married Mary Anne, the youngest of the Sutton sisters, and had one child, Marianne, before he died, the year Ouida was born. The fact that it was still illegal to marry one's deceased wife's sister doesn't seem to have distressed the sensible families concerned, but may have prompted Ouida, years later, to write this description of a member of the House of Lords:

Rugby don't mean to do any harm; he thinks himself a pillar of the State, and subscribes to the Carlton, and presides at county meetings, and is always present to vote against marriage with a deceased wife's sister; but I do understand how the sight of this excellent youth, with his guns and his friends and his keepers, does tend to make a mild socialist of the worthy British farmer who pays rent to him.

Although Ouida's home circle consisted of a widowed grandmother, widowed aunt, grass-widowed mother, four girl cousins, and William, her diary doesn't give the impression of having been written by someone restricted to feminine society. Small boys abounded at the junketings she records, and although she doesn't say so—for, although unusually explicit, Ouida had no reason at this time to be aggressive—it is clear that the little girl was popular with friends and relatives, that where domestic affection was concerned she got as good as she gave. Though she was thin and plain, with a large nose and unattractive voice, this fact didn't worry her, for the excellent reason that she was unaware of it. Vitality, intelligence, a warm heart, beautiful eyes, and pretty hands and feet, prevented her from feeling inferior to her cousins; and it should be remembered that depressing accounts of her looks, though probably accurate detail by detail, leave out the imponderable element in personality that, allied to unusual talent, attracted the interest of most, and the friendship of many, of the more remarkable men and women with whom she later came into contact.

Happy, loving, and diligent—at eleven she wrote in her diary: "I must study or I shall know nothing when I am a woman"—she soon started making up stories. As a small child she used to cut out cardboard figures of knights and ladies, paint them gorgeously, and then use them as marionettes with which to act out even more gorgeous stories to herself. She never doubted that she would one day be a rich and famous writer, able to keep her parents and grandmother in

luxury, and to equip herself appropriately for the passionate love bound
to come her way. Although sometimes dreamy, Ouida was never
vague and, luckily for her, the possibility of making her dreams come
true was far greater at this period than had been the case even a few
years earlier. For this Mr. Mudie was partly responsible.

Until this period the popularity of Walter Scott's novels had enabled
publishers to charge a guinea and a half for a three-volume novel; so
when Charles Edward Mudie opened the first popular lending library
in 1842 this caused a revolution, first in the country's reading, then in its
writing habits. Previously, only the upper classes could afford to buy
new books, the middle classes relying for fiction upon novels issued in
monthly parts, at a shilling each—a form of publication which continued until the founding of, among others, magazines like All the
Year Round, London Journal, Leisure Hour, Once a Week, Good
Words, Bentley's Miscellany (in which Ouida made her debut), and,
in the sixties, London Society, Temple Bar, Belgravia, Cornhill,
Argosy, and Tinsley's Magazine, all of which provided serialized
fiction.

In order to make novels more generally available, Mudie decided
that his subscribers should for one guinea a year be able to read any of
the three-volume novels he stocked: "the nice handsome books that
none but the élite could obtain, and with them a feeling of being on a
footing of equality with my Lady this and Lady that." The shadow of
the young person deplored by Dickens fell over this enterprise, since
the test as to which books should be stocked was the irrelevant question:
"would you or would you not give that book to your sister of sixteen
to read?" As a result, Meredith's "The Ordeal of Richard Feverel",
Mrs. Anne Edwardes' "The Morals of Mayfair", and some of Charles
Reade's stories, were among the books banned. Present-day standards
of censorship do not permit us to laugh at such idiocy. Mudie both
created and satisfied a huge market for novels, particularly those deal-
ing with upper-class social life and, as a result, women who were obliged
to earn their livings began to see in writing an alternative to the
lugubrious prospect described by Harriet Martineau as "teaching or
being the feminine gender of the tailor and hatter". A hundred pounds
a year was the most a governess could earn then.

Equally important in the country's reading habits were the newly-
founded Daily News and Punch. Costing only fivepence, when the
Times cost sevenpence, the Daily News was edited for a time by
Dickens, backed by Bradbury and Evans, the owners of Punch, and by
Joseph Paxton, a most attractive character who had started work as

gardener to the Duke of Devonshire, and who built the Crystal Palace for the Great Exhibition of 1851. Dickens paid his reporters seven pounds a week instead of the usual five, and engaged the famous Lady Blessington, at five hundred pounds for six months, to write the fashion news. The paper eventually became as influential in England then as Paris-Match in France, or Life in America, now. First contributors to Punch included Thackeray and Douglas Jerrold, the witty author of "Mrs. Caudle's Curtain Lectures". It was there that Thomas Hood's provocative "Song of the Shirt" appeared, anonymously, in 1843. John Leech, the great cartoonist, John Tenniel, illustrator of "Alice in Wonderland" and "Through the Looking-Glass", and George du Maurier, whose stately beauties created as well as derived from a type —his Duchess of Towers is said to have been drawn from the beautiful Lady Ida Sitwell—all worked for Punch, making it a genuine mirror of the age, complete with typical middle-class interior decorations: tassels, fringes, whatnots, pompoms, potpourri, lace antimacassars, patterned velvet, bric-à-brac, wax flowers, mother-of-pearl, red, green, yellow and purple plush, vases of rushes and peacock's feathers, plenty of mahogany, ormulu, dens and snuggeries in which pipes and cigars were smoked (cigarettes became popular only after the Crimean War, during which British soldiers acquired the habit from the Turks), and conservatories in which romances, started during a waltz, polka, quadrille, or game of croquet, came to a head.

During these early years Ouida's only unhappiness was caused by her father's frequent absences. In her diary she notes: "I am sure that when our darling Papa gets into his beautiful France we must not hope for him for some months that's the badness of it." But these absences seemed less abnormal then than they would seem now that identity cards, visas, radio and television have made disappearing a comparatively skilled job. The temperance song, "Father, dear Father, come home to us, do", reflected, as popular songs so often do, a common state of affairs. Ouida's mysteriously Cheshire-Cat-like father, to us so odd, in fact provided one of her few conventionally Victorian attributes. This did not, however, make his absences easier for her to bear. The child saw her mother's grief, felt her own and, having a nature unsuited to resignation, kept struggling to find a rational explanation for her father's irrational behaviour.

But although Louis Ramé caused his wife and daughter grief, he also gave each something of supreme value to her: to Madame Ramé a child whom she adored; to Ouida food for the imagination that was to provide her grandmother, her mother, and herself with the income

her father failed to produce. Not that failure was a word Ouida associated with her father in those days. Everything about darling Papa, so
kind, so clever, so loving when present, enthralled her. His French
blood, unspecified activities, fascinating conversation, pleasure-loving
ways, and mysterious comings and goings, made of him a personage
who might have walked out of one of her future novels—and in 1878
he walked into her thirteenth, the controversy-arousing *Friendship* in
which the heroine describes her father, the Count D'Aresnes, as:

> A man of many ambitions, of no achievement. A political con-
> spirator, his life was spent in the treacherous seas of political intrigue,
> and he at the last perished in their whirlpool. Little was known of
> him—by his daughter almost nothing. . . . Her father had come
> and gone, as comets do. . . . He would kiss her carelessly, bid her do
> a problem or write a poem, stay a few days, and go. . . . He ceased
> to come. . . . His death was mysterious, like his life. He passed away
> and made no sign.

In addition to more picturesque qualities, Louis Ramé had a sense of
humour; but this Ouida didn't inherit. As she once said of herself *I
have some wit but no humour.* One of his few recorded remarks is,
of a Mrs. Gummidge-like acquaintance, "she's never so happy as when
she's miserable"; and he must have been disarming, since Madame
Ramé's diary, reporting a domestic crisis among friends, says "when
one of the daughters ran away they sent for him to break the news to
her father because he was so violent a man none of his family dare
approach him. When Monsieur Ramé went to tell him, all he said was:
'God bless my soul! I did not think the girl had so much spirit in her.' "
It was thanks to her father that, as a child, Ouida spoke and read
French and, as an adult, was able to write in that language, as in Italian,
which she taught herself. He encouraged her love of reading, particularly of history, and, unlike Augustus Hare's mentors, didn't bother
her with Foxe's Book of Martyrs or enquiries as to the minutiae of
Jonah's trip from Joppa to Nineveh. Instead, he encouraged her to
read Balzac—whose dynamic genius affected her nascent talent more
deeply than did any other contemporary author; Stendhal, whose
"Chartreuse de Parme" appeared the year Ouida was born—and who,
far from being the intellectually fashionable author he is now, was then
still admired only by his "happy few"; and such lesser but fascinating
writers as Charles Nodier and Paul Féval. Nodier was himself as
romantic a character as any invented by the most extravagant novelists:
the son of a defrocked Oratorian turned revolutionary, he had been

brought up—chiefly on Homer—by an aristocrat, and worked as a librarian in the Illyrian Provincès, where he found the material for his delightful "Trilby ou le Lutin d'Argail". In addition to introducing Ouida to contemporary French authors, her father explained the principles of Free Trade, and so aroused in her a lively, resolute, and durable interest in current events, thanks to which her viewpoint was never merely parochial.

Had her father not directed her powerful energy outwards, Ouida might have become a prisoner to introspection. Her first biographer, Henry James' friend Elizabeth Lee, writing immediately after Ouida's death, noted that as a small child: "Sometimes in her walks she would pick up a stone lying by the wayside, take it home, and make a sort of pet out of it, saying it was lonely and uncared for." There is something about this that suggests Gelsomina, the touching, half-witted heroine of Fellini's film "La Strada", the little creature who plants seeds during a wayside halt and listens, her ear pressed against the "telegraph trees".

But her father's stories kept Ouida looking outwards, and when she was seven Louis Napoleon provided a new instalment to one of these that made him play in her life the part Davy Crockett plays in that of today's children. After attempting a coup d'état at Strasbourg in 1836, Louis Napoleon had been deported to America—the days when a visa to America was a prize were still far off. But he had managed to get back to Europe the following year in order to visit his mother Hortense, ex-Queen of Holland, and author of the still popular song, "Partant pour la Syrie", who was then dying in Switzerland. When the French government asked the Swiss to expel him, thus almost provoking war between the two countries, Louis Napoleon went to London, where he planned another coup d'état. This was attempted in Boulogne in 1840 and, failing more spectacularly than the previous one had done, caused Louis Bonaparte to be condemned to life imprisonment in the fortress of Ham—a sentence which he greeted with the enquiry: "Combien de temps dure ici la perpétuité?" Six years later he escaped, disguised as a workman and carrying a plank. Once in London, where he was a great success socially, and welcome at the Athenaeum, the Army and Navy, the Junior United Services clubs, and Lady Blessington's salon, he announced that he would soon be Emperor of the French—and in this capacity intended to avenge Waterloo by driving the Austrians out of Italy.

Few people took this declaration seriously, but even fewer held it against him. Most of those with whom he associated wished to see the Austrians removed from Italy, enthusiasm for which was an important part of the atmosphere of Victorian England. Even those who cared nothing for Italians thought that a united Italy would help England maintain the balance of power on the continent, and Piedmont's anti-clericalism attracted all those who deplored popery. Also, the Italian nationalist movement being strongest among the upper and middle classes, refugees were considered socially desirable—and, as Bertrand Russell points out, the patriot of an oppressed country was as attractive to the nineteenth century as the noble savage to the preceding age.

Among the stimulating Italians in London then was Mazzini, who had come there as a refugee in 1837 and founded both an irregularly published newspaper, "Apostolato Popolare", and a Free Evening School, to help the small boys decoyed out of Italy by child-slavers to work as organ-grinders or hawkers of white mice. It was Mazzini's children who supplied Ouida with the point of departure for *In the Apple Country*, one of her collection of stories for children, entitled *Bimbi*, published in 1882 and dedicated to Vittorio Emmanuele, the thirteen-year-old Prince of Naples who, as Vittorio Emmanuele III, was to abdicate in 1946. Mario, the most famous Italian tenor of the century, and one of Ouida's early loves—he was to serve as the model for Raphael de Corrèze in *Moths*, one of her most successful novels—sang at benefits for Mazzini's school.

Awareness of Italy was therefore aroused in Ouida almost as soon as awareness of France. A great political scandal concerning Italy occurred during her childhood, when it was discovered that Mazzini's letters were being opened by the Home Secretary, and the information thus filched transmitted to the Governments concerned. Dickens immediately came to Mazzini's defence, the Times pointed out that the offending Ministry was "the first of late years that had resorted to the meanness of espionage, and condescended to pursue a policy at once unconstitutional, un-English and ungenerous", and Browning wrote "The Italian in England":

> "I am that man upon whose head
> They fix the price, because I hate
> The Austrians over us . . ."

Feeling ran so high that, years later, when Prince Albert suggested Carlyle for a pension, Lord Aberdeen, then Prime Minister, prevented this on the grounds of heterodoxy—but in fact because Carlyle had defended Mazzini, whose views he didn't share, both in the Times and at a private dinner-party at the Barings' house.

To a child of strong passions there was no doubt who was in the right, and Ouida was delighted when, at eight years old, she heard that darling Papa's friend Louis Napoleon had gone home and become President of the second French Republic. His promise to "do something for Italy" was in many minds, for in this year of revolutions Francis Joseph, the new Austrian Emperor, had entrusted his Italian provinces to the aged Marshal Radetsky, who promptly imposed martial law, imprisoned and hanged thousands, and had fifteen Milanese, including two young girls, flogged for hissing an Austrian. It was from these and other events in the Italian war of independence that, later, Ouida drew the plot of *Idalia*, a novel centred around the Balkan adventures of an aristocratic Queen's messenger, which was popular with the public but not with the critics who, being either untravelled or uninterested in continental politics, thought it far-fetched.

Quiet though Ouida's first ten years were domestically, they were not dull. Her affections being satisfied, her imagination was free, and there is much of her own character in that of the child in *Two Little Wooden Shoes* whom she made say:

> I want to know all about the people who lived before us; I want to know what the stars are, and what the wind is; I want to know where the lark goes when you lose him out of sight against the sun; I want to know how the old artists got to see God, that they could paint Him and all His angels as they have done; I want to know how the voices got into the bells, and how they can make one's heart beat, hanging up there as they do, all alone among the jackdaws. . . .

Her lamplit, horsedrawn years gave her a good introduction to life—and then, at eleven, she had her first glimpse of her father's country.

II

THE BEGINNING OF the diary that Ouida wrote between the ages of eleven and thirteen contains three particularly characteristic entries, starting with: "I am getting a great girl—I must study or I shall know nothing by the time I am a woman," which suggests the White Queen's: "Consider what a great girl you are. . . . Consider what o'clock it is . . ." in Lewis Carroll's as yet unwritten "Alice Through the Looking-Glass". Then, noting an old neighbour's death, Ouida writes: *We are very sorry to think we shall never see her again*, the brevity and good sense of which are striking considering how popular long-drawn-out accounts of edifying death-bed scenes were then. Already Ouida not only had feelings, so didn't need to invent them, but was able to express exactly what she felt. The future writer shows in that line, as the future woman shows here:

This month that in the time of our ancestors used to be celebrated for Maypoles and rural feasts, is now not taken notice of even by May flowers except by the poor sweeps. What a pity it is to let all customs slip away! I think we were better then and yet Papa says that we only see the bright side of chivalry, and that there was a great deal of cruelty in the Knights, but still I think when we lived in the rush but out all day long drinking nothing but water and not eating fricassées and ragouts must have been much better for Hygeia . . . than eating Soyer's sauces and pampered and peppered dishes and drinking hot inflaming spirits and sleeping in a room with not one single breath of the dear fresh night excluded from us by stuffs which are purchased at the very cheap price of dozens of our poor fellow-countrymen's hastily washed pale cheeks, their spirits subdued and at last sinking into a long and tedious decline leaving their widows and children desolate only for the sake of giving to their richer fellow creatures what renders them pale and wan in their turn.

Not the least surprising point in this paragraph is that the eleven-year-old Ouida should have heard of Alexis Soyer. The most famous cook of his time, he had been working for the Prince de Polignac in 1830, when Louis XVI's brother, Charles X, was deposed in the July Revolution and succeeded by his cousin Louis-Philippe. Having only just escaped being massacred, Soyer took refuge in London, and was chef at the Reform Club from 1837 to 1850. During the latter part of the Crimean war, he was sent out to improve the army food system. Ouida's reference to him proved that her father didn't favour boiled mutton and rice pudding either physically or mentally. But epicurism was far less characteristic of her than was the fighting spirit that justified the remark she made to Sir Sydney Cockerell only five years before her death: *I often think that Ireland would have suited me.* Age increased this fighting instinct, but the child, still safe in her home circle, could write:

Oh how much better is it to strive by kind words to gain anybody over from wickedness, than to strike one hardly by cold criticism and sarcasm and to have no effect—no, no, gentle words are best I hope I shall remember that. Papa offered me half a guinea the other day to learn some of La Fontaine's fables, how silly, now I learn them for nothing—for nothing? it is knowledge and knowledge is power.

In the same passage she says that she prefers Florian to la Fontaine, an unusual taste. The second best-known French fable teller, Jean-Pierre Claris de Florian, was Voltaire's great-nephew, and his novels helped develop the taste for pastoral romance that led Marie Antoinette to play at rusticity at Versailles.

Papa was at this time ever present in Ouida's thoughts:

> Papa says I learn things quickly but that I forget things too soon, and yet Papa says, and everybody else, that I have a good memory, and so I think I have . . . so it must be that I don't give my whole heart and soul to things I am learning. . . . I'm thinking about my cousins when M. Wanostrocht, Bouilly or Fenélon are talking to me about Mme de Stael, M. Bartelmy, verbs and pronunciation. . . .

Next month, we are told:

> On the sad 13th June dear dear Papa went away to the smokey metropolis. Oh how unhappy we were when he went only to London, but now after having received a letter from him that says he is in Boulogne what can we do? I suppose we must live on hope but 'Hope deferred maketh the heart sick'. . . . In a letter I had from him the other day he told me to put down at what time I got up. I never I think am up before seven and sometimes after. Papa dear is this too late?

Louis Ramé does not seem to have been justified in demanding Spartan habits from those nominally dependent on him; but the early rising he taught his doting daughter stood her in good stead later when, settled in Italy, she found acute pleasure in working in her Tuscan garden at sunrise. Like Colette's first husband, Monsieur Willy, Louis Ramé had the power to stimulate in others talents like those he himself possessed but, through some defect of temperament, was unable to use. Luckily for Ouida she was not, this time, long separated from her father, for on July 23rd she wrote in her diary:

> We are at last to see dear Papa for we received a letter today telling us we are to go to Boulogne this week or next, how beautiful it will be to see him and to see France, it will be so nice, so delicious.

To Madame Ramé this trip seemed as adventurous as one to the Congo would do to a woman of similar background today—and, indeed, it took longer than a flight to Africa would take now. But Ouida was overjoyed. Not even seasickness, which only a Nelsonian spirit can get the better of, could quell her delight. Everyone she met in the course of it was very nice, very pleasant, very clever, or very handsome, and in some cases all four—a state of affairs less common in her adult life:

> On the 3rd of August we set sail for France . . . we travelled down with some very pleasant people who were also going to Boulogne. It was a very rough sea, we were *très très* malade; we met dear Papa at the jetty we were so delighted to see him. We did not go to church for we were not well enough, we were also in great consternation about our box for we had lost one of our truncks but last night we heard it was found at Paris. The Comte de Briasse told us of it. . . . We went last night to the Etablissement. It was very pretty . . . and I was enchanted with Mr. Goold I danced with a very nice little boy. . . .

Like the young Queen Victoria, Ouida dearly loved to dance, and throughout this visit to France showed her unusual capacity not only for knowing what she wanted, but for enjoying what she had wanted when she got it. At no time in her life did she look a gift-horse in the mouth, except in order to notice what an attractive mouth it had. As a result, her account of this trip makes it sound like an episode from "The Young Visiters". Later, frustrated longing for love was to develop Ouida's capacities for unhappiness and bitterness, but at this time she was a very attractive child and, despite her passion for reading, not one of those tiresome characters, so prevalent in autobiographies, who are found, with monotonous frequency, curled up in window-seats with good books. Unlike Sir Osbert Sitwell's great-grandfather, who referred to Boulogne as a semi-penal settlement, she wrote:

> I like Boulogne very much it is a pretty lively place always plenty of life going on and you can have a ball any night you please they dance every night but Mondays Wednesdays and Fridays are the regular ball days when they have a band. The scenery round Boulogne is very pretty to go round the ramparts is a very nice walk you go a great part of the way under avenues of trees, it would take a large army and mighty strength to pull down these ramparts. . . . We have been introduced to and have called upon the Princess Lettitia Boneparte she has a daughter about my age a very nice little girl or rather big girl for she is much taller than I am.

That a poor school teacher should have been on sufficiently friendly terms with the exotic Laetitia Bonaparte to take his wife and daughter to call on her as soon as they arrived in France suggests, more than do any other recorded facts about Louis Ramé, that he was indeed involved in both Bonapartism and Carbonarism. The Princess Laetitia-Christine Bonaparte, a woman of considerable looks and character, forty-six at this time, was the sixth child of Napoleon's younger brother Lucien, whose second marriage to Madame de Bleschamps was so deplored by Napoleon as to have driven Lucien to retire to Italy and naturalize his children as Italian citizens. At the age of seventeen, Laetitia Bonaparte had been married to Sir Thomas Wyse, a distinguished Irishman considerably older than herself, who had promised to take her to St. Helena to see her uncle, a promise which Napoleon's death prevented him from fulfilling. The marriage was not a happy one and, at the time when Ouida made her curtsey to her, Madame Bonaparte-Wyse was separated from her husband. Of her five remarkable children, Ouida now met two. The elder was Marie-Studolmine-Laetitia Bonaparte-Wyse, recently married to the Comte de Solms, an unusually beautiful, passionate, entertaining, trying character, and a gifted novelist and journalist. The Comtesse de Solms subsequently married the Italian minister, Count Urbain Rattazzi, and so was part of Ouida's Florentine life. Ouida's friend Lady Paget, writing her memoirs half a century later, describes the Countess Rattazzi as what now sounds like a typical Ouida character: "Madame Rattazzi was the beautiful daughter of Laetitia Buonaparte and Mr. Wyse, a long-time H.B.M. Minister at Athens. She first espoused an adventurer calling himself Count Solms, but soon separated from him and led an untrammelled life at Paris and Baden Baden." A whole period, class, and way of life are held, like artificial flowers in a paperweight, in the phrase "an untrammelled life at Paris and Baden Baden"— a phrase that Ouida was to illustrate with distinction. The other Bonaparte-Wyse child was Adeline, the "very nice little girl", who was a year younger than Ouida, and eleven years later married a liberty-loving young Hungarian General, Estevan Turr, who served as aide-de-camp to Garibaldi and, after Louis Napoleon came to power, was sent on a semi-official mission to Paris to remind the latter not to forget the promises he had made as a Carbonaro. It was while on this mission that Estevan Turr met Adeline.

Both the looks and the circumstances of mother and daughters appealed to Ouida, and it is not surprising that she later resented being told that descriptions of similar characters were "unreal". They were as real to her—and in fact—as anyone in Bury St. Edmunds, to which she felt less and less anxious to return. Not only were there Bonapartes and adventurers living untrammelled lives in Boulogne, despite the "4 English churches" conscientiously noted, but there was also a conjuror called Monsieur Minola:

> A very clever man who does surprisingly clever things and who possesses the wonderful bottle of Houdin which has the magic power of giving to everyone whichever liquer they wish.

Robert Houdin was the greatest conjuror of the period. Five year later the French government sent him to Algiers to try to destroy the influence of the marabouts by bettering their fictitious miracles. So even his "wonderful bottle" had the power to attract visitors, especially English ones, and according to Ouida "the hotels were so crammed full that they had to send out for mattresses for beds and the travellers had to sleep in the dining-room". The crowds didn't prevent Ouida from enjoying herself, and an unadulterated love of pleasure shows in such passages as:

> I enjoy myself very much indeed here, I went last Wednesday to the ball, I danced a great deal, I had five beaux 2 of their names were Victor de Croquenoire and Albert de Courcy and 2 of the Levriers and the other little boy's name I don't know. . . . Yesterday we went to Portel. . . . Mama and I went on donkeys and Papa and Madame de Lagorgette in a donkey gig, it was not a pic-nic it was only a goute . . . we had a regular pic-nic the other day to Souvrain-Moulins on donkeys but that time we had substantial things and champagne and bordeaux it was so nice, we are to go tomorrow to see the children dance and I think to the theatre, I shall like it very much.

To which she adds, with an abruptness that in this context has the effect of a hiccup: "the unbridled ambition of a few men has in all ages been the true cause of the revolutions of empires." Probably dear dear Papa, who greatly disapproved when the coup d'état occurred in France next year, was growing suspicious of Louis Napoleon's intentions. But, if so, he didn't let his uneasiness prevent him making his daughter's first visit to France a memorable one, and it ended in a burst of gaiety:

> I have been to see the dancing, and went to the theatre with the dear Mdlles de Lagorgette and Mme de Lagorgette, Mr. O'Hara papa and mama, a nephew of Mr. Peter's was there so handsome! . . . Sunday was a dull day for we were to go on Monday we did not go to church [this strikes a familiar note] but heard some beautiful

The house where Ouida was born in Bury St. Edmunds.

Sketch by Constantin Guys, made during the Crimean War.

music in the Place Dalton and gave a last adieu to the dear dear
Établissement. Monday. Finish packing up. Sad very sad breakfast,
Mme Genau gave me a bottle of Casse, and a beautiful bouquet of
flowers, went to the office for a permit got on board, said a sorrowful
good bye to dear dear papa, laid down and floated from the shores
of dear beautiful France.

It never seems to have occurred to either Madame Ramé or her
daughter to reproach dear dear Papa for so often abandoning them;
and once Ouida had seen dear beautiful France, poor dear England,
so far as she was concerned, had had it.

III

BACK HOME, OUIDA found events taking place that reinforced her
father's political lessons. For this was the year when the Austrian
General, Baron von Haynau, recently dismissed from his post as dic-
tator of Hungary, came to London and was assaulted with cries of
"Hyena!" by the draymen of Barclay Perkins' Southwark Brewery—a
sturdy group who objected to the hyena's having flogged Hungarian
women rebels. It was these same draymen who, eight years later, lining
the snowy streets to see the seventeen-year-old Princess Royal drive
by in an open carriage on her way out of England, shouted to Prince
Frederick of Prussia: "Treat her well, or we'll have her back!"

The fact that papa would have approved of the draymen's attitude
only increased Ouida's longing for his presence, and she was entranced
when he decided to spend Christmas at Bury St. Edmunds. The German custom of having a Christmas tree had only recently become an
English one, and celebrations of the kind now taken for granted
and commercialized were still considered essentially foreign. During
this holiday Louis Ramé improved what to the little girl were shining hours by making a liberal out of her, and laying the foundations
of beliefs many of which were to last as long as herself. The child
was mother of the woman, and spoke the truth when, near the end
of her life, she told Sir Sydney Cockerell: "People change as life goes
on, I do not. I think I am exactly what I was when very young, in
opinions and character."

It was a very happy Christmas, and the gravity induced by Ouida's
twelfth birthday ("Now I am twelve years old I really must study. I

hope as I grow in years I may grow in goodness and cleverness")
caused no lessening of merrymaking:

> All my cousins and Arnie dined here and we had capital fun and
> some charades ... went to Dr. Hake's to a juvenile party and enjoyed
> myself much we had games before tea and then dancing and Mr.
> Hake showed us a magic lantern and they dressed up and acted a
> charade and then we had supper and two twelfth night cakes. [The
> custom of eating a special cake, in which a tiny doll is hidden, on the
> day the infant Christ appeared to the three kings still continues in
> France.] It was capital fun on Thursday the 16th I wished dear papa
> and mama many returns of it [their wedding anniversary].

In honour of this anniversary, her cousins acted a play called Strathmore, Willie playing the title role in black velvet:

> It was capitally done my 4 cousins acted lovelyly, they looked so
> nice and such nice dresses I enjoyed it very much there was a little
> dancing before supper, then supper, then after that a great deal of
> dancing I enjoyed the dancing so much. We staid till about two.

This passion for dancing, and her capacity for passion in general, are
curiously—in view of Ouida's intense disapproval of her—like those
of Queen Victoria; and in the case of both women youthful exuberance
concealed great will-power and oddity of character. But the resemblance was a matter of temperament, not of domestic circumstances.
For when Ouida's cousins Sophie and Rolan came for a Christmas
visit "we had some charades in one we were Gebeway Indians and in
another old maids; we were not in bed till halfpast one". After which,
not surprisingly, she "was not able to go to church on Sunday". This
was not the way of life that obtained at Windsor, where the ten-year-
old Prince Edward, exhausted by attempts to force him to resemble his
dear but never absent Papa, was causing Dr. Beecher to complain of
great naughtiness and bad words.

No sooner had the holidays ended than Louis Ramé left on a
mysterious errand, and had still not reappeared in July, when Ouida
was taken ill:

> ... they did not know what was the matter with me all the
> Wednesday and then Mr. Read and Mr. Dalton pronounced it Small-
> pox, but I was not to know anything about its being that, as it might
> have killed me as I had such a dread of it. I remember very little at
> least it seems like a dream only I know I saw very frightful things.

—I might have died but thank God I recovered and without being pitted which of course I don't care about as much as my life but still I shouldn't have liked it. What a quantity of strawberries I did eat to be sure when I was getting better and spungecake too.

At twelve years old, however, her resilience, later to develop into bravery, was immense and no thought of *frightful things* shadows her account of the Great Exhibition in Hyde Park, to which she was now taken as a convalescent's treat. The most attractive feature of this exhibition was the Crystal Palace, described by Thackeray in a May Day ode as:

"A blazing arch of lucid glass
Leaps like a fountain from the grass
To meet the sun. . . ."

Particularly appropriate to the year that saw the repealing of the odious window tax, the Crystal Palace was given its lovely name by Douglas Jerrold of Punch and its form, so unlike the bogus Gothic then fashionable, by Joseph Paxton, who based his design for it on that of the Conservatory built at Chatsworth to house the Duke of Devonshire's giant Victoria Regina lily. The following year this glittering sight was removed to Sydenham, where it continued to serve as a background for German bands, balloon ascents, and fireworks, until it was burnt down in 1936, the year Queen Victoria's great-grandson, Edward VIII, abdicated.

When first displayed, the arch of lucid glass was supposed to symbolise and inaugurate an era of unparalleled peace, enlightenment, and prosperity. But, in fact, the Great Exhibition marked almost the end of the short period of comparative peace that followed Waterloo. Punch ran a picture of the shipwrecked government saved by the Exhibition steamer. It was, incidentally, during the Great Exhibition that Charles Dana, manager of the ten-year-old New York Herald Tribune, and one of the trustees of Brook Farm, asked Karl Marx, recently settled in London, to write bi-weekly letters on European affairs, an offer which Marx accepted. Some of these on the Crimea were later reprinted.

But it was the romantic rather than the sociological aspect of the Great Exhibition that excited Ouida, and an interesting sidelight on the way people thought then can be obtained by comparing her twelve-year-old reactions with those of the thirty-two-year-old Queen Victoria, a persistent diary-keeper, who wrote: "the tremendous cheers, the joy expressed in every face, the immensity of the building, the mixture of palms, flowers, trees, statues, fountains, the organ (with 200 instruments and 600 voices which sounded like nothing) and my beloved husband the author of this 'Peace Festival', which united the industry of all nations of the earth,—all this was moving indeed, and it was and is a day to live for ever. God bless my dearest Albert, God bless my dearest country, which has shown itself so greatly today."

Sincerity, passion, and susceptibility to collective sentiments, are revealed in the young Queen's attitude; Ouida's was dominated by artistic feeling:

> Went to the Exhibition, it is splendid though I admire the nave much more than the transept I declare when the organs are playing and you hear them and look from the gallery it is beautiful, exquisite, I could not put down all the things I liked if I would but my Illustrated London News will give an account of them all and serve as a nice memory. There was a lovely little moving village there, beautiful it was, and oh the statuary too beautiful! Power's Greek Slave and a beautiful little veilled slave and several splendid statues and an exquisite ceilling with Byron painted on it. Splendid! . . . what do I mean by saying I like the nave better than the transept, certainly the latter is far more beautiful, the building far more, but the nave is so fairy-paradisy-like a looking place that when you gaze from the top to the bottom down the immense length it seems surely this cannot be built by men. . . . I wished all people away no-one to jostle against . . . oh, that silver and ebony inkstand with a deer and a fawn and the inkstands formed of stumps of trees all in chased silver—it did not look at all like what it was, it was lovely.

This account of the Great Exhibition ends her diary for 1851, and next year's first entry concerns her thirteenth birthday, marked by a beautiful canary from Arnie, a Shakespeare from dear mama, and more charades—which seem to have played in the social life of that period the part television now plays in the Anglo-Saxon countries. A sartorial note is introduced by: "Fanny and Marian came to tea with Arnie and Willie, the two first were in the Bloomer costume in blue cloth dresses with black velvet jackets blue and white trousers . . . oh it was such fun."

Bloomers had come in soon after bicycles and were a subject for facetiousness similar to that lately applied to Dior's New Look. Mrs. Amelia Bloomer, the spirited American responsible for this fashion, had recently written to the Daily News:

"Sir,

May I be allowed in your columns to ask why the British public is so horrified at the idea of women dressing in trousers, seeing that they have for many years tolerated a number of men from the north of the Tweed wearing petticoats—and shockingly short petticoats too?

Yours,

Amelia Bloomer"

There was no trip to France this year and, perhaps to compensate for this, Madame Ramé took Ouida to stay with the godmother after whom she was named Louise. An old friend of Madame Ramé, Mrs. Harding had been widowed in 1849 and recently married a Mr. Drane of Lee Lodge, Lewisham, a comfortable house in pretty grounds. Visiting here was a great treat for Ouida, who adored her godmother, calling her the Queen, and applying Wordsworth's "a perfect woman, nobly plann'd" to her. Nor was it long before Mr. Drane ranked as the King in the little girl's hierarchy. About her hero-worship for this couple only two facts are slightly unusual. The first is that her childish passion developed into an adult friendship, causing her to write regularly to Mrs. Drane until the latter's death, and to Mrs. Drane's son, Claud Harding, until her own; the second is her refusal, when at an age easily driven to blush and stammer, to be teased or patronised about her emotions. When a visitor said, with the unkind facetiousness of which children have to endure so much: "I can see you have been admiring someone very much all evening", Ouida replied with the tart accuracy that was to make her enemies, "Yes, and very natural too, is it not?"

Natural it certainly was. Mrs. Drane was beautiful, amiable, and kind; Mr. Drane tall, handsome, no less kind; and both the Dranes made much of their guests and provided delightful luncheon and dinner parties, and outings that included the christening of a sweetly pretty baby and donkey rides with Claud, who was six years younger than Ouida: "Oh! such fun we had, dear little Claud rode so nicely, he and I rode together and I think our donkeys were brothers they liked each other's company so much." The Dranes also showered presents on Ouida, including a paint-box, beautiful drawing-books, two boxes of coloured chalk, some charcoal and a steel holder, "oh it was so kind of him and to have a present from *him* that he should think of me, oh he is a darling, he is a perfect, splendid man". There were also Sundays when "we laughed so much all breakfast time I was barely in time for church". No wonder the child thought her devotion to the Dranes natural; what is surprising is her capacity to say so, succinctly.

As stirring as this visit, but differently so, were the Bury St. Edmunds' elections. As impassioned as the Brontës where politics were concerned, Ouida set out in a white frock and red snood to support the liberal candidates, Lord Jermyn and Mr. Bunbury—did Oscar Wilde, one wonders, ever meet this luckless candidate? This is the first time, on record, when Ouida suited her clothes to an occasion. Later, when dressed by Worth, such was her habit. But although "the duck Edward Herbert Bunbury Esq.re spoke well and long", nevertheless "the Conservative stranger Stuart's vulgar speech was received with loud applause!" Despite frock and snood, despite Ouida's having interrupted the feeding of Arnie's rabbits in order to wave red and white roses to passing Bunburyites, Stuart was elected—causing Ouida to add "though he promises an immense deal he is a lawyer and ten to one will not perform them".

But, at that age, her political grudges were evanescent. She had too many other problems in mind, having just decided that if she lived to be a hundred and twenty, and had learned all the European languages, she would then start on Hindustan. Meanwhile her reading included the Illustrated London News (much as she admired Ruskin, she didn't follow his advice to avoid modern books, magazines, and reviews), Chambers' "Papers for the People", "The Last Days of Pompeii", "The Wide Wide World", "Kenilworth", Brewster's "Guide to Science", "Napoleon le petit", "The Cricket on the Hearth", Neale's "Residence in Siam", Macaulay's "History of England", "Rienzi", Samuel Roger's poem "Italy", and Madame de Stael. Her *Extract Book* for this period contains a passage from Rockingham in which she perhaps sensed something of her own future: "Here is the Mediterranean. See all the long line of coast which is bathed by its sparkling waves—Italy, Greece, Palestine, Egypt—all those whom we have learned to admire have trodden those shores and hallowed them by their presence and immortal fame."

But despite Ouida's eager mental activity, despite her affection for her cousins, and appreciation of fun and dancing—especially the Australian polka and a new dance called Pop Goes the Weasel—discontent was stirring in her, unmistakable as growing pains, and exacerbated by Papa's absences. Copying a soothing passage on Contentment from Home Circle into her *Extract Book* she adds longingly: "Surely my dear Papa will like that, oh when will he write to us or come home."

It was at this time that the Duke of Wellington died, and although the Iron Duke was far less important to Ouida than he had been to the little Brontës, she copied an obituary into her *Extract Book*. Heroism attracted her, and change is as disturbing to the very young as to the very old. Even more disturbing than the Duke's disappearance was her cousin Willie's decision to become an actor. Unaware of what, as an intelligent woman, she would later think of such prejudices, the child wrote in her diary:

> He talks most wildly of what he shall do in his profession—profession!—what is it better than slavery? poor fellow as an actor can he ever rise to gentlemanly society? to think what he might have been and what he is!

Ouida was often to write about actors later, but never about the reaction of a middle-class Victorian family to one of its members taking to the footlights. As for poor Willie, who had acted so lovelyly as *Strathmore* in black velvet, either he left the stage or he changed his name, as theatrical posters and papers of the period show no trace of him.

Ouida's adolescent feeling that everything around her was breaking up was increased by the behaviour of Arthur Young, a young sea-captain whom she and her cousins had known as a boy and who now returned full of stories that caused them to play Desdemona to his Othello—"Cats in San Francisco sell for ten dollars (i.e. 2 pound) apiece the Californians being overwhelmed with mice". He so charmed them that they were horrified when Fanny suddenly received a letter announcing the young man's "determination to proceed to Sydney again without coming down or seeing us again to say Goodbye!" It is not clear from Ouida's diary whether Fanny's or Tiny's affections were the ones trifled with, but although she comments "Would he had never come home to cause such sorrow", it is already difficult for her to disapprove of a member of the armed services. She reminds herself: "Poor Arthur! though pitied he MUST be very much blamed"; but it was such as he, with his first-hand experience of shipwreck and earthquake, "Islands 500 miles from Japan", and a block of wood for a pillow, who personified Ouida's childish ideals—so unlike those of the edifying hero of Charlotte Yonge's best-selling novel "The Heir of Redclyffe".

Nothing illustrates Ouida's originality of mind better than her reaction as a child to this novel, in which the high-principled hero, Sir Guy Morville, is destined to "make up for the faults of his ancestors" and therefore decides to spend his honeymoon touring the cathedral towns of England. It was John Keble who first encouraged Charlotte Yonge to write and, since her parents would allow this only if she gained nothing financially, part of the profits from her books were spent on fitting out the missionary schooner "Southern Cross" for Bishop Selwyn. William Morris, Burne Jones, and Rossetti also admired "The Heir of Redclyffe", and during the CrimeanWar it was the book most demanded by wounded officers. So it was clearly in tune with its period as exactly as are Françoise Sagan's books today. But Ouida was already sceptical as to the value of missions, and wrote in her diary:

> England is certainly a glorious land and we have every right to be proud of and to glorify her . . . yet she is not without her faults while talking largely of freedom at home she inflicts servitude abroad on another people no doubt loving their liberty as well as she does herself what right has she to subjugate the Sikhs, those poor people struggling to free themselves are called rebels while doing the self-same things that England would herself under similar circumstances.

Gradually, everything about her home town began to exasperate Ouida. As memories and remnants of the eighteenth century vanished, the notion of respectability as an end in itself spread, imperceptibly at first, then relentlessly as a new fashion that has moved from the glossy magazines to the cheap ones. At a dance at the Salmons, which she enjoyed, she noted that they "came home at two much too early but the people are not fast enough in Bury they do no one thing with spirit". And when floods occurred all over the country the papers never put in anything about Bury "simply because nothing is ever done in the antiquated town with spirit—even the fields won't suffer themselves to be inundated properly—half will be like a river and the rest all high and dry—no, all things in Bury whether animate or inanimate want spirit".

Her general dissatisfaction had been sharpened by an event that horrified and disillusioned her father:

> Louis Napoleon is proclaimed Emperor and this by a people who but 12 months ago elected him President simply because he vowed to keep unchanged the name and statutes of a Republic and now they see this man breaking his oath and forming a style of government far more arbitrary than that of Louis Philippe whom they deposed because they thought his laws illiberal they see this "robber"—for I can call him nothing else,—making all the nation slaves to his will and yet they stand calmly by and listen to his proclamations in which

he calls himself "Emperor of France and Defender of the Holy Sanctuaries" and say "he is the Saviour of our country". There will be no bounds to his ambition if Europe does not rise to check it. Though infinitely lower than his great uncle he proves himself the superior of Napoleon Buonaparte in cunning and dissimilation. [On top of which,] the Contesse de Solms, that I knew at Boulogne has been expelled from France by her own cousin the Emperor so much for Tyranny!

But these shocking doings across the Channel did not lessen her annoyance with her own side of it. Censorious local gossip about her father infuriated her, and she had lost the support not only of Willie but of her other cousins, gone now to live in Derbyshire. In later years her cousins might call on her when they were abroad, and she might see them during her rare visits to England, but they were never again to play an important part in her life.

This separation marked the end of Ouida's childhood—a childhood that presently ceased to seem to her to be her own, as often happens with those lifted by talent, love, or accident into a world remote from the one into which they were born. Completely aware now of her longing to get away, Ouida began to plan. Bury St. Edmunds might be spiritless, but she was not—and at no time in her life did she believe that anything comes to him who waits.

IV

In 1854, while Ouida was beginning to plan her escape from Bury St. Edmunds, the Crimean War broke out. This war, summed up by H. A. L. Fisher as "a contest entered into without necessity, conducted without foresight, and deserving to be reckoned from its archaic arrangements and tragic mismanagement rather among medieval than modern campaigns", was the first large-scale contemporary war in Ouida's experience. It originated, as so many wars have done, in a quarrel between Christians about their religion, in this case between Greek Orthodox and Roman Catholic monks about the custody of certain shrines in Jerusalem, which city then belonged to Turkey. Greek claims were supported by the Tzar, Roman ones by Louis Napoleon, now Napoleon III. Outraged at not immediately getting his own way, the Tzar sent Prince Menschikoff (whose name is now inappropriately associated with a particularly delicious candy sold alongside Chartres Cathedral) with what amounted to a demand that Russia should be given a protectorate over Turkey's Orthodox subjects. The Turks refused; the Russians sunk the Turkish fleet off Sinope; war broke out; and England and France came in on Turkey's side. Cavour, Prime Minister of Piedmont, subsequently persuaded the Turin parliament to send a Sardinian contingent to support Turkey—thus obtaining for Italy the right to express its grievances at the European Council that followed the war.

Both England and France were anxious to keep Russia out of the Middle East, and Turkey had become intensely popular with liberals everywhere for its refusal to hand the Hungarian hero, Kossuth, over to the Russians or Austrians. Five years earlier, Kossuth had declared: "The Russian intervention provoked the indignation of the entire world . . . I trust I am right in saying: it has hardly ever happened in the history of the world that a nation's fight for freedom excited greater sympathy than ours. We fought by ourselves, cut off from the world." Feeling in England was therefore generally anti-Russian. Nevertheless the war was not greeted with unmixed enthusiasm, and a day of National Humiliation marked its outbreak. August Hare mentions having dined off boiled sea kale, "a vegetable which I have ever since associated with that time". How his Aunt Esther must have welcomed both this opportunity to create unpleasantness, and the atmosphere that resulted from people's sobbing in church when the prayers for time of war were read! Confidence in the government was complete at first, but this only made the subsequent disillusionment worse; and though Tennyson glorified the charge of the light brigade, more people thought, with Greville: "the affair of 25th, in which our light cavalry was cut to pieces, seems to have been the result of mismanagement in some quarter. . . ."

It was military, not civilian, reaction that interested the fifteen-year-old Ouida, and the prodigiously vivid accounts of this campaign that she wrote in her first novel, Held in Bondage, owe something to the fact that her beloved London Illustrated News had the acumen to send the great French artist Constantin Guys to the Crimea to make eyewitness drawings. These drawings, which Baudelaire considered the finest account of the war, were as stirring to the Victorian public as Henri Cartier-Bresson's photographs are to us now, and combined aesthetic and social service in the same way.

The war did not prevent Queen Victoria and Prince Albert from visiting Paris in 1855, thus giving encouragement to middle-class travel —though this was not their intention. As it was the first time a reigning

English monarch had been there since Henry VI was crowned in Paris in 1431, this visit filled both French and English newspapers, temporarily ousting the war from front pages. Cards announcing "English Spoken Here" were placed in French restaurant windows, and as much as eighty pounds was paid for the hire of a balcony overlooking the route from the Gare de Strasbourg (now the Gare de l'Est) to the Palace of St. Cloud (burnt by the Prussians in 1870).

The thirty-six-year-old Queen Victoria's opinion of Napoleon III differed greatly from that of Louis and Louise Ramé. She found him "a very *extraordinary* man, with great qualities, there can be *no* doubt. I might almost say a mysterious man. He is evidently possessed of indomitable courage, unflinching firmness of purpose, self-reliance, perseverance and great secrecy: and to this should be added a great reliance on what he calls his *star*, and a belief in omens and incidents as connected with his future destiny. Which is almost romantic, and at the same time he is endowed with a wonderful *self-control*, great *calmness*, even gentleness, and with a *power* of *fascination*, the effect of which upon those who became more intimately acquainted with him is most sensibly felt". The fact that Louis Ramé had shared this view until what he considered as Louis Napoleon's treachery occurred, only increased Ouida's disapproval of the Queen's attitude. Luckily, since she never enjoyed being censorious, she was able to approve wholeheartedly both of thirteen-year-old Prince Edward's vain longing to prolong his stay in Paris, where he was encouraged to dance the Prince of Wales' polka, and of the Queen's enthusiasm for the French Army: "each regiment with its own good, powerful band, and their fine commanding *tambour majors*, their stalwart bearded *sapeurs*; . . . and the very picturesque and smartly dressed cantinières, all cheering . . . then the troops began to *defiler* in quick time, which took three quarters of an hour; a beautiful spectacle, such fine troops! . . . The clothes of all the men are infinitely better made and cut than those of our soldiers, which provokes me much. The drums, too—brass ones—are much finer. Albert regretted, and so did I, that I was not on horseback . . . I had a cantinière called up to the carriage, and looked at her dress and her little barrel. She was very tidy, clean, and well spoken. I wish we had them in our army. They must always be married, and if they wish to remain in the regiment and their husbands die or are killed, they must marry again within the year."

Karl Marx, who thought no better of Napoleon III than did the Ramés, said at this time that the French had changed their motto from Liberty, Fraternity, Equality, to Infantry, Cavalry, Artillery. But Karl

Marx was then in the minority, and Queen Victoria's love for the "dear Zouaves" and "splendid Cent Gardes" reflected, exactly as did Ouida's early novels, the popular feeling of a period when every nice girl loved a soldier. One of the good results of this was a growing concern for army welfare. The Times opened a fund for the sick and wounded in the Crimea and sent Mr. Macdonald out to administer it. A fatuous suggestion from Lord Stratford de Redclyffe that the money would be better employed in building a Protestant church at Pera was very properly ignored.

This war which, according to Nathaniel Hawthorne, gave England a vast impulse towards democracy, increased Ouida's dissatisfaction with Bury St. Edmunds. During the second year of it, the first penny paper appeared. The Daily Telegraph pioneered the use of special correspondents abroad, and the excitement its articles and pictures aroused, the sense that life abroad was lived at a different pace from life at Bury St. Edmunds, seldom left Ouida now, even when she was making up stories among the blackbirds and hawthorns of Hardwick House—one of the few places in England she ever mentioned later with some nostalgia. At last she had realized, though would not admit, that her father could be relied upon for nothing, that self-help must be her motto, as it was that of her period. When at last the war ended, provoking Keats's biographer, Richard Monckton Milnes, to say "we are going to close a discreditable war by an inglorious peace: we shall have 10 p.c. income tax and 0 p.c. benefit to mankind", Ouida succeeded in persuading her mother and grandmother, eighty-four now, but still pretty and active, to leave Bury St. Edmunds for London.

She never saw her birthplace again and when, forty-one years later, Mr. Milner-Gibson Cullum, grandson of the Sir Thomas Cullum who had owned Hardwick in the days when she walked there in a crinoline, wrote to tell her that a memorial tablet had been affixed to the house where she was born, she wrote back, "this tomfoolery in Suffolk annoys me very much. I identify myself with my father's French race and blood, and I shall be greatly obliged if you would do your best to prevent any inscription of the kind you named being put as you say".

That there was no affectation about Ouida's lack of interest in Bury St. Edmunds is proved by the fact that whereas she was able to describe first Belgium, then Italy, with extraordinary vividness after only a few weeks in those countries, she mentioned Suffolk in only one of her novels. There was nothing of the traditional sweet seventeen about her when she faced London as eagerly as young Rastignac had faced Paris, and in much the same spirit: "à nous deux maintenant."

PART II

1857—1871

". . . there are departments of art and literature from which it is impossible to shut woman out. These are not however to be regarded as resources for bread."

Harriet Martineau, "Deerbrook", 1839

V

DURING THEIR FIRST year in London, the three women, and their dog, Beausire, stayed first at 41, Lansdowne Road, Kensington Park, then at Bessborough House, Ravenscourt Park, Hammersmith. It was an anxious but exhilarating time for Ouida. Neighbours gossiped about the virtually manless household, but as England then contained seven hundred thousand more women than men—which partly accounts for the frantic if decorous pursuit of husbands that is often to be found in Victorian novels—this gossip was not very wounding to sensible people, and both old Mrs. Sutton and Madame Ramé were far too sensible to allow what the neighbours might think to drive them into trying to thwart Ouida in her plans for achieving financial independence. In consequence she was free to make the most of her escape from Bury St. Edmunds.

The London of a hundred years ago was bounded by leafy Kensington to the west, Poplar with its ships' masts to the east, Regents Park to the north, and Camberwell to the south. Its gas-lit streets still echoed with the sounds of horses' hooves, cabs' wheels, the muffin-men's bells, barrel organs playing such tunes as "Villikins and his Dinah", Nigger Minstrels, who made their appearance in London about this time, and the cries of bowler-hatted shoe-shines and vendors of shrimps, herbs, sherbet, old clothes, rabbits, matches, and pies, the latter being hawked around in charcoal-heated baskets. Macassar oil for men's hair had lately become very fashionable, hence antimacassars; and the crinoline had been revived by the Empress Eugénie. Few people, whether employers or employees, lived more than three or four miles from their place of work, and Buckingham Palace still had its peeling façade, topped by lions, shields, and the figure of Britannia. According to the Lancet, this still compact city contained six thousand brothels and eighty thousand prostitutes, but, as Disraeli declared his period to be the age of statistical imposture, this estimate was perhaps unduly exuberant, despite the fact that it was supported by "Paul Pry", a disreputable paper that announced "there can be no disguising the fact that at the West End, at Brompton, at St. Johns Wood, Foley Place, Portland Road, Regents Park, and intermediate spots, some of the most magnificent women in London live under the protection of gentlemen". If this was so it was partly due to the frequency with which Victorian women were pregnant. Fertility was fashionable: the Queen, for example, had nine children; Mrs. Dickens, ten and two miscarriages; and Lady Durham died at thirty-five after bearing thirteen children in seventeen years.

But London contained a great deal just then besides sexual habits not, officially, practised in Bury St. Edmunds. The present British Museum reading-room, created by Mazzini's friend, the refugee Antonio (later Sir Anthony) Panizzi, was opened this year, causing David Masson, one of Milton's biographers, to write:

"Had you seen this fine hall before it was made,
All ye London sons of the book-making trade,
I am sure every time that your ticket admits ye,
You would lift up your hands and bless old Panizzi."

Another important opening was one by the pre-Raphaelite painters, who aimed at conveying "true and high ideas through the medium of true and rightly elaborated details". Recently published books included Elizabeth Barrett Browning's novel in verse "Aurora Leigh", the complete edition of Baudelaire's "Les Fleurs du Mal", Charlotte Brontë's posthumous "The Professor", Mrs. Hamilton's "The Exiles of Italy", a popular novel with a pro-Mazzini hero who belonged to the Society of the Friends of Italy, which greatly influenced Ouida, as did G. A. Lawrence's best-seller "Guy Livingstone". There also appeared Flaubert's "Madame Bovary", which as a serial had been prosecuted for obscenity, and Thomas Hughes' "Tom Brown's Schooldays", which was translated into French, German, Italian, Greek, and Russian. Incidentally, the first edition of "Tom Brown's Schooldays" was printed as being by "an Old Boy", a character who thus made his first, but by no means last, appearance in English life.

As stirring as the Crimean War, and more obviously horrifying, was the Indian Mutiny, which now began with a massacre of the English at Delhi. The conduct of Salkeld and the men who ran, each carrying a twenty-five-pound bag of gunpowder, to blow up the Kashmir gate, was as recklessly heroic as that of any of Ouida's early heroes, and provides one of many proofs that her dashing guardsmen, as differently uniformed from today's national servicemen as a peacock is from a guinea fowl, were drawn as much from life as from fancy. Writing of Ouida fourteen years after her death, Norman Douglas—

who had admired and corresponded with her, and twice invited her
to stay with him—said: "those guardsmen who drenched their beards
in scent and breakfasted off caviar and chocolate and sparkling Moselle—
they certainly seem fantastic. They really were fantastic. They did drench
their beards in scent. The language and habits of those martial heroes
are authenticated in the records of their day; glance, for instance, into
back numbers of Punch. The fact is we were all ludicrous formerly. The
characters of Dickens, to say nothing of Cruikshank's pictures of them:
can such beings ever have walked the earth?"

Such beings could and did. One of them, Alfred de Musset, died this
year; another, the romantic Richard Burton, who was to be a great
favourite with Ouida, returning from the Crimea had set out a year
before on the dangerous African journey that resulted in his discovering Lake Tanganyika. "Wider yet and wider shall thy bounds be set"
had not yet been written, but the feeling it expressed was general
throughout the Empire, on which the sun was not just then setting.
Charles Darwin might talk about apes, but most people felt, as did
Disraeli, that they were on the side of the angels.

Particularly stimulating to the politically minded Ouida was the
General Election that followed the defeat of Palmerston's government,
caused by the Chinese war. And to complete her happiness this
year, Louis Ramé came to London to spend his birthday with his
family.

But in spite of the novelty of London life—and Ouida managed to
attend Henley, Goodwood, and Ascot, all of which set her imagination
working as busily as a ticker-machine during a stock exchange crisis—
she put her work first. Feeling responsible for her mother and grandmother, she drove her quill pens as fiercely as the heroes of the Light
Brigade drove their horses. And, at this point, luck came to her assis-
tance.

When the household moved to Hammersmith it had as neighbour
and family doctor a Mr. Francis Ainsworth, who was sufficiently
impressed by Ouida to introduce her to his cousin, William Harrison
Ainsworth, author of popular historical novels, and editor of a monthly
magazine called Bentley's Miscellany, in which Mrs. Henry Wood,
author of "East Lynne", was among those given their first chance.
Ouida promptly sent him several stories, and he as promptly accepted
them.

The first of these, *Dashwood's Drag; or The Derby And What Came of
It*, was serialized in the April and May numbers of Bentley's Miscellany
for 1859, and from then until July 1862 every number contained a story

signed Ouida. These included *Cecil Castlemaine's Gage*, which concerned the beautiful Cecil Castlemaine's (feminine, despite the name) love for Fulke Ravensworth, Envoy from the exiled Stuarts at St. Germain; *Little Grand and the Marchioness*, a piece of rollicking fun-in-the-mess; *Deadly Dash*, the story of how an English black-sheep who had fought a duel too many redeemed himself by dying as a volunteer in the American Civil War (which broke out in 1861); *Sir Galahad's Raid, an Adventure on the Sweet Waters*, the story of a young English diplomat's attempt to snatch a Turkish beauty from her harem, and his discovery that he has been fobbed off with her negro servant; *A Line in the Daily*, an account of regimental high jinks at Norwich; *The Beauty of Vicq D'Azyr*, a crude but valid study of snobbery; *Fitz's Election or Blue and Yellow*, a Dickensian frolic for which Ouida drew on her recollections of the Bury St. Edmunds' elections; *Redeemed, An episode of the Confederate Horse*, another American Civil War story; and *The Marquis's Tactics, or Lord Glen's Wager*; *A Study à la Louis Quatorze*; *The Story of a Crayon Head*; *The Donkeyshire Militia*; *Belles and Blackcock*; and *Fleur-de-lys and the Two Viscounts*.

All these stories were written with tremendous dash and brio, the fact that Ouida had not at that time seen Norwich, Cambridge, Paris, Bohemia, Vienna, Scotland, Chamonix, or a German watering-place lessening neither the accuracy nor the vivacity with which she described these places. Even the most preposterous pages show that she never lacked one of the greatest qualities a writer can possess: readability. Years later, giving the publisher Fisher Unwin a reader's report on one of Ouida's Italian novels, G. K. Chesterton wrote: "Though it is impossible not to smile at Ouida it is equally impossible not to read her." Having been given its head, her imagination was, literally, over the hills and far away.

Her success was such that, in the magazine "Epilogue for 1860", Ainsworth wrote: "we offer not our own opinion but that of a host of critical commentators, when we say that few periodical writers have suddenly achieved a greater success than the contributor who has chosen the fanciful designation of Ouida; whose sketches of society, both in England and on the Continent, are as graceful as they are accurate." Artistic ambition was not the only feeling this sudden success gratified. As Ouida's mother later wrote in her diary, it was "entirely due to Louisa's exertions that we have such a home as we have always had".

But neither the Crimean War nor the Indian Mutiny touched Ouida as did the Italian struggle for independence, of which Massimo d'Azeglio told the Brownings: "It is '48 with matured actors." In 1859 many young Englishmen responded to a newspaper announcement headed EXCURSION TO SICILY AND NAPLES: "all persons (particularly members of Volunteer Rifle Corps) desirous of visiting Southern Italy and of *aiding* by their presence and influence the *Cause of Garibaldi* and *Italy*, may learn how to proceed by applying to the Garibaldi Committee." A minor result of this was that Garibaldi shirts for women—of scarlet French merino, braided with black, and worn with black felt hats trimmed with red and white ostrich-feathers—became as fashionable as Zouave jackets had been in the forties. Augustus Hare's sister, Esmeralda, was in Italy at the time and describes the volunteers singing "Viva l'Italia" and as "so radiant they seemed to be starting for a festival": which, together with her description of the French lancers arriving "with flying colours and splendidly mounted", and being received with flowers and applause since "the Emperor had been waiting for the arrival of this regiment to begin war in earnest", strikes a very Ouida-ish note. The Austrians were defeated at Solferino and Magenta (a fine picture of this struggle has recently been given by Visconti's film "Senso"), and in 1860 Garibaldi and his Thousand liberated Sicily.

The American Civil War broke out the following year, incidentally dislocating the British textile industry. The Manchester Guardian and Daily News supported Abraham Lincoln and the Northerners, but most people in England were pro-South—partly because the problem of slavery was not raised as a major one until the latter half of the war; partly because the Northerners seemed to many Whigs to be trying to force an unwanted form of government on the chivalrous South; partly because England needed cotton and the southern states, from which the cotton came, were for Free Trade, then part of the English middle-classes' religion, while the Yankees, dislike of whom was fanned by Dickens' "Martin Chuzzlewit", were for Protection; also because the romantic exploits of the blockade-runners were backed by the correspondent of the Times and by the Illustrated London News. Nevertheless the Lancashire mill hands, whom the war robbed of their livelihood, supported Lincoln—part of the credit for which is due to the Methodists, always violently anti-slavery.

Among other events of this period, an Atlantic Cable was laid; John Brown was hanged for conspiring with slaves to commit treason and murder; Ferdinand II of the Two Sicilies, better known as King Bomba, died at Lecce of a "loathsome disease" after giving his subjects every reason to revolt; and Cavour said "we have made Italy, now we must make the Italians". Jews were admitted to the British parliament; Worth set up his own establishment in the Rue de la Paix; the first petroleum wells were sunk; Blondin crossed Niagara Falls on a tight-rope, stopping to cook an omelette in mid-air; the first Pony Express—80 riders, 420 horses, 190 relay stations—operated over the 1,950 miles between San Francisco and St. Joseph, Missouri; Richard Burton returned from a three years' expedition during which he had discovered the source of the Nile; and an amiable Liberal politician, Lord Carlingford, announced that since he had clearly established the principle of aerial navigation, it was now only a question of forming a company for bringing his "aerial chariot" out, and then for "the whole world to witness at last the long-sought-for discovery, advancing civilization and administering to the prosperity of nations."

Closely connected with admiration for prosperity was the success of Samuel Smiles' "Self Help". This disarming book, characteristic of its age, class, country, and cheerful industrious author, appeared in 1859, and half a century later had sold a quarter of a million copies in English, and been translated into French, Russian, German, Italian, Swedish, Dutch, Spanish, Czech, Croat, Turkish, Egyptian, Tamil, Murati, Guyrati, Hindustani, Canares, Magyar, Siamese, Armenian and Pali. The Revue des Deux Mondes said that its wisdom might be described as "la splendeur du bon sens"; and one reader wrote, tantalizingly, "I was on the slide downwards, Self Help arrived in the nick of time." Ouida's independent and resourceful character made her admire Samuel Smiles, but although she was an adept at self help she was unfortunately less well equipped to follow the advice given in his later book "Thrift". Capable of immense industry, she was equally incapable of putting away for a rainy day. Her stories had bought her first taste of luxury— and as she began, so she meant to go on.

VI

OUIDA'S FIRST NOVEL, *Granville de Vigne*, was published in book form, with the new title, *Held in Bondage*, in 1861—the year Victor Emmanuel II of Sardinia became the first King of Italy, that the Russian serfs were emancipated, and that the Prince Consort died. Ouida was only twenty-two, but this fact had no commercial value then. Age was not viewed as it is now—very naturally, the expectation of life at birth being much lower than it is at present. Balzac's "Femme de Trente Ans", published in 1844, described a situation likelier to involve a woman of fifty today.

By one of those coincidences common in fact but despised in fiction, the publication of *Held in Bondage* occurred the same year as that of George Meredith's "Evan Harrington", the heroine of which was based on Lucie Duff Gordon's nineteen-year-old daughter Janet, who, as Janet Ross, later became the mistress of a man Ouida was to adore. Janet Duff Gordon's background was as brilliant as Ouida's was obscure. Her father was the handsome and charming Sir Alexander Duff Gordon; her mother Lucie Duff Gordon, daughter of John Austin, the distinguished writer on jurisprudence, was as clever as she was beautiful, translated from German and French, suggested the character of "The Princess" to Tennyson, and died in Cairo, where she had gone for her health and accomplished admirable welfare work. When the thirty-year-old Meredith fell in love with the sixteen-year-old Janet she was good-looking, a fine horsewoman, and already very spirited. Henry Taylor, a writer and member of the Colonial Office, told the Duff Gordons teasingly that Janet was pleasant when pleased, but that he could not help thinking that if anyone were to inconvenience her at a moment when she had a pointed instrument within reach, she would be "hasty and inconsiderate" in her manner of showing her resentment. To which he added, jokingly, that he considered her a potential homicide.

Ouida was later to share this view, non-jokingly, but at the time her imagination was occupied by the military, her first novel being full of the feeling expressed by the popular Irish writer, Charles Lever, in "Tom Burke of Ours", that "there is, perhaps, no species of society so striking and so captivating to the young man entering on life as that of a military mess". *Held in Bondage* is a first novel relatively free from autobiographical elements and displaying unusual pace and vitality. It tells the story of a group of cavalry officers known as the Dashers, and in particular of Granville de Vigne, who "hunted with the Pytchley, stalked royals in the Highlands, flirted with maids of honour, supped in the Bréda Quartier, had dinners fit for princes at the Star and Garter, and pleasant hours in cabinets particuliers at Venours and Maison Dorée". In other words, a life not unlike that presently made fashionable by the Prince of Wales. It was de Vigne who, in the midst of the horrors of the Crimean campaign, said "How horrible it is, Arthur, not to be able to wash one's hands!"—thus showing himself one of the first employers of the stiff upper lip and modest understatement that, far from being a permanent feature of the English character, were introduced in the nineteenth century by the rise of the middle-classes and the transformation and growth of Public Schools. Neither Lord Melbourne ("this damned morality will ruin everything") nor Mrs. Gummidge ("I'm a poor lost lorn critter") had the slightest tendency to understate their feelings.

But although he gave the book its original title, De Vigne's charms were moderate beside those of his friend Colonel Sabretasche, of whom the young author wrote:

> Had I been a woman [the book was written in the first person and as if by a male narrator] that beautiful face would have done for me irretrievably, as, according to report, it had done for a good many. Reckless devil-may-care the man looked with the recklessness of one who heeds nothing in heaven or earth; a little hardened by the world and its rubs, rendered cynical, perhaps by injustice and wrong; but in the eyes there lay a kindness and in the mouth a sadness that betokened better things. He might have been thirty, thirty-five, forty. One could no more tell his age than his character, though, looking at him, one could fancy it true what the world said of him—that no man ever found so faithful a friend, and no woman so faithless a lover, as Vivian Sabretasche.

Despite their charms, both gentlemen have a hard time with the ladies. De Vigne is trapped into marriage with "the Trefusis":

> Magnificent she looked in some geranium-hued dress, as light and brilliant as summer clouds, with the rose tint of sunset on them, and large white water-lilies in her massive raven hair, turned back à l'impératrice off her low brow, under which her eyes shot such parthian glances. One could hardly wonder that De Vigne offended past redemption the Duchess of Margoldswarzel, ruined himself for life with his aunt, the Marchioness of Margueterie, annoyed beyond hope of pardon the Countess of Ormolu, the five heiresses, all the county princesses-royal, all the archery-party beauties, and, careless of rank, right or comment, opened the ball with—the Trefusis.

Unfortunately the Trefusis turns out to be an adventuress whose real name is Lucy Davis, and only the discovery that she is a bigamist frees de Vigne to marry the gentle Alma Tressillian, who proves to be

Sabretasche's daughter by his fickle Italian wife—whose timely death enables Sabretasche to marry the charming Violet Molyneux.

Written with tremendous imagination and gusto, *Held in Bondage* was immediately successful, especially with the army, which is understandable, since Ouida's attitude was then surprisingly near to Kipling's: "there aren't better stuff to make soldiers out of nowhere than Englishmen, God bless 'em! but they're badgered, they're horribly badgered." Its success even rivalled that of "East Lynne" ("Dead, dead, dead, and he never called me mother") and "Lady Audley's Secret". Its plot appears far-fetched now, since its conventions are not ours, but its improbability did not strike Victorians, who were shortly to be taking sides passionately over the Tichborne case—which concerned a butcher from Wagga-Wagga who came to England to impersonate a baronet's drowned heir and successfully deluded the dead boy's mother. And, although Ouida herself wrote in the preface to the 1870 edition of the book: "I hope that no reader will form any judgement upon me as a writer from this very immature and imperfect romance," her first novel was full of passages indicating a forceful and unusual imagination, such as this:

We went to the Crimea gladly enough ; most of us had a sort of indistinct panorama of skirmishes and excitement, of breathless charges and handsome Turkish women, of dangers, difficulties, and good tough struggles, pleasant as sport, but highly spiced ... we thought of what our governors or grandsires had done in the Peninsula, and longed to do the same—we did not guess that as different as the bundles of linen, with wrinkled, hideous features, that the Tartars called women, were to the lovely prisoners from the convents of Flaming Badajoz, would be the weary, dreary, protracted waiting while the batteries strove to beat in the walls of Sebastopol. ... When I think of them all, my dear friends, whose bodies lie thick where the sweet wild lavender is blowing over the barren steppes of the Chersonese this summer's day, I remember wrathfully, how civilians, by their own warm hearths, sat and dictated measures by which whole regiments, starving with cold, sickened and died. ... Winter in the Crimea—the Crimea of 1854–55. The very words are enough to bring up again to memory that sharp, stinging wind, of whose concentrated cold none can imagine in the faintest degree, save those who have weathered a winter in tents on the barren steeps before Sebastopol. Writing the very words is enough to bring up before one the bleak, chill, dark stretch of ground, with its horrible roads turned to water courses, or frozen like miles of broken glass; the slopes, the vast morasses of mud and quagmire, or trackless wastes of snow; the hurricanes, wild as a tropical tornado, whirling the tents in mid-air, and turning men and horses roofless into the terrible winter snow, of howling wind, of pouring ink-black rain, in which the men in the trenches and the covering parties and pickets, watched with eyes that must never close, and senses that must never weary; the days when under those pitiless skies officers and men shared alike the common fate, worse clad than a beggar, worse cared for than a cab-horse; —all rise up before one as by incantation, at those mere words winter in the Crimea.

The fact that a great many people now know a great deal more about this campaign than was the case at the time is largely due to Mrs. Woodham Smith's superb study, "The Reason Why"; readers of which will realize how unusual was the quality that enabled an un-travelled and unmarried girl of twenty-two to see through recruiting-poster slogans to what the war really meant then.

As soon as the serialization of *Held in Bondage* ended, that of Ouida's next novel, *Strathmore*, began. This was one of her most melodramatic productions. It concerns handsome Lord Strathmore of White Ladies, a hitherto unsusceptible character who falls in love with an adventuress named Marion Lady Vavasour and Vaux. Adventuresses abound in Ouida's early novels, as they appear to have done in that portion of Victorian society which yearned to get into the recently named Marlborough House set presided over by the Prince of Wales. With most professions still shut to women, being an adventuress was the nearest many gifted ones could come to paralleling the achievements of the explorers whose adventures were so much admired.

Since wicked Lady Vavasour and Vaux makes a point of creating jealousy, she soon provokes a quarrel between Strathmore and his best friend Bertie Erroll, better known as Beau Sabreur—a name P. C. Wren was years later to use as the title of a best-seller that inspired many an English schoolboy with a longing to join the Foreign Legion. After killing Erroll in a duel, Strathmore discovers that worthless Lady Vasour is not really married to the now dying Marquis de Vaux, and he therefore determines to ruin her socially. He also discovers that Erroll's young Hungarian wife—hitherto unacknowledged, lest Erroll senior disinherit Bertie—has died of grief, leaving a daughter, Lucile. Strath-more, who is clearly related to Mr. Rochester, brings Lucile up, they fall in love with each other, and, after a series of very complicated complications, marry. Lady Vavasour repents and ends as a St. Vincent de Paul nun.

This absurd but richly coloured book contains an excellent description of Prague and a passage that is interesting because obviously based on the doings of Richard Burton:

> For a year Strathmore was not seen in Europe. Rumour, which must ever lie rather than keep silence, babbled now and again remembrance of him; he had been seen in Luxor; he had been met on the Amazon, or the Ganges; he had been heard of as dwelling at Damascus, and studying the buried learning of the East; he had been slain in a midnight fray with dragomans close by the gates of the kings of Europe—these were among the things that rumour babbled of him.

Meanwhile rumour was doing some babbling about Ouida. People were beginning to wonder about the identity behind the "fanciful designation of Ouida". It was even said that the author was a woman who had been divorced. "We want to know from whom," Madame Ramé pertinently noted in her diary. "She is said to be Miss Evans, the author of 'Adam Bede', on whom great scandal rests—scandal to which I give little credence, knowing any about Louise or myself to be perfectly false; therefore in all probability it may be so of her. Still, knowing that the highest in the land might be proud to call Louise their wife both from her talents and her virtues, it is hard to think vile and scandal-loving people should have power to injure her."

In fact, the reputation created by the scandal-loving people probably did Ouida more good than harm. It provided her with glamour of the sort conjured up today by the kind of travel advertisements that attract people to interesting places for silly reasons. Soldiers, explorers, diplomats, and sportsmen were among her earliest admirers and, thanks to her prodigious assimilative faculty, proved of the greatest use to her. William Tinsley, who published her first book, wrote: "it is often wondered by readers of her novels how it is that she obtains such a masculine grasp of character. . . . I am told that occasionally she used to invite young officers of the Guards, and young gentlemen of a sporting tendency, to dine with her and her mother. After dinner, when they lighted up their weeds and pipes, she would say, 'Now, gentlemen, suppose my mother and myself are out of the room. Seat yourselves; smoke and drink as if you were at the club; talk as if you were in the smoking-room there; never think about us.' . . . I have seen the menu of a dinner for a number of persons, and at the back of the card, in Ouida's bold handwriting, is written thus: on est prié d'attendre et de fumer."

Nor were young gentlemen of sporting tendency her only admirers. Madame Ramé's diary notes: "Went to Burlington Street. Mr. George Bentley congratulated Louise very warmly upon the success of *Strathmore* and told her she must eventually take the highest position. He spoke with great sincerity. We also went to Beaufort House; there the printer told her how greatly it had sold." Most important of all, *Strathmore* brought her the friendship of Baron Tauchnitz, a clever and excellent-hearted German publisher, who included the novel in his collection of English books.

Chandos, her third novel, and the last she wrote in Hammersmith, had a Disraelian hero, Chandos of Clarencieux, a wealthy artistic aristocrat too impractical to defend himself against the machinations of his man of business, John Trevenna, who is in reality, though Chandos doesn't know this, his envious bastard brother. Financially ruined by Trevenna, and with his engagement to frivolous Lady Valeria St. Albans broken, Chandos goes abroad, lives in poverty, makes a reputation as a poet, and finally marries the beautiful half Italian Castalia, who turns out to be the daughter of his friend, the Duc d'Orvale, just killed fighting for Italian independence.

Prefaced by Sir John Harington's:

> "Treason doth never prosper; what's the reason?
> For if it prosper, none dare call it treason."

this book, like all Ouida's early adventures in wonderland, is full of fascinating passages, such as this Cruikshank-like description of London:

> In all the narrow streets about Westminster there were the roar of traffic and the glare of midnight; the throngs were jostling each other, the unscreened gas-jets of the itinerant stalls were flaring yellow in the stillness of the air. The screaming of the ballad-singers pierced shrilly above the incessant noise of wheels, the shouting of coster-mongers, butchers, oyster vendors, and fried-fish sellers added its uproar to the pandemonium, and the steam and stench of hot drinks and of rotting vegetables was blent with the heaviness of smoke borne down by the tempestuous oppression of the night.

More surprising is this evocation of a place she had not yet seen:

It was sunset in Venice,—that supreme moment when the magical flush of light transfigures all, and wanderers whose eyes have long ached with the grayness and the glare of northward cities gaze and think themselves in heaven. The still waters of the lagoons, the marbles and the porphyry and the jasper of the mighty palaces, the soft grays of the ruins all covered with clinging green and the glowing blossoms of creepers, the hidden antique nooks where some woman's head leaned out of an arched casement, like a dream of the Dandolo time [one of Ouida's heroes, Dandolo was a twelfth-century Doge who defeated the Pisans, headed Crusades, and took Constantinople by storm], when the Adriatic swarmed with the returning galleys laden with Byzantine spoil, the dim, mystic, majestic walls that towered above the gliding surface of the eternal water, once alive with flowers and music and the gleam of golden tresses, and the laughter of careless revellers in the Venice of Goldoni . . . everywhere the sunset glowed. . . . Then a moment, and it was gone. Night fell with the hushed shadowy stillness that belongs to Venice alone; and in the place of the riot and luxuriance of colour there was the tremulous darkness of the young night, with the beat of the oar on the water, the scent of unclosing carnation-buds, the white gleam of moonlight, and the odour of lilies-of-the-valley blossoming in the dark archway of some mosaic-lined window.

Another description reflects the liberal feeling of the time, the feeling so finely expressed by the Brownings:

There was a great tumult rising through Venice; swelling at the first from a distant quarter, it had been borne nearer and nearer through the silence of the city of the waters, the tumult as of a surging sea, as of the roar of sullen winds—the tumult of a people, long-suffering and launched at last against their oppressors. The sound had not penetrated the depth of the church aisles; only its low muffled echoes could reach there, and they had been unheard by those who stood in solitude, lost in the misery of their own passions. In the clear gold morning, in the luxuriance of colour and of beauty, in the warmth of the fragrant air, in the hush of the tranquil streets, revolt had risen as it had risen in the great northern hive of labour; but here, in the "sun-girt south" it rose for liberty; there in the gaunt, smoke-stifled Black Country it rose for wages. [At this moment

Karl Marx, a refugee semi-resident at the British Museum reading-room, was studying the relationship between liberty and wages.] They were but the youths whose hearts were sick and whose lives were aimless, like the life of Leopardi, the children of eighteen or twenty summers, whose blood was kindled and whose souls were pure with patriot fire; who would have flung themselves away like dross to cut the withes from their Venetia; whose ardour thought the world a tournament, where it sufficed to name "God and the Right" to conquer and to see the foe reel down; who fed their eager fancies on the memory of Harmodius and Aristogeiton [two sixth-century Athenian friends who murdered Hipparchus, younger brother of the tyrant, Hippias, were both killed, and subsequently regarded as patriotic martyrs and given supreme honours], and who refused to see that the nations of their own day adored the Greeks in story, but called a living patriot an "agitator" if he failed, and sent him to the cell, the scourge, the death of felons. It was the boy-hood of Venice that had risen. The past day had been an Austrian festa for an Austrian chief, and the music, the laughter, the glitter, the salvoes of artillery, the wreaths of flowers, all the costly follies, had driven the iron deeper into the souls of those who closed their shutters to the sound of revelry, and mourned, refusing to be com-forted, desolate amidst the insolence of the usurpers' magnificence and mirth. The festa, following on the arrest of a songstress beloved of the city, who had been seized for singing an ode of liberty, had broken their patience down, had driven them mad, had made them believe once more in their old sublime fatal blindness, that a pure cause and a high devotion would prove stronger than the steel and the granite of mailed might. They expiated the evil as it is ever expiated; they were made the burnt sacrifice of their own creeds.

They met with little mercy: in the sight of their foes they were but seditious malcontents, to be shot down accordingly, or pinioned alive like young eaglets taken for a caravan cage. The soldiers of Austria made swift work with them,—so swift that the hundreds who had risen with the dawn with the shout of "liberta" upon their lips as with one voice, and the noble insanity of the liberators' hope beating high in their fearless breasts, were, almost ere the first echo of the chaunt had rung through the silent highways to wake the slumbering spirit of the Free Republic, shot down, cut down, well-nigh as quickly as seeding grasses fall beneath the scythes,—were driven as the deer are driven under the fire of the guns, yielding never, but overborne by the weight of numbers and the Trained skill of veteran troops, never losing their courage and their resistance and their scorn, but losing order and adhesion, and seeing their young chiefs fall in the very moment of their first gathering, seeing their long-counted enterprise, their long-watched opportunity, their long-cherished hope of union and strength and victory, fade and wither and perish under the upward course of the bright morning sun.

For Ouida's generation the Italians' struggle struck the note that the Spanish War was to strike for a later generation, and the Hungarian rebellion for a still later one. The year *Chandos* was published the Austrians left Venetia, after being defeated at Sadowa.

On December 20th, 1865, Madame Ramé wrote in her diary: "This day recalls sad thoughts; where now is the one whose birthday it is? Are my forebodings right that we shall never see him again? I wish my dear Louise could think with me on that point. True, he came so unexpectedly in '63 that there is no wonder she thinks he may come any day again. My own ideas are very different." Madame Ramé's forebodings were justified. Louis Ramé was never seen again—unless, as is possible but, in the absence of records, merely a matter of conjecture, Ouida visited Paris and saw him there. A letter to Baron Tauchnitz, telling him of the dramatisation of *Idalia* in 1867, contains the sentence: "I do not go to Paris yet, as the accounts I hear are not very attractive of the Exhibition," which shows that visiting Paris was by then among Ouida's habits.

The only other account of Louis Ramé at this time occurs in Lady Paget's "Scenes and Memories", in which she mentions a friend's having said of Ouida: "She never knew whether he was dead or alive, as he belonged to many secret societies, and the last she saw of him was one day, shortly after having published her first novel, *Idalia*. She was sitting on a bench in Kensington Gardens, he suddenly appeared out of the bushes and congratulated her on her achievement." This, however, contains several inaccuracies. *Idalia* was not Ouida's first but her fifth novel, published when she was twenty-eight; and it is most unlikely that her father would have burst from the bushes, which—since he couldn't have guessed which bench she would choose—would have involved shadowing her, instead of going to her home where he would have been very welcome to a share of her prosperity. Elizabeth Lee, Ouida's first biographer, and the only one who wrote at a time when many of Ouida's friends and relatives were alive, calls this story apocryphal, and no subsequent information has proved her wrong.

It was believed by his English relatives that Louis Ramé died in the Commune street-fighting of 1872. But this is unproved. As Ouida was thirty-three in 1872, her mother must have been at least fifty, and since her father was "considerably older" than Susan Sutton—his marriage certificate states he was a widower, so Ouida may have had French brothers and sisters of whose existence she was unaware—he was probably over seventy at the time of the Commune. The Archives de la Seine's list of deaths in the Paris area from 1860 to 1872 mentions only one Louis Ramé, a two-year-old who died in 1862 in the rue D'Enfer, and was the child of Louis Auguste Ramé and Cesarine Portier. These archives contain omissions, since they had to be reconstituted after the burning of the city hall in 1871; but so few Ramés are listed for the entire period—twenty-two in all, eighteen of whom were women—as to suggest that Ramé is not a Parisian name.

The distinguished Bonapartist scholar, the Vicomte Fleuriot de Langle, thinks that Ramé may well be one of·the many soldiers' patronymics coined by Napoleon's armies; while a marginal entry pencilled in a book in the Alençon public library asserts that Louis Ramé was the pseudonym of Eugène Sue, author of "The Wandering Jew". The latter is a particularly attractive notion, Ouida's talent being of exactly the kind one might expect from Sue's daughter, but, unfortunately, Eugène Sue died in 1857—six years before Louis Ramé vanished for the last time from his English family's life. The anonymous writer probably meant to imply that Ouida was Sue's daughter in a literary sense, as she might also be said to be Balzac's—and the fact that Eugène Sue was a Bonapartist and devoted to Laetitia Bonaparte, and in particular to her daughter, the future Madame Rattazzi, may have somehow got linked up with the rumour that Louis Ramé was a Bonapartist agent. Perhaps Ouida's assertion that her father came of noble Breton stock was, like many of her most improbable-sounding statements, accurate; certainly no romancing was needed to make Louis Ramé into a character as mysterious and eccentric as any conjured up by his daughter's imagination.

Despite his incorrigibly irregular conduct, neither his wife nor his daughter ever ceased to love Louis Ramé, and in 1866 Ouida's longing for him was sharpened by the fact that the simulacrum of a family for which she worked so hard began breaking up. At the beginning of the year her dog Beausire was taken ill and often kept them awake all night by his barking. Madame Ramé wrote in her diary, in a style that proves Ouida resembled her mother as well as her father: "No doubt the dog has his reasons, poor fellow, and wants us to understand him.

I only wish I could do so, for of course one's sense tells one that no dog so intelligent would be so uncomfortable unless something to his canine sense influenced him." When the dog died, in March, she wrote: "Noble Beausire died, both Louise and myself fell ill after the dear dog's death."

Ouida's love of animals was, like all her feelings, violent. But it was neither sentimental nor merely the result of an unmarried woman's instinct to lavish on animals some of the emotion no man wants. Even during her happy childhood she showed a tendency to react as did the little girl who, when asked if she felt a need to do something for her fellow creatures, said "my fellow *animal* creatures, yes"; and, like her love for her godmother, this feeling endured throughout Ouida's life —and was largely responsible for her death; nor did she fail to give practical expression to it: she battled ferociously against vivisection and for the Society for the Prevention of Cruelty to Animals.

Beausire was still being mourned when old Mrs. Sutton died. She was ninety-four, and her death gave Ouida and Madame Ramé more freedom, but they did not see the matter in that light. As loving a granddaughter as she was a daughter, Ouida missed the pretty white-haired, blue-eyed old lady in whose house she had been born, and who had done so much to enliven her childhood and make up for dear papa's defaulting ways. Fourteen years later she wrote from her Florentine home to Claud Harding: "I am glad you remember dear grandmama. What a lovely old lady she was!—and beautiful even in death. Save her, whom I loved dearly, all that early life has quite faded into a dream, sometimes I cannot believe that I was ever out of Italy. It seems impossible."

It was in 1866 that her longing for more vivid surroundings sent Ouida in the direction that was to lead to Italy. After leaving Hammersmith, mother and daughter finally settled for "fine apartments" in Welbeck Street. But these didn't anchor Ouida, and the year that *Under Two Flags* brought her fame of the rare, extravagant, "Bonjour Tristesse" kind she began staying at the Langham Hotel (opposite the site of what is now the B.B.C.). This new hotel, run by an ex-colonel of the Confederate Army, and favoured by the Prince of Wales, who attended the opening and said it reminded him of the Astoria, New York, suited Ouida perfectly. Having installed her mother and her new dog, Sulla, a magnificent Newfoundland given her by Hamilton Hume, the Australian-born explorer, in rooms to which candlelight at all hours, and quantities of flowers, gave what she considered a homelike air, she was able to devote most of her time to writing, and to indulge in the pleasures of entertaining without the tedium of house-keeping. She was also able to order her clothes from Worth of Paris.

Madame Ramé, her presence as sure a guarantee of respectability as a hall-mark is of the authenticity of silver, attended all the dinners during which Ouida combined work with pleasure. Her regular guests included: Richard Burton, the explorer, who looked like a handsome Arab and stained his under-eyelids with kohl; his wife, Isabel, whose passion for animals appealed to Ouida; Colonel Meadows Taylor, who served in the Army of the Nizam of Hyderabad, was put in charge of some of the ceded districts of Deccan after the mutiny, wrote more than half a dozen books, such as "Confessions of a Thug", containing highly coloured and accurate pictures of India, and died in Menton in 1876; Major Brackenbury, the Times' military correspondent; Colonel Pemberton, another Times correspondent, killed in the Franco-Prussian war; Whyte-Melville, who joined the 93rd Highlanders at seventeen, retired from the Coldstream Guards as a captain ten years later, volunteered for the Crimea, was appointed major of the Turkish irregular cavalry, wrote very successful novels of fashionable and sporting life, and was killed hunting in 1878; Bierstadt, the American landscape-painter, and the poet Longfellow; Lieutenant-General Sir Edward Bruce Hamley, who had served in the Crimea, was later Commandant of the Staff College, and wrote a score of books on literary as well as military subjects, including one on Voltaire—and whom Henry James remembered, twenty-seven years later, as having justified his conception of one of the finest types, "that of the cultivated soldier, of the lover of letters who was also apt for action"; George Lawrence, author of the best-selling novel "Guy Livingstone"; Hamilton Aïdé, the English poet and novelist, born in Paris of an Armenian father and an English mother, who studied at Bonn and served in the British army before concentrating on literature; James Robinson Planché, a well-known playwright and antiquary, of Huguenot descent, who was made Somerset Herald at this time; Major-General Breckin-ridge of the Confederate Army, later Vice-President of the United States; Serjeant-at-law Ballantine who was concerned in a number of famous cases—the Muller murder trial, the Tichborne case, and the defence of the Gaekwar of Baroda, who offered him twenty thousand guineas to visit India; Algernon Borthwick, who succeeded his father as editor and owner of the Morning Post and was created Lord Glenesk in 1895; Bulwer Lytton, the Byronic author of "The Last Days of Pompeii", whose dashing personality and feeling for melodrama were

Life Guardsman, 1860.

The Villa Farinola, Scandicci, where Ouida lived from 1874 to 1888.

greatly admired; and charming Sir Alexander Duff Gordon, whose
daughter was to help break Ouida's heart ten years later.

Lady Paget once suggested that Ouida had a gift for "forcing
people to come to her"; but it is unlikely that either young guards
officers or civilians of unusual calibre, none of them reduced to putting
up with boredom for the sake of a free meal, would have attended the
parties of a plain unmarried woman unblessed by social assets, unless
they enjoyed themselves. That they did enjoy themselves is likely if
the atmosphere resembled that described by Ouida in *Idalia*:

> The access of vivacity and abandon which a considerable amount
> of wine drunk and the introduction of tobacco invariably produce,
> flowed into the conversation; its gaiety grew very gay, and though
> there was still nothing that was licentious, there was a tone in it not
> customary before women of rank; the anecdotes had a Bréda aroma,
> the epigrams had a Jockey-club flavour, the equivoques were fitted
> for a little gilded supper cabinet in the Maison Dorée. . . .

Apart from their enjoyment of good food, drink, tobacco, and freedom from the obligation to make conventional small talk, the gentlemen of sporting tendency all admired Ouida. Her often-repeated
remark "Je n'écris pas pour les femmes. J'écris pour les militaires" was
imprudent but not, at this period, inaccurate. *Under Two Flags*, her
greatest success to date, was serialized in a military periodical before
appearing in book form, and was dedicated, with their permission, to
Colonel Poulett Cameron, a distinguished Indian officer, and to the
explorer, Hamilton Hume.

A rapidly moving, highly coloured, frequently preposterous, and
frequently touching novel, *Under Two Flags* concerns the adventures of
the Hon. Bertie Cecil—an Hon. if ever there was one—of the 1st Life
Guards, better known as *Beauty* in the Brigades. Ouida's description of
the Hon. Bertie's rooms provides an engaging picture of popular
standards of luxury in the London of the sixties—particularly if
supplemented by contemporary Punch drawings. It also exhibits a
feeling for luxury not unlike that displayed by Balzac in "La Maison
Nucingen" when he describes a fashionable young man about town
in the eighteen-thirties with his tilbury, his "tiger", and his
mistresses:

> A guardsman at home is always, if anything, rather more luxuri-
> ously accommodated than a young Duchess, and Bertie Cecil was

never behind his fellows in anything; besides he was one of the cracks of the Household, and women sent him pretty things, enough to fill the Palais Royal. The dressing table was littered with Bohemian glass and gold-stoppered bottles, and all the perfumes of Araby represented by Breidenbach and Rimmel. The dressing case was of silver, with the name studded on the lid in turquoises; the brushes, boot-jacks, boot-trees, whip stands, were of ivory and tortoiseshell; a couple of tigerskins were on the hearth with a retriever and blue grey hound in possession; above the mantelpiece were crossed swords in all the variety of gilt, gold, silver, ivory, aluminium, chiselled and embossed hilts; and on the walls were a few perfect French pictures with the portraits of a Landseer, of a steeplechaser by Henry Hall, one or two of Herring's hunters, and two or three fair women in crayons. [Landseer had recently caused a sensation by exhibiting at Burlington House a portrait of Skittles, the famous demi-mondaine.] The hangings of the room were silken and rose-coloured, and a delicious confusion prevailed through it pell-mell—box spurs, hunting-stirrups, cartridge cases, curb-chains, muzzle-loaders, hunting-flasks, and white gauntlets being mixed up with Paris novels, pink notes, point-lace ties, bracelets and bouquets to be despatched to various destinations, and velvet and silk bags for bank notes, cigars, or vesuvians, embroidered by feminine fingers and as useless as those pretty fingers themselves. On the softest of sofas, half dressed and having half an hour before plashed like a water-dog out of the bath, as big as a small pond, in the dressing-room beyond, was the Hon. Bertie himself, second son of the Viscount Royallieu, known generally in the Brigades as "Beauty". The appellative, gained at Eton, was in no way undeserved. When the smoke cleared away that was circling round him out of a great meerschaum-bowl, it showed a face of as much delicacy and brilliancy as a woman's, handsome, thoro'bred, languid, nonchalant, with a certain latent recklessness under the impassive calm of habit, and a singular softness given to the large, dark hazel eyes by the unusual length of the lashes over them. [Fortunate Hon. Bertie, able to indulge in scent, turquoise-studded dressing-cases, French pictures, point-lace ties, and startling eyelashes without anyone misundertanding him!] His features were exceedingly fair, fair as the fairest girl's; his mouth very beautifully shaped; on the whole, with a certain gentle, mournful love-me look that his eyes had in them, it was no wonder that great ladies and gay lionnes alike gave him the palm as the handsomest man in the Household Regiments—not even excepting that splendid golden-haired Colossus, his oldest friend and comrade, known as "The Seraph".

(In Balzac's "Albert Savarus", written in 1842, he explains that the fashionable use of the word "lionnes" comes from Alfred de Musset's famous poem, "Avez vous vu dans Barcelone . . . c'est ma maitresse et ma lionne"; and "Les Lionnes Pauvres" was the title of a play by Emile Augier, showing up the morals of the second Empire and displaying the phenomenon of middle-class prostitution on the stage for the first time.)

The Hon. Bertie's affections being disengaged at the beginning of the book, he is having a love affair with the Lady Guenevere. This is briefly described in terms that, although deliciously shocking to some of Ouida's first readers, were not in the least inaccurate—as can be seen if the state of society they evoke is compared with that conjured up by so subtle a novel as Miss Sackville West's "The Edwardians", not to mention many a diarist's accounts of the practical-joke-studded houseparties then being planned all over England in order to "keep the Prince amused", a task apparently of the greatest magnitude. Neither Bertie nor Lady Guenevere cares deeply for the other but:

> Both of them wore the masquerade dress to perfection. . . . Nobody was ever so indiscreet as to call it anything else [but friendship], and my lord was too deeply absorbed in the Alderney be uties that stood knee-deep in the yellow straw of his farm yard . . . ᵗo trouble his head about Cecil's attendance on his beautiful countess. . . . They corresponded in Spanish; they had a thousand charming ciphers; they made the columns of the Times and the Post play the unconscious role of medium to appointments; they eclipsed all the pages of Calderon's or Congreve's Comedies in the ingenuities with which they met, wrote, got invitations together to the same houses, and managed signals for mute communication; but there was not the slightest occasion for it all. It passed the time, however, and went far to persuade them that they were really in love, and had a mountain of difficulties and dangers to contend with; it added the "spice to the sauce", and gave them the "relish of being forbidden". Besides an open scandal would have been very shocking to her brilliant ladyship.

When scandal does threaten, the Hon. Bertie unhesitatingly sacrifices himself to save both Lady Guenevere's undeserved reputation for chastity, and his weak younger brother's undeserved reputation for probity. Supported by his faithful batman Rake—half Sancho Panza, half Jeeves—who sticks to him through thick and thin, Bertie sets out for North Africa, Ouida's descriptions of which were enthralling to readers with no cinemascope to familiarize them with foreign parts:

In the straight white boulevards, as in the ancient winding streets, under the huge barn-like walls of barracks, as beneath the marvellous mosaics of mosques, the strange bizarre conflict of European and Oriental life spread its panorama. Staff officers, all a-glitter with crosses, galloped past; mules, laden with green maize and driven by lean brown Bedouins, swept past the plate-glass windows of bon-bon shops; grave white-bearded sheiks drank petit verres in the guinguettes; Sapeurs, Chasseurs, Zouaves, Cantinières, all the varieties of French military life mingled with jet-black Soudans, desert kings wrathful and silent, eastern women shrouded in haick and serroual, eagle-eyed Arabs flinging back snow-white burnous, and handling ominously the jewelled hilts of their cangiars . . . gas lights were flashing, cigar shops were filling, newspapers were being read, the Rigolboche was being danced, commis-voyageurs were chattering with grisettes, drums were beating, trumpets were sounding, bands were playing, and, amid it all, grave men were dropping on their square of carpet to pray, brass trays of sweet-meats were passing, ostrich eggs were dangling, henna-tipped fingers were drawing the envious veil close, and noble oriental shadows were gliding to and fro through the open doors of the mosques, like a picture of the Arabian nights, like a poem of dead Islamism—in a word, it was Algiers at evening.

Here Bertie proceeds to join the Foreign Legion, after dicing as to whether to choose the French or the Arab side. Before long *Beauty* of the Brigades is known as *Bel-à-faire-peur* of the 2 ème Chasseurs, and has won the devotion not only of the wildest of his companions but of Cigarette, the tough little waif with a heart of gold who is the Legion's mascot:

Her mother a camp follower, her father nobody knew who, a spoilt child of the army from her birth, with a heart as bronzed as her cheek, and her respect for the laws of meum and teum nil. Yet with odd stray, nature-sown instincts here and there of a devil-may-care nobility, and of a wild glee that nothing could kill—Cigarette was the pet of the Army of Africa, and was as lawless as most of her patrons. Cigarette was a resolute little democrat; she had loaded the carbines behind the barricades in an emeute in Paris before she was ten years old, and was not seldom in the perplexity of conflicting creeds when her loyalty to the tricolor and the guidons smote with a violent clash on her love for the populace, and their liberty. . . . She was pretty, she was insolent, she was intolerably coquettish, she was mischievous as a marmoset, she would swear if need be like a Zouave, she could fire galloping, she could toss off her brandy or her vermouth like a trooper, she would on occasion clench her little brown hand and deal a blow that the recipient would not covet twice, she was an enfant de Paris, and had all its wickedness at her finger tips, she would sing you guingette songs till you were suffocated with laughter, and she would dance the can-can at the Salle de Mars with the biggest giant of a Cuirassier there. [The can-can was performed in England for the first time on Boxing Day of the year *Under Two Flags* was published. It was danced by Finette, a Creole whose real name was Josephine Durwend, a handsome gypsy-like woman, who had been Whistler's model. The Prince of Wales was among those who relished it, so much so that a few nights later he took Princess Alexandra to see it.] And yet with all that she was not wholly unsexed, with all that she had the delicious fragrance of youth, and had not left a certain feminine grace behind her, though she wore a vivandière's uniform, and had been born in a barrack, and meant to die in battle; it was the blending of the two that made her piquante, made her a notoriety in her way; known at pleasure, and equally, in the army of Africa, as "Cigarette" or L'Amie du Drapeau. . . . In her sight the survivor of the Army of Italy was sacred; sacred the eyes which, when full of light, had seen the sun glitter on the breastplates of the Hussars of Murat, the Dragoons of Kellerman, the Cuirassiers of Milhaud; sacred the hands which, when nervous with youth, had borne the standard of the republic victorious against the gathered Teuton host in the Thermopylae of Champagne; sacred the ears which, when quick to hear, had heard the thunder of Arcole, of Lodi, of Rivoli, and, above even the tempest of war, the clear still voice of Napoleon; sacred the lips which, when their beard was dark in the fullness of manhood, had quivered, as with a woman's weeping, at the farewell, in the spring night, in the moonlit Cour des Adieux.

(Ouida must have inherited this feeling for the Army of Italy from her father, rather than acquired it from the British and American officers at the Langham.)

Fond as he is of Cigarette, the Hon. Bertie doesn't realize she loves him, and his emotions are presently absorbed by the arrival of a party of visiting firemen in the shape of English milords, one of whom is his erring brother, now Lord Royallieu, the other his former friend "the Seraph", now Marquis of Rockingham. With them is the beautiful Princess Corona, whom Bertie doesn't recognize as the Seraph's sister, Lady Venetia, whom he knew as a child—and who, having no sooner been married to a man not of her choosing than she was widowed, is still a virgin. The troubled friendship that springs up between the princess and the soldier leads to Bertie's striking his perfidious commanding officer, and as a result he is condemned to death. Frantic with grief, Cigarette rides to Algiers to get the Marshal's pardon and arrives back just in time to gallop across the firing squad—thus being killed in her successful attempt to save Bertie. After Cigarette's death, Bertie's brother confesses his misdemeanours and Bertie returns to England, home, and beauty in the shape of the Princess, soon his loving wife. But it is Cigarette who has the last word, as Lord and Lady Royallieu contemplate the grave on which is written:

CIGARETTE
Enfant de l'Armée, Soldat de la France

With the possible exception of frivolous Lady Dolly in *Moths*, Cigarette is Ouida's most remarkable female character, a genuinely original and moving figure whose untidy curls, boyish ways, tough language, and capacity for devotion have often since been borrowed by writers who have never heard of Ouida. That the type is still irresistible is illustrated by the recent and deserved music-hall success of Zizi Jeanmaire; and that Cigarette's military exploits are not altogether far-fetched is shown by this description of a flesh-and-blood contemporary written by Augustus Hare's brother, Francis, who served as aide-de-camp to Garibaldi: "The Contessa della Torre was exceedingly handsome. She wore a hat and plume, trousers, boots, and a long jacket. She was foolhardy brave. When a shell exploded by her, instead of falling on the ground like the soldiers, she would stand looking at it, and making a cigarette all the time. The hospital was a building surrounding a large courtyard, and in the centre of the court was a table where the amputations took place. By the side of the surgeon stood the Contessa della Torre, who held the arms and legs while they were being cut off, and when they were severed, chucked them away to join others on a heap nearby. There were so many, that she had a heap of arms on one side of her and a heap of legs on the other. The soldiers, animated by her example, often sang the Garibaldian hymn while their limbs were being taken off, though they fainted away afterward. . . . When the war was over the Contessa della Torre retired to Milan. Her first husband, the Count della Torre, she soon abandoned; her second husband, Signor Martino, a rich banker, soon abandoned *her*. Lately she has founded a society for the Conversion of the Negroes of Central Africa, of which she appointed herself patroness, secretary, and treasurer; and, obtaining an English clergy list, wrote in all directions for subscriptions. Of course many clergy took no notice of the appeal, but a certain proportion responded and sent donations, which it is needless to say were *not* applied to Central Africa."

The sales of *Under Two Flags* were increased by the fact that a volume of Ouida's early short stories was now attacked in the Pall Mall Gazette by Lord Strangford, a well-known philologist. The savagery with which he set about breaking a very gay butterfly on a rather drab wheel defeated its own purpose and—as when François Mauriac devoted an editorial to Françoise Sagan—people hurried to buy the condemned book rather than attend to the condemnation. Not even a philologist could prevent young Miss Ramé of the Langham from tasting success and enjoying it.

VIII

ALTHOUGH OUIDA HAD now acquired honourable professional standing, an entertaining social life, and an adequate income—she soon earned more than the fifteen hundred pounds a year that Bulwer Lytton's son considered the minimum on which a gentleman might ask a gentlewoman to share his life—she made no attempt to relax. She enjoyed her social life, but more as grist to her mill than for its own sake: to a greater degree than at any other time in Ouida's life, work came first with her.

Her fifth novel, *Idalia*, had a hero typical of her imaginative exuberance at this period. A dashing Queen's Messenger, Sir Fulke Ercel-donne (whose name was probably suggested by that of Thomas the Rhymer of Ercildoune, the thirteenth-century Scottish seer) has a job that many diplomats now at loggerheads with bureaucracy might envy. Nothing could be less suggestive of form-filling-in than this programme:

The constant travel, the hard riding, the frequent peril, the life of cities alternating with the life of adventure—these were to his taste. And while in the capitals of Europe there was not a woman who could beguile, or a man who could fool him: the Mexican gauchos found in him a rider fleet and fearless as themselves; the French Zephyrs knew in him a volunteer, fiery and elastic as any their battalions held; the fishers of Scandinavia had lived with him through many a blinding, icy, midnight sea-storm; the Circassians had feasted and loved him in their mighty mountain strongholds; and the Bedouins welcomed as one of themselves the Frank, who rode as they rode, without heeding the scorch of the brazen skies and sands; who could bring down a vulture on the wing whirling right betwixt his sight and the burning sun, a black speck on the yellow glare; who could live like themselves, if needs be, on a draught of water and a handful of maize or of dates, and who cared for no better bed than their desert solitudes, with his saddle beneath his head, and the desert stars shining above.

In the course of his duties in the Carpathians, Sir Fulke narrowly escapes being murdered by Conrad Phaulcon, a Greek of ambiguous background. His cry of "tell them I destroyed the papers", as he loses consciousness, is not only in the best tradition of Victorian adventure stories, but in one still valid: when Togliatti, head of the Italian communists, was shot at in 1948, he devoted all his failing energy to keeping hold of his briefcase. At this point Idalia saves Sir Fulke's life by taking him to a convent where the nuns nurse him—but can tell him nothing of the woman whose beauty now haunts him. When, at last, he finds her again he discovers that she is a revolutionary aristocrat with immense charm, and an indefinably ambiguous social background. In some respects Idalia is a forerunner of the Princess Casamassima and, like Henry James' heroine, she owes something to the extravagant Princess Belgiojoso, a great lady who fought for Italian freedom, raising troops and leading them into battle, and who died four years after *Idalia* was published—and also to Jessie White, an Englishwoman who served as a nurse in Garibaldi's army, and was so fanatical that Mrs. Browning said her conversation suggested "scaffolds looming in the distance".

Sir Fulke follows Idalia to Capri—Ouida was one of the first novelists to describe Capri and the Blue Grotto—but thanks to the machinations of Victor Vane, a suitor whom Idalia has repulsed, she is betrayed to the reactionary party, imprisoned, ill-treated, but eventually rescued by Sir Fulke, who is now tormented by doubts as to the nature of her relations with Conrad Phaulcon. It is not until Idalia and Sir Fulke are recaptured, and in danger of death, that she tells him Conrad is her father:

> I thought him a God, a hero, a patriot. He was a communist, an agitator, an adventurer; but I knew none of those names. I thought mankind was divided into the oppressors and the oppressed, into the haters and the lovers of liberty.

Fortunately Idalia and Sir Fulke are rescued and united, but not before:

> moving through the gore-stained, artillery-trodden maze of Lombardic fields, where in some unrewarded skirmish young, eager, patriotic lives had been shot down by the troops of Austria, gasping to their latest breath "Italia fara de se!" he had stood beside some shattered wreck of brightest manhood that had fallen there, down head-first into the yellowing wheat, and when he had thought all life was dead in that broken mass, above which the tangled corn stalks nodded and met in summer winds, he had caught a last sigh in which the name of Idalia was blent with that of Italy, and died together with it down the Lombard breeze.

Idalia was dramatized by George Roberts and produced at the St. James Theatre on April 22nd., 1867, with the beautiful Miss Herbert as Idalia, Charles Wyndham as the Queen's Messenger, and Henry Irving as Conrad Phaulcon. The struggle in the Balkans was transformed into the Italian struggle for independence—an indication of popular taste: George Meredith, whose novels Ouida admired—in 1891 she asked Tauchnitz why he didn't publish more of them—had just written "Vittoria", a novel set in Italy during the 1848 rising. The scenery was of the splendid solid kind now associated with Drury Lane, in London, or the Chatelet, in Paris: the gorge of Gonda contained a mountain torrent of real water; and an army of Zouaves, each carrying a lamp, graced the scene of the eve of Solferino.

Despite its superficially extravagant character, this immature novel contained at least one passage in which Sarajevo, 1914, could be seen as the future can be seen in tea leaves:

> Matters are getting very serious eastward; everywhere over there the people are ripe for revolt; I expect Venetia, and Galicia, and Croatia, and all the rest of them, are meditating a rising together.

... England, France, Austria, and Russia are all disturbing themselves after the affairs of this out-of-the-way nook, conceiving that with Greece in insurrection, and Italy in a transition state, and Poland quivering afresh beneath her bonds, even Moldavia might be the match to a European conflagration.

After this came *Tricotrin*, in 1869, this being the name of a French strolling player who has adopted an abandoned waif, Viva, who—it much later transpires—is the daughter of Coriolis, a heartless actress. Love of pleasure leads Viva to desert Tricotrin for Paris, where the good and distinguished Duc de Lira falls madly in love with her, marries her, and soon dies, leaving her the fortune for which, despite her genuine affection for the man, she married him. A dazzling widow, she falls in love with Lord Eastmore, who is really Tricotrin's brother and who, on discovering his long-lost brother's story, would despise Viva for ingratitude if Tricotrin did not arrive in the nick of time— just before getting killed in a political street-fight.

After this came *Puck*, as great a success as *Under Two Flags*. Whyte Melville wrote to Ouida: "I have just finished *Puck* and congratulate you indeed. To my fancy it is the best of yours, good as the others are. It has all their imagination and dramatic power, with a vein of the most beautiful sympathy and feeling running through it, and a true poetry in the descriptions that is entirely independent of language, although clothed in the most beautiful and appropriate words. It is quite a work even a *man* might cry over, and that one would read many times and like better each time. In short, I think it is a first-rate, first-class, first-flight novel." *Puck* was the story of a Maltese terrier whose adventures take him from a cottage in the Peak district during his puppy days to London and the care of first a gossip writer, then an actress, Laura Pearl (a recognizable portrait of Skittles' contemporary, rival, and colleague, Cora Pearl), to Laura's protector Lord Beltran, and to a little actress called Nellie, who is something of a cockney Cigarette. After being stolen by dog-snatchers (like Elizabeth Barrett Browning, Ouida detested these horrid haunters of the Victorian scene) Puck is taken first to Italy, then to France, and then back to England, where Lord Beltran's young wife Gladys, a great classical actress, has her heart broken by Laura Pearl, whom Puck recognises as the country-girl who ill-treated him when he was a puppy.

Dedicated to her dog Sulla, and providing a rattling account of London's half-world, *Puck* contains several passages of editorializing in which Ouida's own vehement personality is apparent:

If you find any touch of egotism, as of vanity, in these pages, you will kindly remember that in these early days of my education I heard a great number of religious autobiographies. It is remotely possible that their influence may still colour my style . . . if it be a party of both sexes, ask people that are a little in love with each other, for people a little in love are always eager to shine; but banish all grandes passions; they have an eloquence of their own indeed, but they are very stupid society at a dinner table . . . that endless warfare with starvation and ruin which is all that the very poor know the world of life to mean . . . it seemed to me that life was but a sequence of tender ties, formed only to be ruptured and leave the poor heart aching . . . you want a good deal of barbarism and a good deal of faith in an age, to get a really great stage out of it. . . . Do all reviewers live in a nutshell, and absorb themselves in an eternity of knitting, and muffins and threepenny whist, that they persist in declaring there is no romance in real life?

Folle-Farine, Ouida's eighth novel, and the last of her forty-seven books to be written in England, was the story of a Norman miller's half-gypsy granddaughter, hence the nickname Folle-Farine, who after a childhood of ill-treatment, which has made a beautiful savage out of her, falls passionately but unwillingly in love with Arslan, a starving Norwegian painter. Enthralled by his art, as well as by him, Folle-Farine does all she can to help him, but it is not enough. He goes to Paris, and is likely to starve there, but Folle-Farine follows him, and in despair becomes the mistress of a rich man in order to ensure Arslan's success. Once his gifts are recognised he, not knowing what he owes her, despises Folle-Farine, who consequently kills herself. The descriptions of Norman peasants are excellent:

they understood that there was a world beyond them, but they remembered it only as the best market for their fruit, their fowls, their lace, their skins. Their brains were as dim as were their oil-lit streets at night; though their lives were content and mirthful, and for the most part pious.

But Ouida had exhausted her first vein of inspiration and felt, like Folle-Farine:

what she wanted was to live. Live as the great moon bird did that she had seen over these pale, pure, blue skies, with its mighty wings outstretched in the calm grey weather; which came none knew whence, and which went none knew whither; which poised silent and stirless against the clouds; then called with a sweet wild love-note to its mate, and waited for him as he sailed in from the misty shadows where the sea lay; and with him rose yet higher and higher in the air; and passed westward, cleaving the fields of light, and so vanished;—queen of the wind, a daughter of the sun; a creature of freedom, of victory, of tireless movement, and of boundless space, a thing of heaven and of liberty.

It was not westward that Ouida wanted to go, but southward. Despite the comfort and prestige of the Langham, despite the military and sporting friends, she had had enough of London. It has been suggested that the reason for this was her failure to "get into society", and her unhappy love for the Italian tenor, Mario. But since she was young, famous, and reputedly eccentric, all that she wanted of society came to her. And as for her love for Mario, the then sixty-one-year-old son of the General de Candia, while she was undoubtedly full of ecstatic admiration for this handsome and charming singer (after his farewell performance in "La Favorita", she flung on to the stage a bouquet containing an ivory cigar-case enscribed with an altered quotation from Dante:

> Pietosi dissero gli Dei
> Oda la terra una volta la musica
> Del Ciel, e labbre toccaro di . . .
> Mario)

there is no evidence that her feelings were more than schoolgirlish ones, like those she entertained for Mr. Drane at Bury St. Edmunds. Had she not used Mario for the hero of one of her most successful books, *Moths* (written eight years later, when she was passionately, justifiably, and tragically in love with another man) it is possible that onlookers, who though they may see some of the game do not always succeed in making sense of what they think they've seen, would have attached less importance to this. What more probably drove her to move was a feeling, instinctive as that which drives birds to emigrate, that her imagination was not getting something, she scarcely knew what, that it needed, and could find elsewhere. In addition she had had bronchitis and needed a change of air.

In earlier years she would have gone to France. But this was not possible then, for France was at war, Napoleon III having been tricked

by Bismarck's tinkering with an official telegram into declaring war on
Prussia over the Spanish Succession. Since Bismarck's repulsive behaviour was not made public until years later, many hitherto pro-French
people, like Ouida, were disgusted with Napoleon. In the September of
1870 she wrote to Baron Tauchnitz: "You have cause indeed for
triumph and my poor France for bitter repentance of the submission
she gave to a corrupt and emasculated government."

At Balmoral, Queen Victoria's preacher seized the opportunity for
a sermon on French decadence. Among the decadent ones was the
brilliant young French painter, Bazille, who was killed in the war;
Manet, who served in the National Guard; Degas, in the artillery; and
Renoir, in the chasseurs à cheval. A further instance of this insular and
frivolous attitude towards France was provided by someone who signed
himself, most appropriately, "amateur critic" and wrote, complaining
of the production of Boucicault's melodrama *Formosa, or the Railroad
to Ruin*: "I have hitherto always fondly believed that this was one of
the best recognised and not least important distinctions between the
dramas of the two nations, that however necessary it may be to exercise
caution in Paris, one can in London always take one's unmarried sister
or country cousins to a theatre without risk of prostitution, in all the
paint, powder, costly jewellery and superb dresses, being flaunted
before them." To which the manager, Mr. Chatterton, a calm and
sensible man, replied that for the last seven years he had lost money
producing Shakespeare, Byron, Milton, and Goethe—the pit and
gallery being full in each case, but the stalls and boxes empty—and "I
am neither a literary missionary nor a martyr, I am simply the manager
of a theatre, a vendor of intellectual entertainment to the London
public, and I found that Shakespeare spelt ruin, and Byron bank-
ruptcy." Still young enough to be intransigent, Ouida must have felt
she had had enough of this.

IX

OUIDA'S LAST YEARS in London, most of which she spent writing,
were as turbulent as usual as regards public events. During this time
Russia sold Alaska to America for two cents an acre; the Dominion of
Canada was established; Prussia annexed Schleswig-Holstein; revolu-
tion in Japan was followed by the Mikado's assuming power; Isaac
Butt founded the Home Government Association in Dublin; Australia

received its last shipload of convicts from England; diamonds were discovered in South Africa; public executions were abolished in England, partly thanks to Dickens' "Letters on Capital Punishment"; trains were provided with an outside cord that rang a bell in the driver's cabin, thus offering some protection against the railway murders that played a prominent part in contemporary fears if not in fact; Papal Infallibility was proclaimed by seven hundred and sixty-four prelates, the only objector being the intrepid Bishop Fitzgerald of Little Rock, Arkansas; General Hope Grant introduced Field Manœuvres which, together with the Volunteers' Annual Field Day at Brighton, encouraged public interest in the army; Landseer's lions took up their positions in Trafalgar Square, the Daily Telegraph calling them "splendid, tremendous, authentic, magnanimous animals"; the circulation of the Daily News was tripled as the result of Archibald Forbes' electrically telegraphed messages from the Franco-Prussian war-front; W. E. Forster's Education Act was introduced to England; the Suez Canal—due, like Panama, to de Lesseps' genius—was declared open by the Empress Eugénie, after religious ceremonies performed by both Ulemas and Catholics; and Disraeli remarked that religion would give the new electorate something to take sides about.

Fashion was influenced by Strauss waltzes; by Fabergé trinkets—the great jeweller assumed the direction of his family business in 1870; and by the importance now attached to women's stomachs—"a *ventre* of gutta-percha is the remedy for these natural defects" (flat stomachs). The first lifts were being installed, and an early form of refrigeration on ships; and theatregoers flocked to Meilhac and Halevy's "Frou-Frou", and to "The Grand Duchess of Gerolstein", in which the lead was played by Hortense Schneider, a notorious charmer courted at various times by Bismarck, the Tzar, the Kings of Prussia, Portugal, Bavaria and Sweden, and the Prince of Wales.

Interested by her London life, but still as irremediably eager for something else as she had been in Bury St. Edmunds, Ouida set out for a continental holiday in August, 1871—the August during which a statutory Bank Holiday was observed for the first time. The Franco-Prussian war had ended only a few months earlier, but although Thiers had suppressed the Commune with a ferocity that reminded people of the excesses of Robespierre, and Mazzini had remarked that, by seizing Alsace-Lorraine, Germany had made another war inevitable, tourists were once more welcome across the Channel.

First Ouida went to Brussels, staying at the Hotel de l'Europe and making excursions to Antwerp, Bruges, and the Ardennes. Both her assimilative power and her delight in all she saw were shown by *A Dog of Flanders*, a very successful book which she wrote this year:

Antwerp, as all the world knows, is full at every turn of old piles of stones, dark and ancient and majestic, standing in crooked courts, jammed against gateways and taverns, rising by the water's edge, with bells ringing above them in the air, and ever and again out of their arched doors a swell of music pealing.

There they remain, the grand old sanctuaries of the past, shut in amidst the squalor, the hurry, the crowds, the unloveliness and the commerce of the modern world; and all day long the clouds drift and the birds circle, and the winds sigh around them, and beneath the earth at their feet there sleeps—Rubens. . . . Flanders is not a lovely land, and around the burgh of Rubens it is perhaps least lovely of all. Corn and colza, pasture and plough, succeed each other on the characterless plain in wearying repetition, and save by some gaunt grey tower, with its peal of pathetic bells, or some figure coming athwart the fields, made picturesque by a gleaner's bundle or a woodman's faggot, there is no change, no variety, no beauty; and he who has dwelt upon the mountains or amidst the forests feels oppressed as by imprisonment with the tedium and the endlessness of that vast and dreary level. But it is green and very fertile, and it has wide horizons that have a certain charm of their own even in their dullness and monotony; and amongst the rushes by the water-side the flowers grow, and the trees rise tall and fresh where the barges glide with their great hulks black against the sun, and their little green barrels and vari-coloured flags gay against the leaves.

A month or two later the Ramés travelled through Germany and the Tyrol—where Ouida wrote to Baron Tauchnitz: "I was delighted with the autumnal splendour of the German forests as I passed through them into the Tyrol." This was the year Heinrich von Treitschke, the champion of the Hohenzollerns and of Prussia, who longed for Germany to conquer the world, became a member of the Reichstag. But though Ouida gave Germany her visual attention, she gave it little else. For in October, 1871, she entered Italy for the first time.

PART III

1871—1882

"No exhalations damp the spirits choke,
That feed on ether temp'rate and serene;
No yellow fogs, or murky clouds of smoke
Obscure the clearness of this joyous scene."
> Charles Greville. Written in a carriage between
> Naples and Mola di Gaeta. 1830.

"Italy is a land full of presences. It has produced many great statesmen, brilliant artists, admirable musicians, superb poets. Each of these has left something of his spirit in Italy. Scarcely any other country has preserved so much of a richly varied past. If it were not for the courage and vitality of the Italians, they would be dwarfed by their own history."
> Gilbert Highet, "Poets in a Landscape".

X

MOST TRAVELLERS WHO remember seeing Italy for the first time
will understand Ouida's feelings as she crossed the snow-topped
Dolomites and came down through dark-green forests and light-green
pastures, past stretches of rock the colour of Jersey cattle, into valleys
full of fruit trees, fields of rice, plains of wheat, and so into the old
walled cities that to western Europeans evoke the beginning of civilization as they know it:

Every old Italian city has this awe about it—holds close the past and
moves the living to a curious sense that they are dead and in their
graves are dreaming; for the old cities themselves have beheld so much
perish around them, and yet have kept so firm a hold upon tradition
and upon the supreme beauty of great arts, that those who wander
there grow, as it were, bewildered, and know not which is life and
which is death amongst them.

Ouida came, saw, and was conquered. It was love at first sight, and
durable love. Like the child Osbert Sitwell thirty years later, she
suddenly realised "this was how I had always hoped the world would
appear. . . . Here there was no necessity to struggle for breath with an
encompassing and enveloping fog: here, on the contrary, was serene
and aromatic air, scented on the mountains with herbs and in the valleys
by orange blossom". Even today, when many of Italy's main highways
are bedaubed by the inaccurate assertions and perfect silliness of adver-
tisement-hoardings, when both the serenity and the aromatic qualities
of the air have been affected by the ubiquitous Vespa—even today there
are no towns in Italy entirely without beauty, and many entirely free
from ugliness. To those accustomed to the industrial north the shock
is tremendous.

The first Italian city to excite Ouida's imagination was Bologna,
darkly beautiful and somewhat sinister with its medieval towers, its
sombre Romanesque and Gothic churches, its arcaded streets with shop-
windows in which fruit and sausages glitter like tropical fish in a dusky
aquarium, and the exquisitely severe colonnaded vistas that make it

easy to understand why the Bibbienas, whose home this was, became the greatest scene-designers of the eighteenth century. Between Bologna and Florence the route winds through mountains exactly like those that in fifteenth-century Italian paintings so often provide the backgrounds for Holy Families, benevolent lions cheek by jowl with smug lambs or elegant unicorns, and pellucid rivers from which bright-eyed fish stare up at scarlet-clad cardinals.

Emerging from these Ouida was able to look down on Florence cupped in its lovely valley, surrounded by the silvery olive trees first introduced into this landscape by the Medicis, to whom the city owes so much: down on the small perfect city bisected by the golden-green river Arno, its superb bridges still unharmed by war, its roofs and ramparts richly brown as Siena earth or red as dark roses in faded tapestry, its tawny palaces with flower-seller's displays banked up against their walls under the great iron rings for tethering horses and the smaller iron rings for holding torches, its box-hedged cypress-dominated green gardens populated by marble statues and, appearing to float over everything. Brunelleschi's solid yet ethereal dome. In *Pascarel*, the first novel Ouida wrote in Italy, she describes her arrival in Florence, and it is clear from this that her first sight of it filled her not only with joy and awe but with the disturbing sense of recognition that sometimes accompanies one's first encounter with a place or person destined to be of great importance to one:

> The past is so close to you in Florence. You touch it at every step. It is not the dead past that men bury and then forget. It is an un-quenchable thing: beautiful and full of lustre, even in the tomb, like the gold of the Etruscan kings that shines on the breast of some fair living woman, undimmed by the dust and the length of the ages. [The Etruscan tombs, familiar to many people now—at least in photographs—had only just been rediscovered.] The beauty of the past in Florence is like the beauty of the great Duomo. About the Duomo there is stir and strife at all times; crowds come and go; men buy and sell; lads laugh and fight; piles of fruit blaze gold and crimson; metal pails clash down on the stones with shrillest clangour, on the steps boys play at dominoes, and women give their children food, and many maskers grin in carnival fooleries; but there in their midst is the Duomo all unharmed and undegraded, a poem and a prayer in one, its marbles shining in the upper air . . . other, though not many, cities have histories as noble, treasuries as vast; but no other city has them living and ever present in her midst, familiar as

household words . . . every line, every road, every gable, every
tower, has some story of the past present in it. Every tocsin that
sounds is a chronicle; every bridge that unites the two banks of the
river unites also the crowd of the living with the heroism of the
dead. . . . The beauty of the past goes with you at every step in
Florence. Buy eggs in the market, and you buy them where Don-
atello bought those which fell down in the broken heap before the
wonder of the crucifix. Pause in a narrow by-street in a crowd and
it shall be the Borgo Allegri which the people so baptized for love of
the old painter and the newborn art. Stray into a great dark church
at evening time, where peasants tell their beads in the vast marble
silence, and you are where the whole city flocked, weeping, at midnight to look their last upon the face of their Michael Angelo. Pace up
the steps of the palace of the Signoria and you tread the stones that
felt the feet of him to whom so bitterly was known, "Com'e duro
calle, lo scendere e'l salir per l'altrui scale". . . . Amidst all her commerce, her wars, her hard work, her money-making, Florence was
always dominated and spiritualized at her noisiest and worst, by a
poetic and picturesque imagination.

Once inside the walls of the city where she was to live for twenty-
three years, and which she was to leave against her will, Ouida and her
mother settled at the Hotel de l'Italie (now the Hotel Excelsior Italia)
in the Piazza Ognissanti, on the right bank of the Arno, two bridges
down from the Ponte Vecchio, and almost opposite the Porta S.
Frediano district, where Pratolini's poor lovers were later to live.
Ouida's passion for nature and art would have made her love Florence,
in which the two are so exquisitely dovetailed, even had there been no
human beings to retain her there. Henry James, to whom Ouida's
opiniated vitality was particularly repellent, grudgingly wrote: "the
best and most sincere thing about her I seemed to make out was—or
had been—her original genuine perception of the beauty, the distinction
and quality of Italy." (This grudging spirit later provoked Norman
Douglas, who loved Ouida's independence, and honoured her
feeling for the oppressed, to describe Henry James as a derivative
intellectualist, lacking in sex.)
    To her delight in Florence was soon added that which she took
in its cosmopolitan society, which was eager to welcome a writer as
famous as many, and richer than most, of the foreigners then in Italy.
The fact that Ouida was reputed to be eccentric discouraged no one
at this stage, since eccentricity was still associated with foreign milords

and was smiled at and admired in this city which had been Italy's capital for a decade and only just ceded its position to Rome—with considerable annoyance, for just as Romans still declare that "the Orient begins at Naples", so the Florentines judge Rome. Only a few years earlier, Lady Paget had written: "Florence has always been celebrated for the odd foreigners who got into society, and now that it was a capital, it became necessary to be a little more careful . . . we always went by the rule the Queen established that a woman who lived with her husband was to be received. . . . In Florentine society of that day there were always about nine men to one woman."

The first King of Italy, Victor Emmanuel, Il Re Galantuomo, had made no attempt to develop the social life of his Florentine court. A fine sportsman, keen mountaineer, and vigorously devoted to women, he spent most of his leisure hunting the steinbock or chamois in the nearby mountains, only now and again making an uneasy appearance at receptions at the Medici-built Pitti Palace. So what Walpurga, Lady Paget, called *real society* in Florence consisted of about a dozen women and fifty men. When one of these women arrived at a party she was conducted to a seat and had a gilt Chiavari chair placed in front of her so that she might put her feet on the crossbar, thus protecting them from the cold marble floor. Gentlemen then gathered round the lady, like wasps around honey, the size of the gathering indicating the quality of the honey. Ladies who habitually arrived after midnight were known as *les dames d'après minuit.*

Being so small a group, *real society* was constantly shaken by the gossip and intrigues common to institutions, particularly when, as in this case, all the members of the institution have plenty of money and leisure and an exalted idea of their social position. Twenty years later pretty Mabel Dodge, writing of Florentine society from the disarming viewpoint of a Scott Fitzgerald character visiting a Henry James world, explained: "there were always some people who were cutting somebody else. Unless one lived in a remote castle too far to move in and out of society there, or unless one chose to remain perfectly aloof and indifferent, one had to become embroiled in bickering intrigues, take a side, be converted to the opposite one, carry tales, repeat secrets, constantly hear horrors against one's friends and, in fact, live in a very highly charged human atmosphere." This explains Ouida's later strictures on the group that inaccurately called itself polite society; but for the moment, entranced by the loveliness of her surroundings and the novelty of her amusements, she was unaware of any cause for fault-finding. As for the highly charged human atmosphere—she liked that, had in fact left

Bury St. Edmunds because the atmosphere there was insufficiently charged for her.

The first important difference between her social life in England and the one she led now lay in her choice of friends. In London she had neither made, nor tried to make, friends with women other than Richard Burton's wife, Isabel, whose passions and eccentricities matched her own in intensity if not in kind. But in the women she met in Florence Ouida instinctively recognised the anything-but-raw material her talent required, and she soon formed a circle of female acquaintances, several of whom became loyal and lifelong friends.

The closest of these were Emilie de Tchiatcheff, a Scottish woman connected with the Dalhousie family and married to the Russian writer and explorer, Pierre de Tchiatcheff, who had a salon and headed Anglo-Florentine society; Princess Anna Corsini and the Marchesa Isabella Piccolletti, both distinguished hostesses; and Lady Orford, a woman of eighteenth-century character who championed Ouida with wit and discernment, and whose sharp tongue affected nineteenth-century Florence much as that of Margot Asquith affected twentieth-century London. Lady Orford dressed in the fashion of thirty years before, powdered her hair, chain-smoked Caporal cigarettes, had fine manners, and quick wits, and received every Sunday after midnight. Ouida described her in *Friendship*, a novel published seven years later, as the Marchioness of Cardiff:

The Marchioness of Cardiff loved to call herself an old woman. But she had kept three things of youth in her—a fair skin, a frank laugh, and a fresh heart. She was a woman of the world to the tips of her fingers; she had had a life of storm and a life of pleasure; she turned night into day, she thought no romance worth reading save Balzac's and Fielding's, she did not mind how wicked you were if only you never were dull. She was majestic and still handsome, and looked like an empress when she put on her diamonds and sailed down a salon. On the other hand she would laugh till she cried; she would do an enormity of good and always conceal it; she honoured unworldliness when she saw it, though she regarded it as a kind of magnificent dementia; and, with all her sharpness of sight, the veriest impostor that ever whined of his misery could woo tears to her eyes and money from her purse. She always wintered in Rome, and never lived with Lord Cardiff. He and she were both people who were delightful to everybody else, but not to each other. She was a Tory of the old school and a legitimist of the first water; she believed in

Divine right, and never could see why the Reform Bill had been necessary. Nevertheless, Voltaire was her prophet and Rochefoucauld her breviary; and though she saw no salvation outside the Almanach de Gotha, her quick wit almost drove her at times near the wind of Democracy. Anomalies are always amusing, and Lady Cardiff was one of the most amusing women in Europe.

That this is a good likeness can be proved by comparing it with the description written by Lady Paget in her memoirs: "Lady Orford was one of the ladies whose doors never opened before midnight. Only once a year, when we announced our advent, her guests were convened for an earlier hour, and smoking was not allowed. A supper table, covered with plates of sandwiches and bottles of Marsala, was set out at one end of the long room, and a great many men and very few women filled the room. Ouida in her book *Friendship* paints Lady Orford to the life. She appears in it as Lady Cardiff. When I knew her she still had a fresh complexion and abundant flaxen hair, always amply powdered to preserve the colour. It was she who told me that if I wished to keep the auburn colour of my hair I ought always to powder when in Italy. I need not say that this was impossible to follow in those days, when powdering and painting were as much tabooed in England as they are now (1923) the fashion. Lady Orford's two charming and well-brought-up daughters also walked about with powdered heads, looking like little Dresden Figures. Whatever the mistakes may have been which banished Lady Orford from English Society I always found her, besides being most excellent company, kind, good natured and charitable, ever open-handed and warm hearted to those in distress." (Living abroad still seems to have had a Botany Bay favour for the upper classes. It is difficult to understand why, since so many lived abroad from choice.) "She paid, at that time, £1,500 a year out of her small fortune to Lord Orford for the right of keeping with her the two daughters whom he disowned. When, some years after this, Maud, then married to Prince Griffonia, died of diphtheria, Lord Orford forced her to continue to pay the ransom. Lady Dolly, the second, married a Neapolitan, the Duke del Balzo. She distinguished herself in the summer of 1885, by being the only lady of rank who remained at Naples through all the time the cholera reigned there, visiting the hospitals and doing all she could to alleviate the misery."

With this seductive rake as her mentor, Ouida was introduced to precisely the life of which she had dreamed in Bury St. Edmunds, precisely the life she had already so colourfully described in her early novels. There was a fancy-dress ball at the Comte de Talleyrand's to which the majority of the guests went dressed as their most distinguished ancestors; there was the famous hunt "Corso" to which everyone including Ouida wore pink coats, followed by a huge dinner-party at Doney's; there was an expedition to Milan to see Garibaldi make one of his last public appearances; there was a trip to the San Rossore Grand Ducal park near Pisa, where could be seen the last of the camels introduced in the seventeenth century by Ferdinand de Medici; later there was the excitement generated by visits from Queen Victoria, the Duke and Duchess of Teck, and Queen Victoria's fourth son, Prince Leopold, Duke of Albany, who became one of Ouida's admirers. Even had all this not sufficed to anchor Ouida in Florence, an encounter which she made on All Saints' Day of this year would have done so.

For it was then that, just as she had fallen in love with Italy, so she fell in love suddenly, violently, and lastingly, with an Italian ten years older than herself. The Marchese Lotteria Lotharingo della Stufa aroused in Ouida the greatest passion of her life; and although he broke her heart ten years later, turning her into that conventional but none the less tragic figure, a lonely spinster frenetically concerned with animals, he also brought her great joy and helped her to do her best work. Unusually handsome, sweet natured, and charming, he belonged to a family that had settled in Florence in 1210, and his ancestors included not only soldiers but the Blessed Girolamo of the Minori Osservanti di S. Francesco, and the Blessed Lotteringo, one of the seven Florentine nobles who used to meet daily to sing the Ave Maria in the Chapel of St. Zenobio, where Giotto's tower now stands, and who were responsible for the building of the church of SS. Annunziata in 1250. A many-sided man of various interests, he was at this time gentleman-in-waiting to United Italy's first king.

XI

OUIDA'S LOVE FOR this delightful man was very different from her childish excitement over Mario. Though far more violent, it was also far more rational, since the Marchese was free to marry her, and for several years—during which they lived within a short walking distance of each other and met daily—he showed her enough attention to make others beside herself think he wanted to do so.

In addition to the beauty, charm, and distinction that made him as enchanting to Ouida as one of her own heroes, he had qualities of mind unusual for his class and type. Few people, seeing these two meet for the first time, can have imagined that the Ramés and the della Stufas had much in common as regards their social background; but in fact they shared an important matter, namely involvement with the Bonapartes. Like Fabrice in "La Chartreuse de Parme", and like many liberal-minded Italian aristocrats, the Marchese's father had admired Napoleon, considering him as fundamentally an Italian who, though he came as a conqueror, had taught Italy the value of political unity. In consequence he volunteered for service with the French army, losing three fingers in the retreat from Moscow. So the name of Bonaparte had echoed through della Stufa's childhood as it had through Ouida's, conjuring up dramatic pictures of heroism, and arousing in both of them a responsiveness to panache, and some of the ambivalent feelings towards Napoleon that are reflected in Alfred de Vigny's "Servitude et Grandeur Militaires", and Alfred de Musset's "La Confession d'un Enfant du Siècle". Incidentally, there is something inexplicable about the recurrence of the Bonaparte motif that stamps Ouida's life as definitely as bees stamp First Empire furniture; and anyone who has studied the death-mask of her strong idiosyncratic face may have noticed the physical likeness that unaccountably linked her to this remarkable family.

Another quality shared by della Stufa and Ouida was an extreme love of nature. The Marchese's ancestors had been soldiers and courtiers, but also farmers, cultivating the land around the fine old house (in which the family still lives) since 1450; so he was not only ready but eager to give Ouida as much information about local animals, birds, and plants as she could have given him about those of the Suffolk countryside. Nor were della Stufa's interests purely local. Four years earlier he had made a trip to Burma with an Englishman, Doctor Clement, in order to study the possibility of constructing a railroad from Mandalay to Rangoon; and he was as obsessed as the White Knight by inventions which, in his case, ranged from the first petrol-driven engine to a washing-machine.

The first excursions this only superficially ill-assorted pair made together were designed to help Ouida find views to paint. Sometimes they drove, but more often they walked: Ouida dressed—this was a period of flounced dresses for golfing and befurred ones for archery— in a walking-outfit of grey poplin, the skirt just touching the ground, and a fashionable Alsatian hat of black velvet, tied beneath the chin; while della Stufa, in a neat country suit with knickerbockers, carried her painting materials. Vallombrosa was among the places they visited, and Ouida's pleasure in seeing it was so intense that she probably thought of Milton, who went there as a young man and remembered it, with longing, when he was blind. She greatly enjoyed painting, and a graphologist who was recently shown her writing guessed it to be that of a painter. (After Ouida's death, Lady Paget sold many of her pictures for the benefit of the Anti-Vivisection Society.) Henry James considered her pictures bad, but the Marchese admired them—and while she painted he gave her an enormous amount of information about Italy in general and Italian peasants in particular. As Ouida's feeling for kind hearts was even stronger than her feeling for coronets, this information eventually helped her to write about Italian politics with enough sense and sensibility to get herself into trouble with some of the authorities.

But despite the impact on Ouida of Italy and love, despite the fervour with which she threw herself into social life, and despite the difficulties incidental to working in hotels or furnished rooms, she managed to get plenty of writing done. The year after her arrival in Italy she published *A Dog of Flanders*, a collection of four short stories which appeared first in Lippincotts' Magazine and was illustrated by a Florentine, Enrico Mazzanti, when in book form. The title story, inspired by Ouida's visit to Belgium, concerns a peasant child who dreams of being a painter such as Rubens, and his dog, who dies with him of cold and starvation. *A Branch of Lilac* describes a travelling actor's love for a worthless flirt, which leads him to join the franc-tireurs after the French defeat of 1870. This story is particularly interesting for its picture of the fighting in France:

> I remember in that ghastly time seeing a woman put the match to a piece whose gunner had just dropped dead. She fired with sure aim: her shot swept straight into a knot of horsemen on the Neuilly road, and emptied more than one saddle.
> "You have a good sight," I said to her.
> She smiled.
> "This winter," she said slowly, "my children have all died for want of food—one by one, the youngest first. Ever since then I want to hurt something—always. Do you understand?"
> I did understand: I do not know if you do. It is just these things that make revolutions.

The third story, *A Provence Rose*, also contains echoes of the Franco-Prussian war; and the last one, *A Leaf in the Storm*, provides a picture of a Norman village before and after the Prussian invasion that would require few alterations to make it as true to 1940 as to 1870. The Prussians' burning of the village, in particular, is very like that of the Nazis' burning of Oradour—and greatly distressed Baron von Tauchnitz. He begged Ouida to omit the lines "The soldiers kicked aside the warm and quivering body. It was only a peasant killed", asking his dearest Miss de la Ramé to believe that the Germans were not so barbarous as she thought. But although she appreciated his generosity in admiring the stories, she would not alter a word. "Surely," she pertinently, but uncompromisingly, asked, "a victorious nation can afford to endure adverse opinions? The severity with which the war was conducted was no doubt strictly politic and logical, and from a German point of view perhaps justifiable, but nothing can extirpate to the dispassionate observer many actions in it for which there was no military precedent—the burning of the villages and hanging of franc-tireurs were to me most inexcusable in any campaign, and I frankly own that the ending of the whole question in such an enormous financial fine is of heavy ill-omen to the future of the world. However, on those points you and I will agree to differ, and I promise faithfully not to weary you with any statement of these perverse views when I have the very great pleasure (I hope ere long) of welcoming you, my dear Baron, to Florence."

The Baron accepted this. He was a man of exceptionally fine nature, and since Ouida, like most of the public, was unaware of Bismarck's machinations, she could not then deny that provocation had come from France; but she did interpolate: "Pray do not say that the French Nation wished the war. It was the effort of Ollivier [chief minister during the liberal administration that took office in 1870] and Napoleon to bolster up a waning dynasty; it was like all L.N.'s policy, a gambler's risk—he threw and lost—and, alas! the country pays the penalty." To which the Baron replied: "There cannot be the least doubt that our differing opinions about Germany and France will—as to me—never touch our personal relations. On the contrary, I hope that our cordiality will last forever." And it did last as long as they themselves lasted.

By the public in general *A Dog in Flanders* was much admired, Lord Lytton writing to Ouida that the stories were full of grace of style. But Ouida felt herself less personally involved in its reception than she had done in that of previous stories, for she was now absorbed in writing one of her best novels.

Entitled *Pascarel*, it is a declaration of love to Italy. The dedication says that whoever doesn't care for Florence will be bored by the book, but for once Ouida underestimated herself. Wilfrid Scawen Blunt considered *Pascarel* the best description of Garibaldian Italy in English literature, and it is delightful not only to those who love Florence, but to those who would love Florence had they been there. Nor does Florence stand alone. Almost every town in Tuscany is included in Ouida's large and brilliant canvas, and she has captured the fierceness, the animal vigour, of Italy as well as its beauty. The plot of *Pascarel* concerns the adventures of Nella and her brothers, the children of a dead Italian opera singer and of an English nobleman and gambler who for months on end leaves them without news of him, in Verona, with old Mariuccia, their nurse:

> I adored my father with very little reason for it, for I saw him perhaps six days in the year, and each time I saw him I received about six careless words. But he was so handsome, so easy, and so good-humoured, so indifferent to every created thing or any possible future, that he seemed to me the very perfection of humanity.

The boys grow up and go, one to sea, one to fight, and so out of Nella's life. When old Mariuccia dies, at carnival time, the young girl is befriended by a troop of Commedia dell'Arte actors, led by the brilliant and attractive Pascarel, last of a now ruined line of nobles. The little company works its way from Verona to Florence—enabling Ouida to give not only a moving picture of Italy in the days of Garibaldi, but a very exact one of the lives of poor touring actors only a few degrees better off than those Fellini recently conjured up in his film, "La Strada":

> There is nothing upon earth, I think, like the smile of Italy as she awakes when the winter has dozed itself away in the odours of its oakwood fires. . . . The springtide of the north is green and beautiful, but it has nothing of the radiance, the dreamfulness, the ecstasy of spring in the southern countries. The springtide of the north is pale with the gentle, colourless sweetness of its world of primroses; the springtide of Italy is rainbow hued, like the profusion of anemones that laugh with it in every hue of glory under every ancient wall and beside every hill-fed stream. . . . Come out here in the young months of summer and leave the highways. . . . The sheaves of Arum leaves that thrust themselves out from every joint of masonry or spout of broken fountain. The frame of roses that burns on every hands-breadth of untilled ground and springs like a rainbow above the cloud

of every darkling roof or wall. The ocean spray arbutus and acacia shedding its snow against the cypress darkness. The sea-green of the young ilex leaves scattered like light over the bronze and purple of the older growth. The dreamy blue of the iris lilies rising underneath the olives and along the edge of the fields . . . the soft, pretty, quiet pictures where mowers sweep down with their scythes the reedy grasses on the river banks; where the gates of the villas stand wide open with the sun aslant upon the grassy paths and the vines; where in the gloom of the house archways the women sit plaiting their straw, the broad, shining fields before them all alive with the song of the grilli; where the grey, savage walls of a fortress tower on the spur of the mountains, above the delicate green of young oaks and the wind-stirred fans of the fig trees; where the frate, in broadleaved hat of straw, brushes with bare sandalled feet through the bright acanthus, beaming a Rabelaisian smile at the contadina who goes by him with her brown water-jar upon her head; where deep in that fresh, glad tumult of leaf and blossom and bough, the children and the goats lie together, while the wild-thyme and the trefoil are in flower, and the little dog-rose is white among the maize; where the sharp beak of the galley-like boat cuts dark against the yellow current, and the great, filmy square nets are cast outward where the poplar shadows tremble in the stream . . . only now and again there is some headless helmet in the grass or the dog-roses blossom above a dead warhorse; or a cherry tree, red with fruit, lies on the ground, its stem broken under a rain of bullets.

As for the people . . . the more I dwelt among them the more I loved them. There is no other people on the face of the earth so entirely lovable, even with their many faults, as the Italians. But what is known of them by other nations?—hardly anything at all. That the Italian patrician may be little understood outside the pale of his own immediate associates, it is not difficult to conceive. His confidence is rarely bestowed; and the pride which fences him in is at once the most delicate and the most impenetrable that a man can place betwixt himself and the outer world. But it is strange . . . that the Italian of the people, as seen in his streets and fields, by his hearth, and his market stall, is as little understood and as invariably misrepresented . . . the Italian, even in the lowest strata of social life, has a repose and a dignity in him which befit his physiognomy . . . see a stonebreaker, or a mason, or a boatman asleep in the noonday sun, and you will surely see attitudes no sculptor could wish bettered for his marble. . . . True, you will do ill to make mock of him; high or low, it is the one unpardonable sin which no Italian will pardon . . . and he has a lightning-like passion in him which may smite his neighbour to the earth in a trice about a cherry-stone, or a broken broom, or any other casus belli of the hour. But . . . how bright he is, how gregarious, how neighbourly, how instant, and graceful in courtesy, how eager and kindly in willingness; how poetic his glee in song and dance, and holy day and pageant; how absolute his content upon the most meagre fare that ever held body and soul together; how certain his invariable selection of a pleasure for the eye, and the ear, rather than one for the mouth and the stomach.

Did Ouida think of her cousin Willie when she wrote about his profession?

When they grew up in Italy, all that joyous band—Arlecchino in Bergamo, Stenterello in Florence, Pulcinello in Naples, Pantaleone in Venice, Dulcamara in Bologna, Bettramo in Milan, Brighella in Brescia—masked their mirthful visages and ran together and jumped on that travelling stage before the world, what a force they were for the world, those impudent mimes! "Only Pantomimi?" . . . free speech was first due to the Pantomimi—They hymn Tell and chant Savonarola, and glorify the Gracchi, but I doubt if any of the gods in the world's Pantheon or the other world's Valhalla did so much for freedom as those merry mimes that the children scamper after upon every holiday.

To be with Pascarel near Florence makes Nella supremely happy— until she discovers that her colleague, the jolly commonplace little Brunotta, whom she had taken for Pascarel's sister, is unrelated to him, but was formerly his mistress. Jealousy, combined with Brunotta's treacherous suggestion that Nella is a burden to the company, drives her to run away, and in her absence Pascarel is arrested on a trumped-up charge of sedition. When at last they are reunited, Nella's jealousy is not appeased, so Pascarel searches Europe for her father and on finding the latter rich again, thanks to an unexpected inheritance, sends Nella to her father to assume her rightful social position. But by now Nella hates the life for which she once longed, and when she learns that her mother and father were never married she flings away the inheritance to which she has no legal right, and sets out to find Pascarel and the way of life that suits her. He is away fighting with Garibaldi, but at last they are reunited. Into this violent lyrical book, the happiest Ouida ever wrote, she put many of her new feelings:

All the greatest gifts that have enriched the modern world have come from Italy. Take those gifts from the world, and it would lie in darkness, a dumb, barbaric, joyless thing. . . . The faith of Columbus of Genoa gave to mankind a new world. The insight of Galileo of Pisa revealed to it the truth of its laws of being. Guido Monacco of Arezzo bestowed on it the most spiritual of all earthly joys by finding a visible record for the fugitive creations of harmony ere then impalpable and evanescent as the passing glories of the clouds. Dante Alighieri taught to it the might of that vulgar tongue in which the child babbles at its mother's knee, and the orator leads a breathless multitude at his will to death or triumph. Teofilo of Empoli discovered for it the mysteries of colour that lie in the mere earths of the rocks and the shores, and the mere oils of the roots and the poppies. Arnoldo of Breccia lit for it the first flame of free opinion and Amatus of Breccia perfected for it the most delicate and exquisite of all instruments of sound, which men of Cremona, or of Bologna, had first created . . . Brunelleschi of Florence left it in legacy the secret of lifting a mound of marble to the upper air as easily as a child can blow a bubble, and Giordano Bruno of Nola found for it those elements of philosophic thought, which have been perfected into the clear and prismatic crystals of the metaphysics of the Teuton and the Scot.

But, although she did not know it, Ouida was now in the position of the fairy-tale princess who has been given every gift but the essential one. Happily absorbed by della Stufa, and seeing him absorbed by her, it did not occur to her that past loves might have claims on him. Her adolescent stories had been full of dashing males with mistresses, but she had no experiences of mistresses in fact—and her relationship with della Stufa was strongly established long before anyone told her that until her arrival he had been what was politely called the *cher ami* or *cavaliere servente* of Mrs. Ross, the Duff Gordons' authoritative twenty-nine-year-old daughter, who had settled in Florence four years earlier, after six years in Egypt, where her husband worked as a banker. She sometimes wrote for the Times, and she and her husband enjoyed travelling. During Ouida's early days in Florence the two women were on sufficiently amiable terms for Ouida to make Mrs. Ross a present of a white Maremma hound—which she would certainly not have done had she known that Mrs. Ross was the Marchese della Stufa's mistress.

As it was, she had no idea that, as her first biographer put it, "it is probable that a connection of old standing formed a bar to matrimony on his side".

In these early days, before either she herself or Mrs. Ross had done anything to provoke a scandal, Ouida's own relations with della Stufa were very happy ones. She adored him and, although those who disliked her subsequently alleged that she only imagined his feelings for her, there is no reason why an attractive, honourable, and much-sought-after man in his position should have constantly chosen Ouida's company if this didn't please him. He may, like many another man or woman to whom the act of charming is as instinctive as breathing, have led her to believe that he felt more definitely than was the case; but he certainly displayed sufficient feeling to justify Ouida in thinking her love returned. After most of her papers were stolen, she asserted that she had sixty-three letters from him, all beginning *ma chérie*; and later Lady Paget said that these letters were very poetic, and that in one he compared Ouida's mind to a clear rivulet flowing over dead leaves which looked golden in the water—which illustrates Ouida's possession of the transforming power that, as a child, she had so admired in Houdin's Magic Bottle.

Her first biographer, after mentioning the "connection of old standing that formed a bar to matrimony", says that some of della Stufa's friends thought he had been attracted by the notion that Ouida was rich, and withdrew when he discovered his mistake. But, apart from the fact that he would not have required ten years to discover that he had overestimated her income, Ouida *was* rich: she was earning five thousand pounds a year, which was worth fifty thousand of today's money, and income tax was negligible. It has also been suggested that Mrs. Ross—who was far more sophisticated than either della Stufa, who obeyed Plato's behest that "every man ought to be both as passionate as possible and as gentle", or Ouida, who was throughout her life as single-minded as Queen Victoria—began by favouring this alliance; but in view of their respective upbringings it is unlikely that either Mrs. Ross or della Stufa would have adopted a "Wings of a Dove" attitude. The fact that Ouida was rich would certainly not have discouraged a man born in circles where marrying in order to consolidate family estates was considered far more estimable than marrying merely to gratify a passing inclination; but nor would it have automatically prevented the gentle della Stufa from being drawn to the dynamic Ouida. For if he enthralled her by his likeness to the lover of whom she had dreamed, she fascinated him by her originality and by her

conversation, so unlike that to which he was accustomed when standing around ladies with their feet on the cross-bars of their Chiavari
chairs—and her prestige, at a time when she was often compared, by
people who were not fools, to Balzac and George Sand, was as exciting
to him as his social position to her. It was not until Ouida's obvious
vehemence, combined with Mrs. Ross' iron-willed objection to it,
threatened to make him socially ridiculous that his respect for con-
vention made him take fright.

XII

OUIDA'S FIRST YEAR in Florence was followed at the beginning
of 1873 by three months in Rome, della Stufa being there on duty.
Everything about this visit, made at the happiest time of her life, en-
chanted her, beginning with the journey, which she described four
years later in *Ariadne*:

It is so beautiful, that highway to Rome across the land from
Etrurian Arezzo; the Umbrian soil is rich and fresh, masses of oak
clothe the hills, avenues of oak, and beech and clumps of forest trees
shelter the cattle and break the lines of olive and of vine; behind are
the mountains, dusky against the light, with floating vapours veiling
them, and half hiding some ruined fortress or walled village, or
some pile, half palace, half prison, set high upon their ridges; and
ever and again, upon some spur of them or eminence, there is some
old grey city, mighty in the past and still in fame immortal; Cortona,
with its citadel like a towering rock, enthroned aloft; Assisi, sacred
and grey upon the high hill-top; Spoleto, lovely in her ancientness
as any dream, with calm deep woods around, and at her back the
purple cloudswept heights that bear its name; Perugia Augusta,
with domes and towers, cupolas and castles, endless as a forest of
stone; Foligno, grand and gaunt, and still desolate, as all these cities
are, their strength spent, their fortresses useless, their errand done,
their genius of war and art quenched with their beech fires; one by
one they succeed one another in the long panorama of the Apennine
range; wood and water and corn and orchard, all beneath them,
and around them, fruitful and in peace, and in their midst, lone
Trasimene, soundless and windless, with the silvery birds at rest

upon its silvery waters, and here and there maybe a solitary sail, catching the light and shining like a silver shield amidst the reedy shadows.

Then after Trasimene come the wild bold gorges of the Sabine mountains; wooded scraps, bold headlands, great breadths of stunted brushwood, with brooks that tumble through it; rocks that glow in the sun with the deep colours of all the marbles that earth makes; deep ravines, in which the new-born Tiber runs at will; and above these the broad blue sky, and late in the day the burning gold of a stormy sunset shining out of pearly mists that wreath the lower hills; then the wide level green plains, misty and full of shadows in the twilight, white villages hung aloft on mountain edges like the nests of eagles; then a pause in the green fields, where once the buried vestals were left alone in the bowels of the earth, with the single loaf and the pitcher of water, to face the endless night of eternity; then "Roma", says some voice as quietly as though the mother of mankind were only a wayside hamlet where the mules should stop and drink.

Despite the sense, that one still has there, of the nearness of the surrounding countryside, Rome was very unlike a wayside hamlet just then, being full of political excitement, to which Ouida responded as a circus-bred horse responds to music. Augustus Hare, writing from Rome in March, observed: "I think a Republic here will soon follow that of Spain. Victor Emmanuel is so hated, and the profligacy of the Court and the cruel taxes are hastening the end. People already shout *Viva la Republica* and bawl Garibaldian hymns all night. I wonder whether you would think the freedom of religious worship a compensation for the moral changes here—the shops always open on Sundays, which were formerly so strictly closed, the churches deserted, stalls for infidel books in the streets, and an ostentatious immorality which was formerly unknown. In the Carnival, in insulting reference to the Pope, a pasteboard dome of St. Peter's was made to travel up and down the Corso in a car, with a parrot imprisoned in a cage on the top, 'pappagallo' being Italian for parrot, and 'Papa Gallo' a nickname given to Pio Nono during the French occupation. . . . There is a stall for Bibles now opposite S. Carlo. A great dog manages it, such a fine beast. He cannot be expected to do all the business, so he just receives the customers and, when anyone wants a Bible, he puts his feet up and barks." Later he added: "Even the most ardent Protestants too are a little shocked that the famous Quirinal Chapel, so redolent of Church History, should be turned into a cloakroom for balls, and the cloak-tickets kept in the holy water basins."

So far as Ouida was concerned, irreverent jokes about parrots, sightseeing in deserted churches, balls at the Quirinal, and Sunday shopping for books sold by dogs, all added to the delight with which she visited Rome under the guidance of one of the most attractive men there. Still young, passionately and hopefully in love, rich and successful, she even enjoyed the lionizing to which she was subjected. For now, and for many years to come, foreigners visiting Italy were liable to ask their friends, "Do you know Ouida? Could you take me to see her?" —and at this time she received such visitors enthusiastically, partly because she felt their admiration symbolised the security for which she had worked so hard, and partly because she thought della Stufa would be impressed by her success, as indeed he was. But she did not allow social life to prevent her studying Rome as ardently as if she had had nothing else to do. Ever since she was a small child she had understood the feeling that made Cicero say "not to know the events which happened before one was born, that is to remain always a boy"; and here, as in Florence, she felt that she was touching the past while living the most exhilarating moment of her own present. Florence remained her favourite city, but that she responded to Rome is shown by her description of it as it was then, when fever still played the dramatic part in Roman life evoked by Henry James in "Daisy Miller". (Even as late as 1895 malaria caused 16,464 deaths in Italy.)

Water is the living joy of Rome.

When the sky is yellow as brass, and the air sickly with the fever mists, and the faces of men are all livid and seared, and all the beasts lie faint with the drought, it is the song of the water that keeps our life in us, sounding all through the daylight and the darkness, across the desert of brick and stone. Men here in Rome have "written their names in water", and it has kept them longer than marble or bronze . . . when one is far away across the mountains, and can no more see the golden wings of the Archangel against the setting sun, it is not of statues or palaces, not of Caesars or Senators, not even of the statues that you think with wistful longing remembrance and desire: it is the water that is everywhere in Rome, floating, falling, shining, splashing, with the clouds mirrored on its surface, and the swallows skimming its foam . . . I wonder to hear them say that Rome is sad, with all that mirth and music of its water laughing through all its streets, till the steepest and stoniest

ways are murmurous with it as any brook-fed forest depths. Here
water is Protean; sovereign and slave, sorcerer and servant, slaking
the mule's thirst, and shining in porphyry on the prince's terrace,
filling the well in the cabbage garden, and leaping aloft against the
Pope's palace; first called to fill the baths of the Agrippines, and
serve the Naumachia of Augustus, it bubbles from a griffin's jaws
or a wolf's teeth, or any other of the thousand quaint things set in
the masonry at the street corners, and washes the peoples' herbs and
carrots, and is lapped by the tongues of the dogs, and thrashed by
the bare brown arms of washing women; first brought from the
hills to flood the green Numidian marble of the thermae, and lave
the limbs of the patricians between the cool mosaic walls of the
tepidarium, it contentedly becomes a household thing, twinkling
like a star at the bottom of deep old wells in dusky courts, its rest
broken a dozen times a day by the clash of the chain on the copper
pail, above it the carnations of the kitchen balcony and the caged
blackbird of the cook.

While she was in Rome two deaths occurred in England that intensi-
fied Ouida's feeling of having cut loose from her past. Bulwer Lytton,
whom she had so much admired, and who had been one of her first
admirers, died in January in Torquay; reading of his burial in Westminster Abbey, Ouida must have remembered the hard-earned
holiday she and her mother spent at the Imperial Hotel, Torquay, the
year before they left England. Ouida had bought a sailor hat and blue
top-coat for the occasion, and worn them for long walks along the
beach with her dog Sulla; and the climax of the holiday had been an
invitation from Bulwer Lytton to visit Argyll House, where Ouida
and her host had raged together against the Dog Act. During this
same January Napoleon III died, and although Ouida certainly did not
regret him, her thoughts of Louis Napoleon were inextricably mixed
up with memories of her father, and of the time when her eleven-
year-old self had set out so gaily to cross the Channel, dance with little
French boys, and curtsey to Bonaparte princesses. Of all the figures
who had helped compose her past only her beloved mother did not
seem ghostly now compared with the reality of della Stufa; but the
loss of two of those ghosts made her feel as if she had woken in the
night to find the bedclothes on the floor—and made her turn more
eagerly than ever to new friends.

It was during this visit to Rome that Ouida first met her future
friend the beautiful Walpurga, Lady Paget, then British ambassadress

there. This friendship was to be very important to Ouida since, in
several respects, Lady Paget's circumstances, looks, and character were
remarkably like those of what came to be considered a typical Ouida
heroine; and intimacy with her naturally encouraged Ouida in the
creation of figures liable to seem unreal to those without personal
knowledge of this type.

Born Ehrengarda Helena Walpurga, Countess von Hohenthal,
daughter of Charles Frederic Anthony, Count Hohenthal, head of his
house and owner of large estates in Saxony, Prussia, and some of the
smaller German Duchies, and of the Countess Loida Emilie Neidhardt
von Gneisenau, youngest and favourite daughter of Field Marshal
Count Gneisenau, the future Lady Paget had had a Spartan and
romantic upbringing in a Saxon castle built by Henry the Fowler in the
ninth century. Orphaned at sixteen, she had become the ward of
Count Adolph von Hohenthal, then Saxon Minister in Berlin. In
1858, when the nineteen-year-old Ouida was scribbling away literally
for dear life, the nineteen-year-old Walpurga von Hohenthal came to
London to take up her duties as lady-in-waiting to the Princess Royal,
who was to marry Prince Frederick of Prussia. Invited to Windsor, the
young foreigner sat between Lord Palmerston and General Grey, who
had taken her in. "There was music the whole time and at the end a
Highlander came round with a bagpipe and walked twice round the
table, it made a horrid noise." Two years later she married Augustus
Paget, British Minister in Copenhagen. "I was married at the Legation
at Berlin. . . . All the Princes and Princesses of the Royal house were
present. The Princess Royal, tho' she was in mourning, insisted upon
giving the breakfast. I wore a dove-coloured moiré-antique dress to
go away in, with a most beautiful green Indian shawl given me by the
Queen, the first one of this colour she had ever given away, as they
were generally reserved for royalties, being much finer than those of
other colours. My white chip bonnet was trimmed with orange
flowers. My brother Maurice had lent us Hohenpriessnitz, where we
remained two weeks. We used to wander about the beautiful woods
and every now and then Mr. Paget went out to stalk a stag as he was
passionately devoted to sport." It was largely through a suggestion
made by young Walpurga Paget to the Prince Consort, while sitting
next to him at dinner, that the marriage between the Prince of Wales
and Princess Alexandra of Denmark was arranged. After six years in
Copenhagen, and a short stay in Portugal, the Pagets had been trans-
ferred to Rome, where Sir Augustus was now ambassador.

In addition to possessing great intelligence and force of character,

Lady Paget was extremely beautiful, with fine bones, auburn hair, green eyes, and something of the dramatic look that made Henry Irving's portrayals of noblemen more convincing than the genuine article. Like Madame de Lieven she disliked mediocrity but was always willing to make great allowances for royalty. Immediately impressed by Ouida, she subsequently showed her very great kindness; but her belief in the importance of class distinctions prevented her from thinking of the writer as her equal, and to this social barrier was added the physical one created by the fact that Lady Paget was an acknowledged beauty of the type most admired then, while Ouida—since the *jolie laide* had not yet been invented—had to depend on her wits for admiration. Lady Paget's ambivalent attitude towards Ouida probably resembled that later described by clever Mabel Dodge in her account of Lady Paget's reminiscences: "These books of hers are full of notes and observations that make us understand what a complex external life these people maintained under their inherited system—a burden of living at once pleasant and protected and privileged, yet burdened, irksome and limited, with everything from birth to death foreseen and accepted, and between all the actors in the pageant that it was, a sort of habitual tacit agreement never to mention or criticize their special fate, or the occasional unpleasant, upsetting accidents of nature . . . of all the Florentine figures of that time, she, I think, had the most perfect form: an exquisite crystallization. And of all the people I have known anywhere, she was most naturally a woman of the great world . . . she grew very affectionate with me, but always there was in her the unconscious certitude of my American outlandishness. There was always between us, the feeling that she took to one in spite of one's race, and she would even try to help me overcome it or make the best of it." In other words, the beautiful young woman was, potentially, a formidable old party.

It may have been an instinctive realization that this was so that intimidated Ouida when she went to see Lady Paget, who described their meeting in these terms: "The first time she came to see me I was lying on my sofa, ill and tired, whiling away my time by looking at the frescoes of the painted ceiling. When this little person was introduced, I rubbed my eyes with wonder. A frail diminutive creature stood before me, clad in trailing damask of black and pale blue. Long brown hair hung down her back, adding to the straightdownness of her appearance. A pair of large innocent, dark-blue eyes gazed earnestly at me and the smallest of gloved hands met mine. But oh! the rest was too fearful. . . . A harsh voice grated on my ear and my first thought was: 'What must not a woman suffer who, with such a thirst for beauty, has been treated thus by nature? Much ought to be forgiven her'. . . . I cannot join in the silly abuse of her books on the count of immorality, because she happens to call a spade a spade, but she never makes vice attractive. Her love of nature, and her sympathy for everything helpless and oppressed she clothes in beautiful and pathetic language. Her knowledge of the world was always nil, for an ungovernable imagination held the place in reality."

Another friend whom Ouida met for the first time during this Roman holiday was Ada Colonna, Duchess di Castiglione, then well known as a sculptress under the pseudonym "Marcello". Born in Switzerland, she was two years older than Ouida, and had made her debut as a sculptor in 1863, when she attracted a great deal of attention by her bust of Bianca Capello. Most of her work was eventually collected in Switzerland at the Fribourg Museum. With her Ouida had a great deal in common, and when she made the heroine of *Ariadne*—which is dedicated to Ada Colonna di Castiglione—a sculptress, it was to this friend that she turned for technical details.

Ouida's imagination might be ungovernable, but it was all she had with which to maintain a hold on reality for her mother and herself and, looking back at the semi-detached house in Bury St. Edmunds from the grandeur of a Roman palace, she must have had a beautiful feeling that everything was going her way.

XIII

BACK IN FLORENCE, Ouida began work on *Two Little Wooden Shoes*, a book suggested by her visit to Belgium. Written with simplicity, it tells the story of the short life of a Belgian girl who, after being abandoned as a baby in the countryside near Brussels, is adopted and raised by a kindly old peasant, whose death leaves her at the mercy of the first attractive stranger she meets. Like all Ouida's work, it is richly coloured by the strong visual imagination that prompted passages such as this slight but effective evocation of Waterloo:

She had always liked to sit out on the quaint wooden steps of the mill and under the red shadow of the sails, watching the swallows flutter to and fro in the sunset, and hearing the droll frogs croak in the rushes, while the old people told her tales of the time when in their babyhood they had run out, fearful yet fascinated, to see the beautiful Scots Greys flash by in the murky night and the endless line of guns and caissons crawl black as a snake through the summer dust, and the trampled corn, going out past the woods to Waterloo.

It also contains the lovely expression "King-haunted Fontainebleu"; and what to those who read Ouida in the hope of being shocked seemed particularly uncharacteristic lines: "there is little talk of love in the lives of the poor; they have no space for it; love to them means more mouths to feed, more wooden shoes to buy, more hands to dive into the meagre bag of coppers."

A small harmonious melodrama, *Two Little Wooden Shoes* was internationally successful, and later inspired the opera "Lodoletta" by Pietro Mascagni, a Leghorn baker's son who, in 1890, composed "Cavalleria Rusticana". Continued success fortified Ouida's determination to take a house in Florence, which she now considered her home; and this year she leased a villa at Scandicci belonging to the Marchese Farinola, grandson of the Marchese Gino Capponi, historian and Dante scholar.

Three miles south of Florence from the Porta San Frediano, Ouida's first Italian home was—and is—a big handsome four-storeyed ochre-coloured villa, part of it dating back to the eleventh century, with a roof of dusky red tiles, and two shapely flights of shallow stone steps curving up to the balustraded marble terrace in front of the door. Fine stables and servants' quarters went with the villa and, best of all from Ouida's point of view, there was a big wild garden full of bird-filled trees, of large exquisitely coloured butterflies, and of darting lizards. Throughout her fourteen years at the villa Farinola—which came to be called the villa Ramé, and is still so called by many of the peasants in the neighbourhood—Ouida delighted in this garden as lovely as any she had described in *Pascarel*:

The delights of an Italian garden are countless. It is not like any other garden in the world. It is at once more formal and more wild, at once greener with more abundant youth and venerable with more antique age. It has all Boccaccio between its walls, all Petrarca in its leaves, all Raffaelle in its skies. And then the sunshine that beggars words and laughs at painters!—the boundless, intense, delicious, heavenly light! What do other gardens know of that, save in the orange-groves of Granada and rose-thickets of Damascus?

The old broken marble statues, whence the water dripped and fed the water-lily; the great lemon trees in pots big enough to drown a boy, the golden globes among their emerald leaves; the magnolias, like trees cast in bronze, with all the spice of India in their cups; the spires of ivory bells that the yuccas put forth; the oleanders, taller than a man, red and white and blush colour; the broad velvet leaves of the flowering rush; the dark majestic ilex oaks, that made the noon like twilight; the countless graces of the vast family of acacias; the high box hedges, sweet and pungent in the sun; the stone ponds, where the goldfish slept through the sultry day; the wilderness of carnations; the huge roses, yellow, crimson, snow-white and the small noisette and the banksia with its million of pink stars; myrtles in dense thickets, and camellias like a wood of evergreens; cacti in all quaint shapes, like fossils astonished to find themselves again alive; high walls, vine-hung and topped by pines and cypresses; low walls with crowds of geraniums on their parapets, and the mountains and the fields beyond them; marble basins hidden in creepers where the frogs dozed all day long; sounds of convent bells and of chapel chimes; green lizards basking on the flags; great sheds and graneries beautiful with the clematis and the wisteria and the rosy trumpets of the bignonia; great wooden places cool and shady, with vast arched entrances, and scent of hay, and empty casks, and red earthen amphorae, and little mice scudding on the floors, and a sundial painted on the wall, and a crucifix set above the weathercock, and through the huge unglazed windows sight of the green vines with the bullocks in the harvest carts beneath them, or of some hilly sunlit road with a mule-team coming down it, or of a blue high hill with its pine-trees black against the sky, and on its slopes the yellow corn and misty olive.

The view from the Farinola is superb. The land in front of the house slopes steeply down to a high stone wall enclosing the villa and its little hill, and beyond can be seen mountains coloured blue by distance, small village-topped hills encircled by vineyards, and olive groves which look like a silvery inland sea when the wind turns the under-sides of their stiff leaves toward the sunlight. From Ouida's viewpoint, not the least of this villa's advantages was its being within a short walking distance of Castagnuolo, the della Stufa estate. It was of Castagnuolo—ancient and deserted-looking outside, but with admirably proportioned rooms connected by open arches and filled with flowers and objects of art—that Ouida thought when writing in *Pascarel*:

The villa was high upon the mountain side—vast, dusky, crumbling, desolate without, as all such places are, and within full of that nameless charm of freedom, space, antiquity, and stillness, that does no less perpetually belong to them.

Where these old villas stand on their pale olive slopes, those who are strange to them see only the peeling plaster, the discoloured stone, the desolate courts, the grass-grown flags, the broken stautes, the straying vines, the look of loneliness and decay.

But those who know them well love them and learn otherwise; learn the infinite charm of those vast silent halls, of those endless echoing corridors and cloisters, and of those wide wind-swept, sun-bathed chambers, of those shadowy loggie, where the rose glow of the oleander burns in the dimness of the arches; of those immense windows wreathed with sculpture and filled with the glistening silver of the olive woods and mountain snows, and limitless horizons; of those great breadths of sunlight, of these white wide courts, of those tangled gardens, of those breezy open doors, of those wild rose trees climbing high about the Aetrurian torso, of those clear waters falling through acanthus leaves, into their huge red conche; of that sense of infinite freedom, of infinite solitude, of infinite light and stillness and calm.

Having chosen her house, Ouida rapidly set about buying furniture and engaging servants; and it was not long before the Farinola looked as described five years later by a visiting journalist, Edmund Yates, son of the actor-manager Frederick Henry Yates, and himself a popular novelist and editor of several periodicals including Temple Bar, Tinsleys, and The World. (While writing for The World he was sentenced to two months in prison for libelling Lord Lonsdale.) After describing the country around Ouida's villa, Yates wrote:

"Passing from the terrace into the vestibule, filled with palms and plants and statues, and having the busts of the old Nerlé in niches in its walls, you look into an immense banqueting-hall, now furnished as a billiard-room. It is carried up the whole height of the villa, and round it runs a gallery communicating with the rooms of the upper storey. Out of this lofty salle, big enough to hold a dozen London houses, opens the ballroom, a lovely room, with pale green walls enriched by white bas-reliefs, and looking on the upper garden. On the left of the vestibule opens what is called the miniature-room from the numbers of old miniatures hanging on its walls, in keeping with the old cabinets, the old china, the metal work, the bric-à-brac of all kinds collected by Ouida in her five years' residence in Italy. . . . Above the windows are two great golden eagles that belonged to Napoleon I; the furniture is all Louis XV. On the right of the entrance hall is another room where Ouida writes in winter mornings at a Venetian writing-table of *cinquecento* work that would enrapture the souls of the *virtuosi* who haunt Christie's; here also are quantities of plants, several of Ouida's own oil-paintings, and plenty of bric-à-brac and many books, chiefly on art and history. The peculiarity of all the rooms is the abundance of flowers everywhere, for Ouida loves them and understands them, and is her own head-gardener. Out of this room is the dining-room, brown and gold and pale blue, with more old china and more flowers. . . . Everywhere these rooms are lofty, and have the arched and vaulted ceilings of medieval architecture. Underneath are the chapel—the sacristy with a fine della Robbia. . . . Outside lie the stables, screened by tall oleanders and arbutus; and the wide wood *stanzone*, where there is perpetually the smell of hay and herbs."

Today the villa Farinola has an abandoned look. Its owners being absent, a bailiff is in charge, and the house is lived in—"occupato ma non habitato"—by eleven peasant families, whose washing provides the sunlit façade with festoons of white flags. The banqueting hall, converted by the Marchese Farinòla into a billiard-room, now shelters ladders, bicycles, rakes, spades, pails, flower-pots, an ancient and elaborate bird-cage, and twists of bast which look like beards left over from a rustic carnival and attract inquisitive pecks from the small chickens who, now and again, dart in to find out whether the cool vast dusky room contains anything better than what they can find in the brilliant sunshine outside. Many of the trees that once provided scent and shade for nightingales are gone now; but the view is as it was in the days when one of the peasants who worked in Ouida's garden asked for a holiday in order to visit his home and explained—pointing at a Piero della Francesca hill clearly visible from the Farinola—that "he was homesick for his own country". Nor are the stables much altered since the days when they lodged Ouida's fast Maremma ponies, Mascherino and Birichino, her Victoria upholstered in oyster grey or dull gold satin, and the white ponies and white-satin-upholstered carriage used on particularly ceremonious occasions.

Charming old Miss Baxter, a Florentine resident who is the grand-daughter of the Dorset poet William Barnes, can remember (1957) her father, who during Ouida's time was a partner in Roberts' the English Chemists, describing the impression of prodigality created as Ouida drove across the beautiful Santa Trinita bridge (destroyed during the

last war and now being rebuilt) and up the fashionable Via Tornabuoni
to pick the Marchese della Stufa up outside the Unione Club, a most
daring thing for an unmarried woman to do then. The fact that the
club's façade was a very sober one made Ouida's ultra-fashionable
Worth clothes particularly noticeable as she sat there, waiting with
unconcealed eagerness.

Founded in 1852, this club was, and is, composed mainly of members
of the nobility—and the presence of a woman anywhere across its
threshold, except in the waiting-room set aside for this purpose, arouses
in its footmen a well-bred consternation expressed by a barely per-
ceptible raising of the eyebrows, a definite lowering of the voice.
Within these precincts a fragment of the nineteenth century still exists,
like a well-honeyed bee in dusky amber; and the club's handsome and
massive photograph album contains likeness after likeness of members
with looks as romantic as their titles, the military ones being every inch
as superb as Ouida's guardsmen of the *First Life*. Towards the end of
the album is the photograph of a magnificent-looking dark-eyed
young man in uniform; on asking which prince was this I was told,
without emphasis, "our present king".

Although her coachman and groom also served her as butler and
footman, Ouida's new way of living cost a great deal, particularly
after she started receiving every Monday from three to six. People
flocked to her house, often without being invited and, as Ouida once
remarked in a moment of revolt against the heartlessness of the nineteenth-century version of café society, the main difference between
Jumbo at the zoo and Ouida at home was that people visited him in
order to give buns and her in order to receive them—and receive buns
they did, since Doneys kept Ouida's receptions abundantly supplied
with tea, wine, and delicious pastries and sandwiches.

Fortunately she was earning a great deal. *Under Two Flags* went into
sixty-three editions in English; and she managed her foreign rights
herself, all her books selling extremely well in France, Italy, America,
Germany, and several other countries from which records are not now
obtainable here. Almost as extravagant as she was generous, and she
was extravagantly generous, Ouida believed that "money must be
spent" and acted accordingly—just as she bought liver and beef for
her dogs on the grounds that "people can't expect to keep dogs for
nothing". Ouida always acted according to her beliefs, and never
expected anything for nothing.

XIV

ENTIRELY AS THE result of her own work, the hostess at the villa Farinola was at last living a life as romantic as any in her novels. The child of eleven had been forced away from "dear Beautiful France", but the writer of thirty-five could take root in her Italian home: could at last forget the dread of insecurity aroused by her father's truancies, and responsible for what would now be called the chip on her shoulder, and which Henry James called her "uppityness". Free to appreciate her sweetheart, spoil her mother, pet her increasing number of dogs, and dazzle new acquaintances by her sharp tongue, soft heart, and ostentatious hospitality, she nevertheless continued to work as hard as ever she had done in London, when her writing was all that stood between poverty and her mother, her grandmother, and herself.

The surroundings in which she worked were ideal: in summer in the open air or in "the garden room", in winter at her cinquecento table, in front of an open fire and a reproduction of Canova's Love and Psyche. She had never enjoyed the daily struggle with words as much as she did now that della Stufa's proximity infused a sense of delight into all she did, just as central heating warms an entire house. It was a place rather than a person that gave the impetus to her new book: but a place, as she couldn't resist mentioning, near the "Villa of the della Stufa who nigh a thousand years before had come over the mountains, Christian Knights and gallant gentlemen, with their red cross and their tawny lions on their shields".

About a mile and a half from the Farinola is a village called Lastra a Signa, surrounded by machicolated medieval walls and three gateways. Many of its inhabitants had never been to Florence, and most of the women worked at plaiting straw for hats. Even now, when an advertisement-scarred main road runs besides its war-damaged ramparts, Signa has considerable charm, with its dim arched-over stone passage-ways leading to tiny gardens; its smell of sun-soaked stone, home-made bread and wood fires; the church, sober within, tinselled without, where children play in the aisles while old women in black lace mantillas pray, beside young girls in brightly coloured orlon sweaters, to a Madonna smiling sweetly down at the rings on her fingers.

The days of its glory are done. It is a gray quiet place which now strays down by the water and now climbs high on the hill, and faces the full dawn of the day and sees the sunset reflected in the mirror of the river, and is starry with fire-flies in midsummer and at noon looks drowsy in the heat and seems to dream—being so very old. The buttressed walls are ruins. The mass-bell swings over the tower roofs. The fortresses are changed to farms. The vines climb where the culverins blazed. White bullocks and belled mules tread to and fro the tracks which the freelances made; and the peasants sing at their ploughs where the hosts of the invaders once thundered.

The hero of Ouida's new novel, the illegitimate son of a village girl by a visiting French artist who quickly abandons her, is called Signa after his mother's birthplace, and gives this name to the book. The plot of *Signa* is melodramatic, but will not seem unrealistic to anyone moderately familiar with police-court news. After his mother's death, the baby Signa is adopted by his uncle Bruno, who, being a bachelor, pays his married brother, Lippo, to raise the child. But unlike Bruno, whose rough ways conceal an excellent heart, Lippo is a suave hypocrite bent on social climbing. He and his wife ill-treat their nephew, who runs away accompanied by his friend Gemma, a pretty little girl who is an instinctive gold-digger. When the hungry children reach a nearby village, Signa, who is unusually musical, plays his fiddle, and Gemma dances, to earn a meal. This attracts the attention of a child-snatcher—these, like dog-snatchers, were real and commonplace figures of the period—who entices them into his company so that he can ship them abroad. Signa is rescued just in time by Bruno, who has at last learnt the truth about Lippo's treatment of the boy; but Gemma, being precociously disgusted by village life, deliberately runs away with the child-snatcher. Bruno quarrels with Lippo and takes Signa to live with him. He adores his nephew and slaves so as to be able to buy land for him. But Signa cares only for music, so Bruno eventually decides—after many struggles with himself and bitter words with the boy—to sell the land so painfully acquired, and devote the money to paying for the production of Signa's first opera. This proves successful, but Signa's subsequent absences abroad separate him increasingly from his uncle:

To those who have traversed far seas and many lands, and who can bridge untravelled countries by the aid of experience and of understanding, such partings have pain, but a pain lessened by the certain knowledge of their span and purpose. By the light of remembrance or of imagination they can follow that which leaves them. But Bruno had no such solace. To him all that was indefinite was evil; all that was unfamiliar was horrible.

An extremely simple young man, apart from his talent, Signa swings uneasily between the country tastes of his boyhood and the troubling new ones of the people now bent on spoiling him. Still unused to success, he meets Gemma, now a great beauty and a famous demi-mondaine. The latter fact is not immediately apparent to him, but when it becomes so the uncompromising quality that helped him become a composer despite his longing to please Bruno, makes Signa turn from Gemma. Accustomed to having her own way, she determines he shall fall in love with her; and when he does so she delights in arousing his jealousy—and eventually drives him to suicide, whereupon the heartbroken Bruno murders her.

Ouida's own feeling for all she was now seeing shows in passages such as this description of Signa's first visit to the Spanish Chapel in the cloisters of Santa Maria Novella in Florence:

> It is all so simple and so foolish there; the warhorses of Taddeo that bear their lords to eternity as to a joust of arms; the heretic dogs of Memmi, with their tight wooden collars; the beauteous Fiammetta and her lover, thronging among the saints; the little house, where the Holy Ghost is sitting, with the purified saints listening at the door with strings tied to their heads to lift them into paradise; it is all so quaint, so childlike, so pathetic, so grotesque,—like a set of wooden figures from its Noah's Ark that a dying child has set out on its little bed, and that are so stiff and ludicrous, and yet which no one well can look at and be unmoved, by reason of the little cold hand that has found beauty in them. As the dying child to the wooden figures, so the dead faith gives to the old frescoes here something that lies too deep for tears; we smile, and yet all the while we say:—if only we could believe like this; if only for us the dead could be but sleeping!

Much of *Signa* is still moving on account of Ouida's deep feeling for Italy and her understanding of children. Whenever she attempts to describe events from a child's viewpoint she is as successful, in a very different way, as the fine American writer J. D. Salinger. Like many very definite persons with a zest for simplifying issues, Ouida had a childlike side to her, though neither her forceful looks nor her vehement intelligence suggested this to superficial observers. In the margin of a page from a proof copy of *Pascarel* that she gave to della Stufa, and which is still at Castagnuolo, she has scribbled in French: "be gentle with me because I am half a child and shall always be so where you are concerned." The poignancy of this faded fragment of long-lost intimacy is increased by the fact that the handwriting, though bold and striking, is much less emphatic than it became after her break with the Marchese.

Her love of animals and her understanding of children brought her several enriching friendships at this time. Soon after her installation at the Villa Farinola, a peasant arrived with a Newfoundland puppy, saying that he must sell it as he could no longer afford to feed it—this gambit was frequently employed by peasants around Ouida, and never failed, even after she had learnt to see through it. The dog was named Fido and had a particularly expansive and loving nature. Before long both Ouida and her mother adored it. But a year later the Cavaliere Tassinari, formerly Grand Chamberlain to the Duke of Tuscany, was walking by the Farinola, heard Fido bark, recognized the dog as one stolen from himself the previous year, and came to claim him. Ouida implored the Tassinaris to let her keep Fido, and the Cavaliere's wife was so touched by Madame Ramé's distress that she persuaded her husband to give way. One of the results of which was Ouida's taking an interest in the Tassinaris' little grandson, Herbert Danyell, whom she often invited to spend the day at the Villa Farinola. She wrote several stories for him, including *The Little Earl*, a forerunner of "Little Lord Fauntleroy", and the enchanting *The Nurnberg Stove*, and taught him consideration for animals, writing to him on one occasion:

"My dear Bertie,
    Don't think I do not like you because I want to see you gentler to animals. You are a bright and clever boy, and ought to understand that animals being so entirely in our power, all unkind use of our strength over them is both mean and unworthy. Try and remember that. Real manliness is always indulgent and never tyrannical. Perhaps long after I am dead you will show this to your children and say, This is what I was told by—
                                                Ouida"

Ouida's feelings were particularly inflamed when the Pope announced that the Holy See could not approve the formation of a society to prevent cruelty to animals, as this would be founded on a theological error, "to wit, that Christians owe any duty to animals".

That Bertie Danyell didn't resent Ouida's advice is shown by his having kept this letter and added: "To Ouida I owe the joy of knowing that there is no such thing as loneliness as long as there are woods and moors and rivers and mountain brooks." To Ouida he also owed his first ride on horseback, in her garden—and the encouraging assurance, when he had to abandon sailor suits for long trousers, that he was not too big for her to continue buying him candy.

Another boy, the Visconde George de Sarmento, admired Ouida so much that when he came to Italy he begged his mother to take him to see "the Magician". There is a Ronald Firbank note about the scene in which the sophisticated small boy eagerly told Ouida all that her books meant to him—and, like many Ronald Firbank scenes, this one contained genuine feelings as well as butterfly colours. For the boy's admiration for Ouida lasted and, as an adult, he became a close friend, to whom she wrote four times a month throughout the last years of her life; and his novel, "A Love Dream", published over the pseudonym George Vane five years after Ouida's death, was set in Hardwick House —in the grounds of which the crinolined child Ouida had wandered, like a miniature Traviata, dreaming obstinately of love and art.

But death seemed very far away to her now, when the affection of children was merely one of many of her life's well-earned pleasures. Above all, her relationship with della Stufa had never given her greater happiness than now, after four years' close friendship; and so far he had neither said nor done anything to dissuade her from the belief that he wanted to marry her. As to whether they were lovers physically, there is now no proof. Ouida's character makes this seem improbable; but the fact that they were unmarried and had two large houses at their disposition, makes it seem possible. Either way, Ouida's feelings could not have been stronger. She loved him as she loved no one else and she had a passionately loving nature.

The situation was not an easy one for della Stufa to face. An honest man, he realized that no matter how eager an unmarried woman without powerful relatives is for a man's company, she cannot obtain it entirely against his will—and it was entirely of his own free will that he had spent so much of the past four years in Ouida's company. Whatever the sentiment, of curiosity, gratified vanity, or pure idleness, that had drawn him to her in the first place, he was now devoted to her; and it is possible that he found her character as absorbing as his mistress's beauty. But even had Mrs. Ross ceased to charm him, it would have been difficult for him to put a stop to this love affair, since he was recognized in the society they both frequented as Mrs. Ross' *cavaliere servente* and, by this time, many of her interests were closely intertwined with his own. Nor would Mrs. Ross have been likely to accept dismissal mildly; both she and Ouida were in some respects more virile than the very gentle man they loved.

It was partly a case of how happy I could be with either, were t'other dear charmer away—and della Stufa is not the first man of estimable character whose anxiety to cause no one pain has resulted in his hurting everyone concerned, including himself.

XV

MORE DETERMINED THAN ever to be a bread, butter, and jam winner, since she now had not only her mother's and her own future to consider but that of her potential husband and his financially burdensome estate, Ouida followed *Signa* by *In a Winter City*, a novel of Florentine high society with a heroine inspired by Lady Paget and a hero by della Stufa.

It is difficult for present-day readers to believe in the authenticity of *In a Winter City*'s beautiful Lady Hilda Vorarberg, but not more so than in that of the reality she so faithfully represents. A paragraph from Lady Paget's "Embassies of Other Days" may clarify this: "There is one thing I am very grateful for to my father, and that is that when I made excursions of a few days with him, he insisted I should learn to do without my maid. I had a mass of hair, and to do this properly was my difficulty; but I surmounted it and have ever after been quite independent of maids. Even when I go to Court, I can put on my tiara and diamonds without help, and this accomplishment, and being so entirely at ease in four languages, have been more useful to me in my daily life than anything else." Ladies who found an ability to put on tiaras and diamonds unaided one of their greatest props in daily life may seem unreal now, but they existed.

Married in her teens to an elderly capitalist who paid her father's debts and had the good taste to fall ill on his wedding day and promptly die, the rich but far from merry widow, Lady Hilda, comes to winter in Floralia. Although she is provided with beauty, money, and distinguished ancestors, Lady Hilda is described with, now and again, a suggestion of irony that may account for Lady Paget's occasional acerbity on the subject of Ouida:

The Lady Hilda sighed. This dreadful age, which has produced communists, petroleuses, and liberal thinkers, had communicated its vague restlessness even to her; although she belonged to that higher region where nobody ever thinks at all, and everybody is more or less devout in seeming at any rate, because disbelief is vulgar, and religion is an "affaire des moeurs", like decency, still the subtle philosophies and sad negations which have always been afloat in the air since Voltaire set them flying, had affected her slightly. She was a true believer, just as she was a well-dressed woman, and had her creeds just as she had her bath in the morning, as a matter of course. Still, when she came to think of it, she was not so very sure.

That is not the way in which the U like being discussed by the non-U. Nor was the description of Madame Mila, Lady Hilda's frivolous cousin, designed to please her friends and relatives:

She was always in debt, though she admitted that her husband allowed her liberally. She had eighty thousand francs a year by her settlements to spend on herself, and he gave her another fifty thousand to do as she pleased with: on the whole about one half what he allowed Blanche Souris, of the Chateau Gaillard theatre.

She had six children, three were living and three were dead; she thought herself a good mother, because she gave her wet-nurse ever so many silk gowns, and when she wanted the children for a fancy-dress ball or a drive, always saw that they were faultlessly dressed, and besides she always took them to Trouville.

She had never had any grief in her life, except the loss of the Second Empire, and even that she got over when she found that flying the Red Cross flag had saved her hotel, without so much as a teacup being broken in it, that M. M. Worth and Offenbach were safe from all bullets, and that society, under the Septennate, promised to be every bit as *leste* as under the Empire.

Despite her inability to feel deeply, Madame Mila is constantly chattering about love, which greatly annoys Lady Hilda, who replies with a speech that may have warned Mrs. Ross that Ouida was no likelier than herself to yield without a fight:

"In love!" she echoed, with less languor and more of impetuosity than she had ever displayed, "are you ever in love, any of you, ever?

You have senses and vanity and an inordinate fear of not being in the fashion—and so you take your lovers as you drink back your stimulants and wear your wigs and tie your skirts back—because everybody does it, and not to do so is to be odd, or prudish, or something you would hate to be called. Love! it is an unknown thing to you all. You have a sort of miserable hectic passion, perhaps, that is a drug you take as you take chlorodyne—just to excite you and make your faded nerves a little alive again, and yet you are such cowards that you have not even the courage of passion, but label your drug Friendship, and beg society to observe that you only keep it for family uses like arnica or like glycerine. You want notoriety; you want to indulge your fancies, and yet keep your place in the world. You like to drag a young man about by a chain, as if he were the dancing monkey that you depended on for subsistence. You like other women to see that you are not too passée to be every whit as improper as if you were twenty. You like to advertise your successes as it were with drum and trumpet, because if you did not, people might begin to doubt that you had any. You like all that, and you like to feel there is nothing you do not know and no length you have not gone, and so you ring all the changes on all the varieties of intrigue and sensuality, and go over the gamut of sickly sentiment and nauseous license as an orchestra tunes its strings up every night! That is what you people call love; I am content enough to have no knowledge of it.

Despite this speech, and despite the fact that Lady Hilda is reputed to be as cold as she is beautiful—she is known to have recently refused the Prince of Deutschland—she unwillingly falls in love with Prince Paolo della Rocca. This is Ouida's first full-length portrait of della Stufa, and its realism confirms the notion that he was the first and last man she loved with a maturity of feeling that could have helped make their marriage a happy one.

When Prince Paolo first meets Lady Hilda, his friends suggest that he marry her for her money. There is nothing disreputable or cynical about this suggestion. He belongs to a class to whom personal inclination seems neither the chief, nor the best, motive for marriage; he is noble but poor. Lady Hilda is noble, so will not dishonour his family, and her money will enable him to carry on the traditions for which he has always been ready to sacrifice his pleasures. But when he finds himself falling in love with her he withdraws, and only discloses his feelings after hearing from her brother, Lord Clairvaux, that if she marries again she will lose her fortune and be faced with poverty—in the shape of the family jewels, eight hundred a year, and a house in Paris. By this time Lady Hilda too is in love but, unable to face giving up her worldly life, refuses him. Disgusted by her frivolity, Paolo departs for Sicily and an attempt to catch a famous bandit who has been murdering the peasants on his estate there.

Anyone who thinks, as did many of the critics with whom Ouida then had to reckon, that this version of big-game shooting is incredible, should read Gavin Maxwell's "God Protect Me From My Friends", an enthralling account of the life and times of Salvatore Giuliano, the beautiful young Sicilian bandit who was killed in 1950, at the age of twenty, in circumstances as mysterious as those of such Elizabethan plays as "The White Devil".

Although successful in his enterprise—thereby becoming a national hero—Paolo catches marsh fever in Sicily and is brought back in what is wrongly thought to be a dying condition. This makes Lady Hilda understand the strength of her love for him, and their reconciliation is swiftly followed by their marriage.

It was Ouida's power to conjure up the atmosphere in which such people lived that prompted Carl Van Vechten to write, in 1923, in his zestful introduction to an American reprint of *In a Winter City*: "Rare flowers, priceless jewels, orphic baubles, elaborate toilets, and exotic foods are carted past the eye until the vision is surfeited, but it is only for the purpose, Ouida almost convinces herself, of showing the reader how empty is the life of the very rich. She has not convinced one reader. Ouida wrote of a life she would have liked to grace, she catalogued jewels she wanted to wear, she described men she desired to embrace. Nor was this merely the unintelligent envy of an outsider. She was enough on the inside to observe the objects of her envious attention at close range and she has set down their existence with an idealization of its power and fascination which, even when she most moralizes over its fatal rottenness, has almost decided me that the life of the idle English is the life for me." In other words she could always, even at her most absurd, dazzle the reader into the willing suspension of disbelief.

But during one of the many hours Ouida was obliged to reserve for work, Augustus Hare was noting in his journal: "I am writing from the old country place of the Lotteria Lotharingo della Stufa. It is reached by driving from Florence through the low vineyarded country for five miles. Then, on the left, under the hills, one sees what looks like a great old barrack, grimy, mossy, and deserted. This is the villa. All outside is decay, but when you enter, there are charming old halls and chambers, connected by open arches, and filled with pictures, china, books, and beautiful old carved furniture. A terrace, lined with immense vases of lilies and tulips, opens on a garden with vine-shaded pergolas and huge orange trees in tubs; and beyond are the wooded hills. The presiding genius of the place is Mrs. Ross (Janet Duff Gordon), who has redeemed lands, planted vineyards, introduced new plans for pressing the grapes—whose heart and soul are in the work here."

Incapable herself of loving other than definitely and single-mindedly, Ouida did not at first grasp the fact that these meritorious agricultural efforts threatened her own future. But, at last, gossip managed to get past the barrier that, like most busy people, she erected against time-wasters—and so not only her time but her feelings were laid waste, and she was forced to realize that, where the man she loved was concerned, she was more than half a child.

XVI

SOON THERE WAS open enmity between Ouida and Mrs. Ross, each fiercely resenting what she considered the other's preposterous tendency to behave as if della Stufa were her property. Mrs. Ross felt, with justification, that she had the prior claim; Ouida felt, with equal justification, that a married woman, with no intention of procuring a divorce, deserved blame for preventing a man from marrying someone else with whom he could be happy. Both were women of strong character, Mrs. Ross the more domineering, Ouida the more impassioned; but the fact that respect for class was considerable in this little world, several of whose most ostentatiously respectable members found it wise to live abroad, provided Mrs. Ross with a distinct advantage over Ouida. Whether or not she had a lover, a well-born woman who "lived with her husband" must be "received": Queen Victoria had said so, and so had Lady Paget.

In so small a circle as that in which both women moved in Florence, there were plenty of idle or malicious people to repeat Mademoiselle de la Ramé's words to Mrs. Ross ("really *most* exaggerated, though I'm *devoted* to her, as you *know*"), and those of Mrs. Ross to Mademoiselle de la Ramé ("it was the *tone* in which she said it, though I'm the *last* person to make trouble, as you *know*"). As a result the behaviour of the unfortunate trio soon provided the equivalent of free bread and circuses. Intimate and loyal friends took sides, but society as a whole, unkind as most groups of not individually unkind persons usually are, gossiped and, through sheer vacuity of mind, did all it could to exacerbate matters.

That Ouida understood as well as idolised della Stufa is shown by a paper in her handwriting that belongs to the present Marchese della Stufa. In this she describes her Marchese first as he was in relation to Mrs. Ross, then as she believed he could be if free to develop his best qualities. In the first account he is described as cultured, charming, witty, good-hearted to the point of weakness, a poor judge of character, and a man whose indulgent attitude toward others' faults makes him appear weaker than he is, weakness being the quality most encouraged in him by his entourage. In the second account, Ouida stresses his feeling not only for art and science, but for his fellow creatures, and the unusual capacity for goodness which would enable him to accomplish great things if it were encouraged. It is clear he was an unusual as well as an unusually attractive man, and the worst part of Ouida's misery came from knowing she had loved and lost someone with precisely the qualities for which she yearned.

But a long time was to elapse before she admitted to herself that she had lost him. There was a good deal of the boy who stood on the burning deck in her, and she would have been overjoyed if all but she had fled. So when, in February, 1877, Mrs. Ross made a business trip to England, and della Stufa was again on duty in Rome, Ouida followed him there. Her mother, who watched all this with anguish, gently pointed out the folly of appearing to be running after him; but Ouida told Baron Tauchnitz that she needed to go to Rome to check certain details for her new novel *Ariadne*, and she probably convinced herself that her journey was really necessary.

Whatever her reasons for being in Rome, Ouida did not neglect *Ariadne*. Her feeling for places was strong and fine and inspiring, and many a Victorian was drawn to Italy by her novels, thereby acquiring a source of lasting happiness. She suffered with her eyes open, and could therefore still write:

There can be hardly any life more lovely upon earth than that of a young student of art in Rome. With the morning, to rise to the sound of countless bells and of innumerable streams, and see the silver lines of the snow new fallen on the mountains against the deep rose of the dawn, and the shadows of the night steal away softly from off the city, releasing, one by one, dome and spire, and cupola

and roof, till all the wide white wonder of the place discloses itself
under the broad brightness of full day; to go down into the dark
cool streets with pigeons fluttering in the fountains, and the sounds
of the morning chants coming from many a church door and
convent window, and little scholars and singing children going by
with white clothes on, or scarlet robes, as though walking forth
from the canvas of Botticelli or Garafalo; to eat frugally, sitting close
by some shop of flowers and birds, and watching all the while the
humours and the pageants of the streets by quaint corners, rich with
sculptures of the Renaissance, and spanned by arches of architects
that builded for Agrippa, under grated windows with arms of
Frangipanni or Colonna, and pillars that Apollodorus raised; to go
into the great courts of palaces, murmurous with the fall of water,
and fresh with green leaves and golden fruit, that rob the colossal
statues of their gloom and gauntness, and thence into the vast
chambers where the greatest dreams that men have ever had, are
written on panel and on canvas, and the immensity and the silence
of them all are beautiful and eloquent with dead man's legacies to
the living, where the hours and the seasons frolic beside the Maries
at the Sepulchre, and Adonis bares his lovely limbs, in nowise
ashamed because S. Jerome and S. Mark are there; to study and
muse, and wonder and be still, and be full of the peace which passes
all understanding, because the earth is lovely as Adonis is, and life is
yet unspent; to come out of the sacred light, half golden, and half
dusky, and full of many blended colours, where the marbles
and the pictures live, sole dwellers in the deserted dwellings of
princes; to come out where the oranges are all aglow in the sunshine,
and the red camellias are pushing against the hoary head of the old
stone Hermes, and go down the width of the mighty steps into the
gay piazza, alive with bells tolling, and crowds laughing, and drums
abeat, and the flutter of carnival banners in the wind; and to get
away from it all with a full heart, and ascend to see the sun set from
the terrace of the Medici, or the Pamfili, or the Borghese woods,
and watch the flame-like clouds stream homewards behind S.
Peter's, and the pines of Monte Mario grow black against the west,
till the pale green of evening spreads itself above them, and the
stars arise; and then, with a prayer—be your faith what it will—a
prayer to the Unknown God, to go down again through the violet-
scented air and the dreamful twilight, and so, with unspeakable
thankfulness, simply because you live, and this is Rome—so home-
ward.

Nor was her view of Rome sentimental. When Ariadne is dis-illusioned by her first sight of the slums, the old cobbler says:

The place is filthy and the people are cruel, and you may well be startled. But do not think that it is all as bad as this. Oh no, Rome is still beautiful; so you will say when you know it well; and the past is all about you in it—only you must have patience. It is like an intaglio that has been lying in the sand for a score of centuries. You must rub the dust away—then the fine and noble lines of the classic face show dearly still. You thought to see Augustan Rome? I know! And your heart aches because of the squalor and the decay and the endless loss everywhere that never will be made up to the world, let the ages come and go as they may, and cities rise and fall. But you must have patience. Rome will not give her secrets up at the first glance. Only wait a little while and see the moon shine on it all in a night or two, and you will learn to love her better in her colossal ruin than ever you have loved the marble and the ivory city of your dreams. For there is nothing mean or narrow here: the vaults, the domes, the stairs, the courts, the waters, the hills, the plains, the sculpture, the very light itself, they are all wide and vast and noble, and man himself dilates in them, gains stature and soul as it were, one scarce knows how, and someway looks nearer to God in Rome than ever he looks elsewhere.

Remembering the happiness of her first visit to Rome, Ouida found it difficult to concentrate on her work. Fragments of her own problems kept forcing their way through the fabric of *Ariadne*, which concerns Goia, a young Italian orphan whose Jewish mother died when she was born, and whose father, a mediocre sculptor, died recently. Goia comes to Rome to find her grandfather. Repudiated by this crotchety old man, she is befriended by Crispin, a kindly old cobbler of unusual character, who notices her resemblance to the Borghese statue of Ariadne, and tries to help her sell the little figures she carves. Impressed by her gifts, Crispin introduces her to his friend Maryx, a sculptor from Provence. The latter undertakes to teach her, and soon falls deeply in love with her. Unfortunately, she then meets Maryx's friend Hilarion, a poet of fickle temperament and noble birth, falls madly in love with him, and becomes his mistress—Ariadne is, incidentally, the only one of Ouida's heroines to become the mistress of the man she loves. When Hilarion deserts Ariadne she pines, and Maryx provokes a duel, but, having promised Ariadne not to injure her lover, fires into the air, and is killed himself. Belatedly realizing Ariadne's worth, Hilarion rushes to Rome—and finds her dying.

This story of a woman who dies for love was published three years after Charles Reade's "A Woman Hater", a novel in which a woman doctor made her first appearance in fiction. European and American women were fighting to obtain the same professional opportunities as men, and for many of them work was presently to provide some of the satisfaction hitherto obtainable only from marriage.

Although Hilarion is not in the least like della Stufa, nor meant to be, he sometimes behaves in a manner that must have made della Stufa hope Mrs. Ross would not read *Ariadne* attentively. For example:

He went to his duchess whom he more than half hated; yet with whom he would not break his unholy relation, because she had that flame in her eyes, and that flint in her heart, at which men whose passions are worn out are glad to strive to rekindle them.

It was Ouida's misfortune, as well as one of the forms courage took in her, that she always tried to defy misery by an overweening manner. In consequence she arrived in Rome prepared to fight—with everyone but della Stufa—and determined not to let herself be unnerved by the sight of beautiful places first seen with him. But there proved to be no need to fight. Romans cared little for the verdict of Florentine society, and her fame brought her more invitations than she could accept. Anxious to be at her best, she pleased or interested most of those she met—and, almost everywhere, della Stufa was a fellow guest. The royal family admired her and, when the relationship between Ouida and della Stufa was mentioned to him, the King suggested that his gentleman-in-waiting would do wisely if he married her.

Probably della Stufa was less influenced by Ouida's success in Rome, or even by the King's attitude, than by the fact that Mrs. Ross was absent and Ouida very much present. Whatever the reason—love, good nature, the inability to come to a decision, or a mixture of all three—he soon began escorting Ouida around Rome as assiduously as ever he had done during her visit there three years ago; and this time a far more sophisticated woman than Ouida would have been justified in supposing his unconcealed attentiveness meant more than ordinary friendliness.

When she dragged herself away in order to go home and finish *Ariadne*, which she had promised her publisher for April, Ouida did so believing that the proceeds of this would be devoted to her husband's house. So she parted from della Stufa happily. He was obliged to remain at the Quirinal, but he wrote to her regularly, and his letters did nothing to discourage her belief that when he returned to Florence it would be to marry her. These were her last weeks of complete happiness, and it was in *Ariadne* that she wrote: "Who can once have laughed in the light of Italy, and not feel the world dark elsewhere ever afterwards?"

XVII

THE MANUSCRIPT OF *Ariadne* despatched, Ouida was free to resume social life, which she did exuberantly, making no secret of the eagerness with which she was expecting della Stufa's return. The fact that her private life at last seemed to her settled, liberated the energy she so often devoted to reacting to public events—although few of these, just then, were of a nature to promote optimism.

In London the liberals had just met to congratulate William I and Bismarck on their strong action against the Roman Catholic church; in Spain the Bourbons were restored to the throne, and in Italy the papal bull *Non Expedit* forbade Italians to take part in politics; Queen Victoria was proclaimed Empress of India, and a revolt against Turkey spread from Herzegovina to Bosnia, Montenegro, Serbia, and Bulgaria, and was terminated by a massacre of the rebels; the Albert Memorial was finished, roller-skating became fashionable, and *Galignani's Messenger*, giving the final report on the oddly-named Committee of Pardons set up in Paris after the Commune, stated that the Paris Courts-Martial and Assizes had convicted 9,537 persons implicated in the 1871 rising: 70 to seclusion, 94 to hard labour for life, 110 to death, 117 to police supervision, 179 to hard labour for a term, 333 to banishment, 1,197 to transportation to a fortress, 1,321 to detention, 2,670 to imprisonment in a house of correction, and 3,446 to simple transportation.

It is unlikely that Louis Ramé was among these unfortunates, but possible—and Ouida was sufficiently accustomed to the unlikeliest possibilities becoming facts in her life for this one to upset her, dragging with it, as water drags seaweed, tangled memories of unreciprocated emotions and unsatisfied longings. At thirty-eight Ouida was still not very different, fundamentally, from the eleven-year-old child who when longing for her father wrote in her diary "hope deferred maketh the heart sick". Memories of that time increased the febrility with which she waited now—accumulating clothes from Worth and food from Doney's, and moving whole conservatories of flowers from one room to another, in an attempt to make of food, flowers, and finery a barrier between herself and defeat.

For the first time in her life her Oliver-Twist-like mind found it difficult to concentrate on reading. Usually she was as voracious a reader as she was prolific a writer, but now every fibre of her being was tense with longing for della Stufa. She had standing orders for new books, but the best current ones—Verlaine's "Romances Sans Paroles", George Eliot's "Daniel Deronda", Henry James' "Roderick Hudson", and Tolstoy's "Anna Karenina"—were no help to anyone trying not to think exclusively of love.

There are more tragic moments in Ouida's life, but none more pathetic than these of waiting for love, like a young girl, on the threshold of middle age. Despite the improprieties attributed to her early books, she herself was still as emotionally innocent, ingenuous, and respectable as the author of shocking "Jane Eyre" had been—and her passion for della Stufa combined the excitement of an adolescent, momentarily unable to visualize anything due to happen after her wedding night, with the intensity of an intellectually mature woman who has found in the man she loves a perfect friend.

Her excitement increased, and with it the frequency with which she referred to della Stufa's homecoming. It was impossible for her not to drag his name into every conversation on the slightest pretext. But gradually it struck her that, among those who loved her, her eagerness aroused not smiling congratulations but unsmiling embarrassment. Panic seized her. But although she often behaved ludicrously, she never behaved like an ostrich—being, in this, the opposite of della Stufa— and, faced with disaster, she asked direct questions loudly and crudely. And so, at last, she discovered what all her Florentine friends, enemies, and acquaintances already knew—that the Marchese had returned two weeks ago. So, unexpectedly, had Mrs. Ross. The next time Ouida saw him she did so without his seeing her. He was driving with Mrs. Ross in the Via Tornabuoni.

XVIII

JUST AS IT had not occurred to the obscure child Ouida to blame dear dear Papa for abandoning her, so it did not occur to the famous woman to blame the man she loved. Nevertheless she had to blame someone. A year later the great Macdermott was to thrill the London Pavilion audiences with a new song:

"We don't want to fight, but by Jingo, if we do,
We've got the ships, we've got the men,
And got the money too!"

—and this was the mood that animated Ouida, helping her, for the moment, to bear her grief.

Determined to keep her flag flying, she gave and accepted more invitations than ever. Even had she been a dull woman, with no value as gossip-fodder, the quality of her food, drink, house, and garden would have attracted guests. As it was, she had no difficulty in surrounding herself with people. But her manner became increasingly high-powered, and senseless waves of anger made her suddenly aggressive. Had she been a child with a nanny, the latter would have said warningly "it'll all end in a big cry". But, unlike those around her, Ouida had never been a child with a nanny; and her mother, who had supported Louis Ramé's vagaries with a patience her daughter had not inherited, could not help her now.

Local gossips, still not sure which of the rivals was the bull and which the toreador, were puzzled by Ouida's renewed passion for society. Surely she was not going to leave it at that? She was not.

At this point Ouida's best course would have been to copy Edward Lear's young lady of Lucca, who when all her lovers forsook her merely climbed up a tree and said fiddle-de-dee, thus disconcerting the people of Lucca. But fiddle-de-dees didn't come naturally to Ouida, and before long anxiety over money was added to her troubles—her sixty-five-year-old banker having defaulted, and eloped with a ballet girl. Unlike those of her heroines who are aristocrats, Ouida could not afford to devote nearly all her time to cultivating her emotions; but she could not refrain from drawing on them for her next novel. This was *Friendship*, and it was to cause more scandal than all the rest of her novels combined.

The plot of *Friendship* is simple and plausible. Lady Joan Challoner, a well-born but snobbish Englishwoman who lives in Rome and is married, beneath her, to a man both shady and complaisant, has acquired as her lover the handsome and melancholy Prince Ioris. A few years later Etoile, a French painter who is Countess d'Avesnes in her own right, comes to Rome on account of her lungs—some of the romantic prestige attached to tuberculosis in Victorian novels was probably due to the fact that only the rich could afford to go to those picturesque places then supposed good for this complaint. Prince Ioris and Etoile meet, and gradually fall in love with each other. Incapable of making it clear to Lady Joan that he is tired of her, Prince Ioris nevertheless determined to leave her—but in an unspecified manner, and at an unspecified time, in this resembling Benjamin Constant's *Adolphe*. Although he tells Etoile the truth about his relationship with his mistress, he cannot bring himself to tell her the whole truth and nothing but the truth. At the back of his mind is the conviction that a vague but yearned-for *something* will enable him to marry Etoile without Lady Joan's making trouble. When, at one point, Etoile wants to write to Lady Joan and clarify the situation: " 'ma femme ne peut pas écrire à ma maîtresse', he murmured in the language which they most often spoke." Thanks to Ioris' dilatoriness, Lady Joan, who has already taken his estate in hand on the pretext of making it pay, is able to involve him in a shady scheme of her husband's for a Messina bridge to unite Sicily to the mainland. (There was a plan of this kind afoot at that time.) The scheme being a fraudulent one, Lady Joan now has a way to blackmail Ioris into doing as she pleases, and on her return from a business trip to England—during which time Etoile and Ioris, together in Rome, have been planning their marriage—she at last succeeds in separating them for good.

Ouida's use of this plot would have caused excitement in Florence even had the characters been less recognisable. Lady Joan, handsome, dark-browed, and given to lounging on oriental divans while smoking cigars is described as "a faggot of contradictions; extraordinarily ignorant, but naturally intelligent; audacious yet timid; a bully, but a coward; full of hot passions, but with cold fits of prudence . . . most people (except artists) carried off the impression that Lady Joan knew a great deal about art. She had a bright, firm, imposing way of declaring her opinions infallible that went far towards making others believe them so . . . perhaps nobody can comprehend how utterly uneducated it is possible to be, who has not lived entirely with the educated classes". The unkindest criticism of Lady Joan is made by Lady Cardiff—a character based on Lady Orford, who did not greatly care for Mrs. Ross: "Clever creature! She really is great fun. Half her life is spent in being so dreadfully afraid people should think she has a lover, and the other half is spent in being so dreadfully afraid people should think she hasn't."

As to Lady Joan's husband, a shadowy figure kept in the background, Lady Cardiff tells Etoile:

Of all lay figures there is none on earth so useful as a wooden husband. You should get a wooden husband, my dear, if you want to be left in peace. It is like a comfortable slipper or your dressing-gown after a ball. It is like springs to your carriage. It is like a clever maid who never makes mistakes or comes without coughing discreetly through your dressing room. It is like tea, cigarettes, postage-stamps, foot-warmers, eiderdown counterpanes—anything that smooths life in fact. Young women do not think enough of this. An easy-going husband is the one indispensable comfort of life. He is like a set of sables to you. You may never want to put them on; still, if the north wind do blow—and one can never tell—how handy they are! You pop into them in a second, and no cold wind can find you out, my dear. Couldn't find you out, if your shift were in rags underneath! Without your husband's countenance, you have scenes. With scenes, you have scandal. With scandal, you come to a suit. With a suit, you most likely lose your settlements. And without your settlements, where are you in Society? With a husband you are safe. You need never think about him in any way. His mere existence suffices. He will always be at the bottom of your table, and the head of your visiting cards. That is enough. He will represent Respectability for you, without your being at the trouble to represent Respectability for yourself. Respectability is a thing of which the shadow is more agreeable than the substance. Happily for us, Society only requires the shadow.

Prince Ioris is described as

very tall and slender, with that look of distinction which, though not always attendant on a great race, is never found outside it; he had high delicate features, and an oval beardless face, a soft olive skin, thoughtful pensive brows, and those eyes which at once allure and command women; he had a beautiful voice, infinite grace and softness of manner, and in aspect might have stepped down off any canvas of Velasquez or Vandyke. Etoile noticed that he was scrupulously alive to every want of Lady Joan's; he bowed his head in resigned silence whenever she contradicted him, which she did twice in every five minutes; he called her madame with strictest ceremony, and addressed Mr. Challoner across the length of the table as "mon cher" with more friendly effusion than seemed needful, on more occasions than were natural. . . . With Ioris gentle impulses were natural. His character had in it that honey of softness which the flies will eat—and tigers and bears as well as flies. Old people lived on him with no other claim than their utter uselessness; hangers-on devoured his substance because he had not resolution enough to cut them adrift; a poor old homeless soul slipt and broke her limb as he was passing, and he took her into his own house and kept her there year upon year; an unwillingness to see pain, and an aversion to wound, were strong in him; Lady Joan found it out and despised it, and laughed at it, and profited by it all at once. "Io's such a fool", she would say—and think him such a fool—and yet all the while love the folly in him from its own utter unlikeness to herself.

Etoile's background is surrounded by mystery. The portrait of her conspirator father has been quoted earlier, and Ouida's conclusions on this subject are characteristic:

There is so much mystery in this world, only people who lead humdrum lives will not believe it. It is a great misfortune to be born to a romantic history. The humdrum always think that you are lying. In real truth romance is common in life, commoner, perhaps, than the commonplace. But the commonplace always looks more natural. In nature there are millions of gorgeous hues to a scarcity of neutral tints; yet the pictures that are painted in sombre semi-tones and have no one positive colour in them are always pronounced the nearest to nature. When a painter sets up his palette, he dares not approach the gold of the sunset and dawn, or the flame of the pomegranate and poppy.

Friendship ends with Etoile's writing, but not sending, Lady Joan this letter:

You need fear me no more; he and I are parted, so you may listen to me for a moment. You are stronger than I; you have known

how to keep him against his will, and how to ruin his strength and
his peace and his fortunes; will you not have pity now? Pity on him.
He does not love you; he was weary of you so long, long ago. When
I met him first, his captivity was bitter and dreary to him; you must
see this—if you would see it—in a hundred signs and ways. I now
ask you to set him free. Not for me. I swear to you that we can
never again be anything to one another, because there is the black
pit of a cruel lie set like a gulf between him and me. I only ask you
for his sake. What is the life you lead him? A life joyless, galling,
faded, unworthy of manhood, robbed of all effort and all hope.
You hurt his honour, you stain his name, you make him a byword
and a jest. You call this friendship—to the world. I tell you that it is
the basest and most cruel passion that ever fed its vanity on the ruin
of another soul. I have surrendered him, and I will never claim him
if you set him free—free to find purer faiths and happier ties than
mine or yours; free to be able to look his future in the face and feel
it is his own—not mine or yours. What can I say to you? How can
I move you? You are a base woman, and you have never loved him
in any noble sense of love one hour; but, sacrifice me as you like,
jest at me, jeer at me, drag my name in the dust, do anything you
will of vengeance on me,—only set him free.

With the exception of Lady Orford, all Ouida's close friends in
Florence begged her not to publish this book. But having failed to
persuade, they stood by her. Meanwhile Mrs. Ross' friends and those
of Mr. Ross—whose part in this imbroglio is a particularly ambiguous
one—began threatening to bring a libel action; nothing, however, came
of this except a deal of excited talk. So high did feeling run—with the
exception of Ouida, everyone involved had almost unlimited leisure—
that according to Horace Annesley Vachell, author of the popular
Harrovian novel, "The Hill", Florentine society was still divided into
Ouida-ites and anti-Ouida-ites when he went there five years later.
This state of affairs was, naturally, favourable to the dissemination of
rumours: that Ouida had caught della Stufa leaving his club, flung herself into his arms and implored him to marry her; that Mrs. Ross had
attacked Ouida with a horsewhip in the Via Tornabuoni; etc.—all
equally untrue, no doubt, but all fulfilling the primary function of
gossip of this kind, which is to combine titillation of the imagination
with self-righteousness.

Naïvely astonished by the virulence of the feelings she had roused,
Ouida wrote to Claud Harding, in whom she had confided since they

were both children: "Everything in Friendship is TRUE as solemnly as I can declare it." It didn't occur to her that, if so, this was unlikely to lessen either the anger of Mrs. Ross or the embarrassment of della Stufa. Soon after arriving in Italy, Ouida had written that no Italian will forgive you for making him look a fool, but, like many born writers, good and bad, she was more perspicacious in her writing than in her behaviour.

Few of those involved in this scandal gave a thought to *Friendship*'s merits, or demerits, as a novel; but eight years later Harriet Waters Preston, an American critic of distinction, discussed it in the July number of Boston's famous Atlantic Monthly, a number which, incidentally, contained part of the serialization of Henry James' current novel, "The Princess Casamassima":

"Italy was destined to do more for Ouida, as an artist, in a larger sense of the word, than to satisfy her ideal of the beautiful in landscape. An experience was reserved for her there, or, more probably, a series of experiences, which vastly enlarged her knowledge of living men and women, and corrected, rudely perhaps, but effectually, her notions of civilized human society in the nineteenth century.

"Whatever one may think of the spirit in which it is conceived, there can be no doubt that the book which goes by the sarcastic name of *Friendship* marks a distinct intellectual advance on the part of the author. In it she clears at one leap the bounds which divide the romantic from the realistic school, and comes down on her old Pegasus, indeed, and with plumes all flying, among the grim observers of our disillusioned latter day. *Friendship* is undoubtedly coarse and crude in parts, but there is no part of it which is not pre-eminently readable, and this is more than can be said of some of the innocuous 'idyls'. As for the identification with real people, over which all tongues were busy, for a time, in the city where the scene of *Friendship* is supposed to be laid, the critic has absolutely nothing to do with them. He who will may see a bit of enraptured self-portraiture in the superfine figure of the peerless Etoile. Strictly speaking, the reader is concerned only with the fact that, though the painting is somewhat overcharged, the figure is really one of extraordinary grace; while there is a certain penetration and subtlety in the analysis of Etoile's nature to which, for whatever reason, the author had not previously come near attaining. How profoundly and unsparingly studied, how consummately, if maliciously, painted, are the figures of Lady Joan Challoner and Prince Ioris! Each is almost a new type for the jaded devotee of fiction, and each leaves behind a singularly vivid memory. The intimate mixture of love and scorn with which Ouida seems to regard the entire Italian people is raised to the power of a consuming passion in her portraiture of Ioris: the gentlest and most helpless of aristocrats; the tenderest, falsest, and most worthless of lovers; the refined, sorrowful, indolent clairvoyant,—appealing and exasperating, fascinating and contemptible representative of a thoroughly exhausted patrician stock. The picture drawn in *Friendship* of the foreign colony in a Continental city, its frivolity and irresponsibility, its meanness, moral and pecuniary, its prostrate subservience to rank, and its pest of parasitic toadies and busybodies, is without doubt an ugly one: but it does resemble the real thing."

Its resemblance to the real thing was certainly great enough to cause a turmoil in Florence, and change the course of Ouida's life.

XIX

So INDISCREET WAS Ouida now that instead of giving della Stufa time to recover from the shock administered by *Friendship*—and to meditate on such truths as it contained—she allowed her craving for his presence to become increasingly obvious. But—and here there occurs one of many passages between Ouida and della Stufa that make this odd, but certainly on neither side superficial, relationship baffling —her extravagant behaviour did not result in his avoiding her. On the contrary. He was soon seeing as much of her as ever he had done before being publicly identified with Prince Ioris.

Since Mrs. Ross must have objected vigorously to this, della Stufa was clearly drawn to Ouida by more than pity; and it is unlikely that when he and she were alone together they could avoid all mention of the book everyone around them was heatedly discussing. They must therefore have spoken not only of their shared past, but of their future prospects—and to have agreed as to the latter well enough for them both to welcome the resumption of their friendship. This remained intact for another three years, during which Ouida wrote two books, one of which, *Moths*, proved her greatest success from a financial and worldly viewpoint.

Mention has already been made of Ouida's fancy as a girl for Mario, the great Italian singer. They were both in Florence now, he a declining, she a still rising celebrity, and as she tried to fight her way out of the misery della Stufa had caused her, her thoughts turned back to the childish emotion that had been as it were the rehearsal for the part in which she was now irrevocably cast. Energetic as ever, she started a novel of which Mario was the hero. Ironically, it brought her European and American fame, and won her back the adulation of many sycophants who had dropped her during the uproar over *Friendship*.

Both in fact, and for purposes of fiction, Mario was as romantic a figure as della Stufa. Lady Paget describes his Florentine establishment as follows: "Sometimes I went to the Villa Salviati, then the property of Mario. It was magnificently furnished with all the rare and costly things he and Grisi had collected in their brilliant career. Gigantic looking-glasses covered the rough, medieval walls. Tapestries, marbles, bronzes were scattered broadcast. Grisi had left off singing, but not spending money." (Grisi was the daughter of one of Napoleon's officers.) "She never drove into Florence with her three little grisettes, as her daughters had been wittily nicknamed, without spending seven or eight hundred francs at the jewellers. At this time Mario still had engagements at St. Petersburg and Madrid, but the wonderful voice was nearly gone. A few years later, immediately after Grisi's death, came the crash and the villa and everything in it had to be sold. When I first went there, they lived in great splendour though it did sometimes happen that, owing to Grisi's unbridled temper, they were left without a single servant in the house. The whole of Florence used to drive to the villa on Grisi's *day*, when the most delightful music was performed, but nobody dreamt of asking her to their house because Grisi was not married to Mario, her husband being still alive. Grisi even then had a fine head, but she was very stout. The three girls, Rita, Clelia, and Cecilia were all pretty and rather like her, but on a smaller scale. At the opera, to which they went every night, Grisi used to fill half the box, and the three little sisters clustered together on two chairs on the other half. Grisi never returned a card. It was the eldest girl who left it with 'Rita di Candia' on it, and above it was written in pencil, 'et Madame', a very clever way of getting out of the difficulty. Before we gave our first ball, Christina Temple Bowdwin came to see me one day and, suddenly sliding down on the floor from the sofa on which we were sitting, she put her arms round my knees and said she had a very great favour to implore—would I ask Grisi and her daughters to the ball? It was the dream of the little girls. I was, of course, delighted to do so and people stared prodigiously at first, but whether it was with horror at the innovation or at Grisi's world-renowned black pearls I did not try to find out, but after this Florence opened its arms to them. Mario, on his return from St. Petersburg, came to thank me. His hair and beard were already snow-white, but he looked so fresh and clean, with his pink cheeks and bright brown eyes, wearing a white waistcoat, a lavender-coloured *batiste* tie and lemon-coloured kid gloves."

Stories of this kind increased Ouida's growing resentment of supposedly polite society—of people who jumped at the chance to enjoy first-rate music without paying for it, but wouldn't invite the sinful music-makers into their own by no means adultery-free homes. Watching the effect of this society on its members, she decided to call her new book *Moths* because "the moths will eat all that fine delicate feeling away, little by little; the moths of the world will eat the un-selfishness first, and then the innocence, and then the honesty, and then the decency, no one will see them eating, no one will see the havoc being wrought, but little by little the fine fabric will go, and in its place will be dust."

Despite Vere, a heroine noble in proportions but ice-cream in sub-stance, *Moths* is one of Ouida's wittiest books. It moves with great rapidity, and the spirit of the excellent opening is maintained to the end:

Lady Dolly ought to have been perfectly happy. She had every-thing that can constitute the joys of a woman of her epoch.

She was at Trouville. She had won heaps of money at play. She had made a correct book on the races. She had seen her chief rival looking bilious in an unbecoming gown. She had had a letter from her husband to say he was going away to Java or Jupiter or some-where indefinitely. She wore a costume which had cost a great tailor twenty hours of anxious and continuous reflection. . . . She had found her dearest friend out cheating at cards. She had dined the night before at the Maison Normande. She had been told a state secret by a minister which she knew it was shameful of him to have been coaxed and chaffed into revealing, she had had a new comedy read to her in manuscript form three months before it would be given in Paris, and had screamed at all its indecencies in the choice company of a serene princess and two ambassadresses as they all took their chocolate in their dressing-gowns.

Nevertheless Lady Dolly is displeased with life—because her daugh-ter, Vere, has just arrived, with her maid, in Trouville, and as Lady Dolly is very pretty and looks far less than her age, which is thirty-four, she has no desire to parade a daughter who is not only beautiful, but looks more than her sixteen years. Although Vere is a prig—"she would go grandly to the guillotine, but she will never understand her own times"—this is natural in a sixteen-year-old severely brought up by an aristocratic Scottish grandmother, and Ouida has given her a childish shrewdness that is at moments very pleasing, as when she says to Lady Dolly's lover, Lord Jura: "You speak as if words cost too much and you were obliged to use as few and choose as bald ones as you can find."

While out exploring the country, Vere meets Raphael de Corrèze, world-famous singer, "I am Raphael de Corrèze; I am the Marquis de Correze if it were any use to be so; but I prefer to be Corrèze the singer. It is much simpler, and yet much more uncommon. There are so many marquises, and so few tenors"—and he and she are immediately pleased by each other. But Lady Dolly obliges Vere to marry Serge Zouroff, a sadistic Russian prince to whom Lady Dolly owes debts that only this marriage will make him cancel. Away in a Polish castle, Princess Zouroff languishes uncomplainingly under her husband's treatment, and longs for Corrèze. When the Zouroffs return to Paris, the Prince, noticing the attachment—still completely innocent —between the princess and the singer, insults his wife in the presence of Corrèze, who promptly slaps him in the face. A duel follows, in the course of which Zouroff shoots Corrèze in the throat, and although he recovers he can never sing again. Vere obtains a divorce—which shuts her out from good society, where all the women have lovers—and is happily united to Corrèze, with whom she retires to the country life they both love.

Into the brilliant and never overdrawn picture of naughty Lady Dolly and her circle, Ouida put all her contempt for the hypocritical society that tolerated Lady Joan's "friendship" for Prince Ioris, but penalized women who had the courage of their emotions; and, although there were personal reasons for her·bitterness, the exactitude of her description is confirmed by the following passage from Sir Harold Nicolson's "Table Talk":

"The Edwardian age will, we may presume, live in history as an age of comfort. It was not. It was an age of fevered luxury; at the same time it was an age of peculiar human ineptitude. People possessed false values, and they endeavoured, fortunately without success, to impose these values upon their children. The whole glittering decade passed in an atmosphere of plethoric friction. It is time that the jade and lobster of the Edwardian epoch were exposed. In the first place, they ate excessively and competitively. No age, since that of Nero, can show such unlimited addiction to food."

The descriptions in *Moths* of Trouville, the fashionable French seaside resort, have some of the qualities of pictures by Boudin, who was painting these beaches at this time; and in Ouida's accounts of social life there are forerunners of those written of Balbec by Marcel Proust, who was nine when *Moths* appeared. But the triumph of the book was Lady Dolly, who is clearly related to some of Somerset Maugham's heartless hussies:

> Lady Dolly was a sweet-tempered woman by nature, and only made fretful occasionally by maids' contretemps, debts, husbands, and other disagreeable accomplishments of life. . . . She had five hundred dear friends, but this one she was really fond of; that is to say, she never said anything bad of her, and only laughed at her good-naturedly when she had left a room. . . .

Lady Dolly's analysis of the reasons for using cosmetics is characteristic:

> "Age has nothing to do with it," said Lady Dolly very angrily. "That is a man's idea. People don't paint because they're old: they paint to vary themselves, to brighten themselves. . . . A natural skin may do very well in Arcadia, but it won't do where there are candles and gas. Besides, a natural skin's always the same; but when you paint, you make it just what goes best with the gown you have got on for the day; and as women grow older what are they to do? It is all very well to say 'bear it', but who helps you to bear it? Not society, which shelves you; not men, who won't look at you; not women, who count your curls if they are false, and your grey hairs if they are real. It is all very well to talk poetry, but who likes de-chéance? It is all very well to rail about artificiality and postiche, but who forced us to be artificial, and who made postiche a necessity? Society; society; society. Would it stand a woman who had lost all her teeth and had a bald head? Of course not. Then whose is the fault if the woman goes to the dentist and hairdresser? She is quite right to go. But it is absurd to say that society does not make her go."

It is pleasant to relate that Lady Dolly remains true to herself throughout the book, which ends:

"She has so much to bear, and she is such a dear little woman!" say all the friends of Lady Dolly. "And it is very dreadful for her not to be able to know her own daughter. She always behaves beautifully about it, she is so kind, so sweet! But how can she know her, you know?—divorced and living out of the world with Corrèze! . . .

Ouida had never known greater success than *Moths* brought her. She received a huge fan mail, and the book's influence can be discerned in Bernard Shaw's early novels and Oscar Wilde's society comedies. It was dramatized and, three years later, successfully produced at the Globe Theatre in London with Mrs. Bernard Beere in the leading part. The libraries couldn't get enough copies of it, but this didn't prevent her English publisher from having the type broken up and a cheap edition prepared within four months of the book's appearance. As a result people paid as much as three guineas for the original edition. Ouida's complaints were acrimonious and justified—as they were when Mudie's threatened to withdraw *Moths* from circulation on moral grounds. No doubt Maupassant would have had similar trouble with "Boule de Suif", published the same year, had Mudie had anything to do with the dissemination of this tiny masterpiece.

A few carping voices were raised, one of which provoked Ouida to reply:

A lecturer in the North of England, lecturing on my novels, remarked with naïveté and incredulity on the number of residences assigned in Moths to Prince Zouroff. Now, had the lecturer taken the trouble to enquire of any one conversant with the world, he would have learned that most great persons of all nationalities have three or four different residences at the least, and that a Russian noble is invariably extravagant in these matters . . . would it not be well if lecturers or reviewers, before calling everything which seems strange to themselves unreal or unnatural, were visited with a wholesome doubt as to whether it might not be their own experiences that were limited?

As to the number of Prince Zouroff's residences she was quite right. Even today, when many of Zouroff's grandchildren are elderly Paris taxi-drivers, while those of Lady Dolly have to open their stately homes to the public in order to try to meet the ravages of income tax, there are still many people with several luxurious houses each equipped with servants. But information of this kind is now spread by illustrated weeklies, so while writers mentioning the fact today may arouse disapproval of the system that permits people who don't work to live in luxury, they are unlikely to be accused by responsible critics of having their facts wrong. But Ouida's experiences were so strikingly different from those of the lesser critics, far more parochial-minded then than now, that her writing frequently aroused in them both envy and prejudice. Fortunately this had no effect on her sales.

The excitement generated by *Moths* improved her social position in Florence. Once more, visitors begged to be introduced to her. Once more, she was treated to flattery, compared with Balzac and George Eliot—the latter had just died saying, conscientious to the last, "tell them the pain is on the left side". Acquaintances who had not yet decided whether to support Lady Joan or Etoile, suddenly began murmuring that there was probably *something* to Ouida's version of the story. Though glad of this, Ouida was not duped by it. During one of their rare separations she wrote to her mother: "I do not in the least deceive myself as to the social adoration I receive, and I don't think they care two straws about intellect:—it is just now the fashion to come to me, and so my room fills with great people."

After *Moths* she produced *Pipistrello*, a collection of six short stories, four of them set in Italy, indicative of her deepening feeling for the problems of the peasants, whom she was now coming to understand. This feeling was presently to drive her to write her finest book, one so unlike *Moths* that it reads as if written by a person of another nationality.

After the humiliations attendant on the publication of *Friendship*, it was exquisitely soothing to Ouida to be able to share the success of *Moths* with della Stufa. Like most people, she was improved by happiness, and della Stufa spent so much time with her that when, three years after *Friendship's* appearance, duty again took him to Rome, she told the Tassinaris: "The days seem so blank and strange here without seeing his face; life is death to me. . . . I always feel so much better when near him." The feeling here is very like that expressed in Queen Victoria's: "I only feel properly *à mon aise* and quite happy when Albert is with me." Despite qualms—"the only thing that makes me doubt about Rome is that it will look like following him"—she could not resist taking another trip to the capital. It was exactly four years since the one during which she had thought her marriage imminent. This time she had no Roman work in progress to provide her with an excuse for her journey and she was as nervous, and therefore as jauntily aggressive, as Charlie Chaplin in one of his early films. But the visit began auspiciously, and she was able to write to the Tassinaris, truthfully:

> He has a wonderfully good position in Rome, and people adore him. He has his suite of rooms in the Palace, and everyone is in raptures over his courtesies and grace. . . . He looked so well at the Royal ball on Monday; they placed me in the seats for foreigners of distinction in front of the throne . . . last night as I drove home from the French Embassy, Rome looked Ariadne's Rome—made of silver and ivory. . . . My rooms look on the Story's garden and I am constantly with them.

An American sculptor and poet who spent most of his life in Rome, William Wetmore Story was an intensely lovable character. He wrote a delightful and erudite study of Rome called "Roba di Roma", and his statue of Cleopatra, which is described by Hawthorne in his novel "The Marble Faun", brought him an offer of three thousand pounds in London in 1862. The Brownings, Hawthorne, and Henry James were among his closest friends, and the latter wrote a biography of him. Lady Paget described him as genial, warm-hearted, and possessed of an excellent manner: "equally civil whether he was talking to a royal princess or an uninteresting tourist." Although Lady Paget was an unusually brilliant woman, it didn't occur to her that some tourists might be more interesting than royal princesses to a man of Story's calibre.

The Storys' company made Ouida feel happy and wanted, and so did that of the Pagets and the de Noailles, both of which families were very good to her at this time; and her spirits were further improved by the Queen's giving her a private audience. But gradually it dawned on her that, despite all the kindness and admiration she was receiving, she was having singularly few private audiences with della Stufa. Something had at last gone irretrievably wrong between them.

Time had either lessened his feeling for her or increased his sensitivity to ridicule. It is possible that, hating unpleasantness as he did, he had counted on this separation to enable him to break with Ouida. Whatever the reason, he was not glad to see her. The obvious and naïve delight with which she greeted him even in public, even at court in the presence of his most strait-laced friends, no longer touched or flattered him—and before long the handsome Italian gentleman-in-waiting began behaving like an English public-school boy whose sister has come to fetch him for a half-term holiday dressed in what the other boys are liable to consider the wrong clothes. Embarrassment, complicated probably by remorse—an emotion particularly prone to make those it seizes on disagreeable—made way for sulks and, at last, courtesies and graces vanished, and the day came when he publicly failed to acknowledge her presence.

Until now Ouida had been helped by her sturdy inability to know when she was beaten. In depriving her of this, della Stufa dealt her a deadly blow. Laying down her arms, she wrote to Claud Harding:

della Stufa is in waiting all this time but he is so fearfully changed that he has nothing of what he once was, save his perfect manner. . . . I go to court and all the great balls, for the sake of 'what the world says', but society is sadder than solitude with him for ever before me. . . . The ball last night at the German Embassy was the grandest, I think, of this year . . . the Royal balls are ill managed and dull, and we all catch cold, the Quirinal is so draughty.

This was the first time Ouida had found a ball dull since the days when, a little girl whose feet itched to dance, she complained of the early hours kept in Bury St. Edmunds. Confronted by disaster, she could, for the moment, produce neither dignity nor tact. All she had left was courage. But that never failed her. Lacking her heroines' convenient ability to avoid suffering by pining and dying, she carried on, grumbling but steady, like one of the old soldiers she understood better than she did courtiers.

But some spring of hopefulness and spontaneity was irremediably destroyed in her. Eccentricity began to seep into her character, colouring it as spilt wine colours a cloth. Her youth was over. She had been thirty-two, and young for her age, when she saw della Stufa for the first time; now she was forty-two, and sick at heart. She felt she had nothing whatever to look forward to, and would not have been consoled had she known that the man she loved had little more. The Marchese della Stufa never married, and eight years later he died of cancer of the throat.

PART IV

1882–1894

"N'est ce pas que ce que tu perds, c'est moins ce qui a été que ce qui aurait pu être, et que le pire des adieux est de sentir qu'on n'a pas tout dit?"

Alfred de Musset, "La Confession d'un Enfant du Siècle"

". . . it is impossible to like some people very much without disliking other people a good deal."

Lytton Strachey on Horace Walpole

"Le moqueur est toujours un être superficiel et, conséquemment, cruel, le drôle ne tient aucun compte de la part qui revient à la Société dans le ridicule dont il rit, car la Nature n'a fait que des bêtes, nous devons les sots à l'Etat social."

Balzac, "La Maison Nucingen"

XX

O UIDA WAS NOW at a crossroads in her life. Had she married della Stufa the marriage might well have been a happy one. Fundamentally, they had many tastes and interests in common; and although Ouida's feelings were always violent they were seldom ephemeral. Her attitude towards her mother proved her aptitude for domesticity and, had she been able to have domesticity within the framework of a marriage that satisfied her imagination as well as her heart, her life would have become not only happier but calmer, with corresponding advantages for everyone around her. Now, thanks largely but not entirely to her own naïveté and extravagance, she had to face not only the pain of unrequited love, and the knowledge that she had made an exhibition of herself, but the spectre—so much nearer to unmarried women of forty then than it is now—of an old age in which she would be able to depend on no one but herself. Both happiness and calm left her, never to return for long, and all that was eccentric in her came to the fore.

Considering Ouida's behaviour at this time, I am reminded of a friend who towards the end of the Second World War was searching the German concentration camps for his parents, who had been deported from France. One of the results of his intense anxiety was that he ate as I have never seen anyone else eat, stuffing himself constantly with any food available, as if to make up for something other than food that was, as constantly, being drained from him. But when at last he found his parents alive, he lost all desire to eat and could hardly swallow until, at last, his ordinarily moderate appetite returned. So now Ouida sought compensation in being immoderate. The passion for lawsuits that was one of her most Latin traits dates from this period, as does her insistence on being known as Mademoiselle *de la* Ramé, now that her pseudonym was "fully as well known from Tobolsk to Tangier as that of Cherbuliez or Alphonse Daudet"—an immodest but, incidentally, truthful statement.

Now that her humiliating defeat was final and widely known, many people other than her intimate friends were prepared to be sympathetic, provided she behaved in the subdued manner they thought appropriate to the lovelorn, particularly the no longer very young love-lorn. But the spirit that had carried Ouida from Bury St. Edmunds to fame and Florence was inimical to restraint. Such intimate friends as Lady Paget, Emilie de Tchiatcheff, Lady Orford, and the Tassinaris, did all they could to protect her at this time—Sir August Paget sent Ouida a special message telling her how much he liked *Friendship* and appreciated its fearlessness—but even more useful than their sympathy was an attack of peritonitis so severe as to have a cathartic effect on her emotions while it lasted.

When she recovered she made one of the greatest efforts of a life remarkable for the amount of effort it contained. She immediately set to work on what was to prove her finest book—one quite unlike any of her preceding ones, and which was to have an effect comparable to that of John Steinbeck's "Grapes of Wrath".

A Village Commune shows the inhabitants of an Italian village struggling in vain against petty bureaucracy. It begins with a plain statement of the subject matter:

> The Commune of Vezzaja and Ghiralda, whose centre is the village of Santa Rosalia, is, like all Italian communes, supposed to enjoy an independence that is practically a legislative autonomy. . . . Anyone who pays five francs' worth of taxes has a communal vote in this free government, and helps elect a body of thirty persons, who in return elect a single person called a syndic, or, as you would call him in English, a mayor. This distilling and condensing process sounds quite admirable in theory. Whoever has the patience to read the pages of this book will see how this system works in practice.

There is very little sexual love in this book, and what there is concerns lovers as poor as those the Florentine Pratolini was to describe half a century later in "A Tale of Poor Lovers":

> Peppo and Viola feared everything, yet knew not what they feared; it is the ghostly burden of dread, that which the honest poor carry with them all through their toiling hungry days, the vague oppressive dread of this law which is always acting the spy on them, always dogging their steps, always emptying their pockets. The poor can understand animal law, and its justice and its necessity easily enough, and respect its severities; but they cannot understand the petty tyrannies of civil law; and it wears their lives out, and breaks their spirits. When it does not break their spirits it curdles their blood

and they become socialists, nihilists, internationalists, anything that will promise them riddance of their spectre and give them vengeance.

Not only the young couple but Peppo's father, Viola's grandfather and aunt, and even Viola's dog, live in terror of Nellemane, a petty bureaucrat who means to go far:

> He was only a clerk indeed, at a slender salary, and ate his friends' tomatoes publicly in the little backroom of the caffè; but he had the soul of a statesman. When a donkey kicks, beat it; when it dies, skin it; so only will it profit you; that was his opinion, and the public was the donkey of Messer Nellemane . . . power is sweet, and when you are a little clerk you love its sweetness quite as much as if you were an emperor, and maybe you love it a great deal more. . . . He saw no reason why he should not become a deputy, and even a minister before he died, and indeed there was no reason whatever. He was only a clerk at fifty pounds a year; but he had a soul above all scruples, and a heart as hard as a millstone.

Norman Douglas shared this opinion of Syndics, as can be seen by the fifteenth chapter of "Old Calabria".

The political and geographical atmosphere of this little world, far more isolated than that of Don Camillo, is suggested by conversation of this kind:

> "What is England?"
> "It is a place where the poor souls have no wine of their own, I think; and they make cannons and cheese. You see their people over here now and then. They carry red Bibles, and they go about with their mouths open to catch flies, and they run into all the little old dusty places; you must have seen them."
> "And why do we want to have anything to do with them?"
> "They will come in ships and fire at us, if we are not bigger and stronger than they. We must build iron houses that float, and go on the sea and meet them."

Thanks to this outlook, such people are easily exploited by those who want their votes:

> Not that the cow-tax, though thundered against by the conservative party, was spoken of either, by any of the ministerials canvassing

in the province; they knew better; they made florid and beautiful speeches full of sesquipedalian phrases, in which they spoke about the place of Italy among the great Powers, the dangers of jealousy and invasion from other nations, the magnificence of the future, the blessings of education, the delights of liberty, the wickedness of the opposition, the sovereign rights of the people; and said it all so magnificently and so bewilderingly that the people never remembered until it was too late that they had said nothing about opposing the cow-tax or indeed any taxes at all, but listened, and gaped, and shouted, and clapped; and being told that they could sit at a European congress to decide on the fate of Epirus, were for the moment oblivious that they had bad bread, dear wine, scant meat, an army of conscripts and a bureaucracy that devoured them as maggots a cheese. . . . Russia and China, he said, were to be left to fight it out, but when the fight was over Italy would allow no treaty to be made that would compromise her rights, and would lay claim to a portion of Mongolia, as a precaution against the influence of France in Cochin-China.

Nellemane's determination that every letter of the most petti-fogging law shall be obeyed leads not only to the ruin of Peppo's father and Viola's grandfather, but to the arrest of the old aunt for vagrancy, and the killing of Viola's dog—which maddens Peppo into attacking Nellemane and getting arrested. All their pleasant harmless lives are wrecked, but it is clear that Nellemane is going to end as a deputy if not a minister.

The effect of this book was tremendous. One of its greatest admirers was the distinguished Neapolitan statesman, Ruggiero Bonghi, who declared that *A Village Commune* should be compulsory reading for bureaucrats. Bonghi's praise was valued not only in parliamentary circles, where he was known to be a man of integrity, and one of the first statesmen to have guessed Bismarck's objectives in 1870; but also at Rome University, where he had taught ancient history; and at court, which he frequented when teaching Queen Margherita Latin. In England, meanwhile, John Ruskin wrote: "There is probably no more oppressed order of gracious and blessed creatures—God's own poor, who have not yet received their consolation—than the mountain peasantry of Tuscany and Romagna. What their minds are, and what their state, and what their treatment, those who do not know Italy may best learn, if they can bear the grief of learning it, from Ouida's photographic story of *A Village Commune*."

Although this courageous book brought Ouida admiration from all
over Europe and America, it also brought her enemies—the veracity of
the book being proved by the type of antagonism aroused. A Miss
Mary Calverley, who lived in Italy, sent the Contemporary Review a
things-aren't-nearly-so-bad-as-that-really letter, in which she suggested
that since Ouida's spelling was often bad her facts must be incorrect.

Much more trying to Ouida than silly quibbles of this kind was the
resentment of some of the Italian nobility and gentry, who so disliked
being told that they "were supine where they were not tyrannical"
that they would have liked to see her expelled from Italy. And even
their vexation was as nothing compared with that of the bureaucrats
Bonghi had set reading *A Village Commune*, and who now saw
reforms looming ahead thanks to the scribblings of a foreign spinster.
One of these syndics, particularly anxious not to have his way of life
altered, first threatened Ouida, then had several roughs fire at her carriage as she was driving from Florence to Scandicci. The noise of the
shots made her ponies, Mascherino and Birichino, bolt—and Ouida's
capacity for being exasperating, touching, and courageous is admirably
illustrated by the fact that she arrived home after this incident complaining furiously that a shock of that kind might do permanent dam-
age to a horse's delicate nerves. That she herself might have been
damaged doesn't seem to have occurred to her. Had she spent the
Second World War in London, Ouida would probably have said of
every bomber she heard overhead "one of ours". As undaunted by
bullets as by insults, she proceeded to add to *A Village Commune* an
appendix which provides an interesting footnote to Italian social
history:

No doubt the public will be tempted to think that the municipal
tyrannies, here depicted, are over-coloured, but I can assure them
that I have not the slightest degree overdrawn the power of those
little communal councils, and the terrible suffering that they entail
upon the poor people of this beloved country.

The system is, as I have said, professedly autonomous, but practically it works in the manner I have depicted. The frightful
taxation of the noble and gentle is bad; the taxation of the commercial interest, of the shipping, and the trades is still worse: but
more cruel by far than all is the municipal extortion by tax, by fine,
and by penalty, that crushes out the very life-blood of the peasant
part of the nation. There are, of course, communes where some good
and wise man is chief proprietor, and then it is fairly well governed.

There are others in which the blacksmith or carpenter is at the head of affairs, and then, though things may go ill, the populace cannot complain. But these are few exceptions, and, in the main part, the twopenny Gessler that I have endeavoured to sketch disposes of its destinies at his will. [Gessler was the tyrannical steward of Albert II of Austria against whom William Tell rebelled in the fourteenth century, thus, according to legend, initiating the movement that culminated in the independence of Switzerland.] It is entirely useless to change the ministries of Italy.so long as this municipal system remains what it is. . . . It is no question here of the Right, or of the Left; it is a question of a method of so-called self-government . . . it is a common remark that Italy wants a Bismarck: she wants nothing of the kind; she wants a minister, temperate, just, indifferent to bombast or display, resolute to destroy corruption, and convinced of the great truth that the first duty of a state is the prosperity of her children. But, alas! When a good man comes, he has no chance . . . to be popular with Parliament and Press, he must talk big of armies, of ships, and of the councils of Europe, and, even if he be premier, it is fifty to one that the great bulk of the populace never even knew his name. . . . As an ounce of example is said to be worth a pound of precept, I will cite the following cases which have come under my eyes in the last three months:

A Contadino was going up a steep hill with some very heavy barrels of wine. Being a merciful man, to lighten his beast he placed two barrels by the roadside, meaning to fetch them later. He was seen by a rural guard, though it was in a wild and lonely part of the hills. He was subsequently summoned and fined ten francs! There is a rule in rural police laws that a man must never let his horse pause in the road to rest; it would be an obstruction.

The wife of a navvy who remains in a city of central Italy while her husband is gone to work in Sardinia is in very great necessity and almost penniless; she had only a few sticks of furniture in a wretched room. One of her children fell ill with fever, and a gentleman sent her a little bed for the sick child. The officers of the law saw the bed going in, and immediately assessed her for eight francs tassa di famiglia. She had not eight pence for bread. They might as well have asked her for a million.

. . . Meanwhile, in the public offices, tens of thousands of dawdling youngsters lounge in for a few hours, and are subsidized at from a thousand to two thousand francs a year, to be entirely useless and grossly impudent.

... It is strange that with the present state of Ireland before their eyes the whole of the public men of Italy should be as indifferent as they are to the perpetual irritation of all the industrious classes at the hands of the municipalities and their organisation of spies and penalties. But indifferent they are; whether Bismarck approve their Greek policy, or Gambetta do not oppose their doings at Tunis, is all they think about; the suffering of a few million of their own people is too small a thing to catch their attention; they think like Moliere's doctor—"Un homme mort n'est qu'un homme mort, et ne fait point de consequence, mais une formalité negligée porte un notable prejudice a tout le corps de medecins."

... My writings have alternately been accused of a reactionary conservatism and a dangerous socialism, so ... I may, without presumption, claim to be impartial; I love conservatism when it means the preservation of beautiful things; I love revolution when it means the destruction of vile ones.

What I despise in the pseudo-liberalism of the age is that it has become only the tyranny of narrow minds vested under high-sounding phrases, and the deification of a policeman. I would give alike to a Capucin as to a Communist, to a Mormon as to a Monk, the free choice of his opinions and mode of life.

The only one of Ouida's contemporaries who was writing on similar lines at this moment was the great Sicilian writer, Giovanni Verga. Born, a year later than Ouida, in Catania, a city with baroque Spanish-style palaces of black lava stone overlooking the Ionian Sea, he began, as did Ouida in Bury St. Edmunds, by writing romantic novels of society life. His first, "Storia di Una Peccatrice", appeared when he was twenty-five, the year Ouida published her second novel, *Strathmore*. Later, like her, he settled in Florence, and "I Malavoglia", his first great novel of peasant life, appeared the same year as *A Village Commune*. Verga's complaints against bureaucracy, and particularly against the effect of conscription on peasant life, were quite as bitter as Ouida's—but whereas hers could be dismissed on the grounds that she was a foreigner, no satisfactory retort could be found to Verga.

Two world wars later, two remarkable Italians were to make beautiful films telling part of the same, still unfinished, story: Vittoria de Sica's "Bicycle Thieves" showing the urban poor, helpless as any peasants in their misery; and Fellini's "I Vitelloni" showing the descendants of Ouida's "dawdling youngsters", the Italian equivalent of

America's mixed-up kids and England's teddy boys. Ouida was seldom
more truthful than when accused of extravagance.

XXI

Despite the success of *A Village Commune*, Ouida continued to
feel like the character in Henry Arthur Jones' current drama, "The
Silver King"—"oh God turn back the universe and give me yesterday"
—and in memory of happy yesterdays at the Quirinal she asked permission to dedicate *Bimbi*, a book of stories for children, to the eleven-
year-old Prince of Naples. The King and Queen had shown Ouida un-
varying kindness—when they came to Florence this year she was one of
the three foreigners invited to the reception they gave at the Pitti Palace,
the other two being the Duc de Dino and the Comte de Talleyrand—
and despite the uproar caused by *A Village Commune* they accepted the
dedication for their son:

A
S. A. R.
Vittorio Emanuele
Principe di Napoli
Speranza dell'Italia
Queste novelle
dettate per lui
consacra riverente

Considering his future, it is melancholy to think of the little prince
enjoying these charming stories—*The Nurnberg Stove*, *The Ambitious
Rose Tree*, *Lampblack*, *The Child of Urbino*, *In The Findelkind*, *Meleagris
Gallopavo*, *The Little Earl*, and *Moufflon*—the year before the birth of
Mussolini, the blacksmith's son who was to do so much to empty the
Italian throne. The book received good notices, the Illustrated London
News comparing Ouida to Browning, and the Manchester Examiner
to George Sand; and it was published in French in the Bibliothèque
Rose, the edition in which the Comtesse de Ségur's famous books for
children appeared.

Ouida's interest in politics had not slackened since the days when she
was a thirteen-year-old Free Trader, waving her red snood to en-
courage the Liberal candidate; and now that della Stufa was no longer

there to centralize her emotions, she devoted more energy than ever to public events.

This was the year when Italy was invited to join Austria and Germany in the Triple Alliance, which she was to repudiate in 1914; when the Panama Canal was being constructed, and the St. Gotthard tunnel opened. The English landed troops in Egypt; Garibaldi died and James Joyce was born; electoral reforms took place in Italy and the Phoenix Park murders in Ireland; and less publicized events included the birth of Virginia Woolf and of Braque, the discovery of the tuberculous germ by Professor Robert Koch of Berlin, and the publication of Nietzsche's "Die Fröliche Wissenschaft".

In view of her subsequent detestation of the Boer War, it is surprising to find Ouida full of admiration for the Egyptian campaign. She even sent to England for a photograph of its leader, General Sir Garnet Wolseley. He was of precisely the type that had appealed to her when she was "that shocking young woman at the Langham Hotel". Born in Dublin, he had joined the army at nineteen, been dangerously wounded in the Burmese campaign, lost an eye and received the Legion of Honour in the Crimea, served in India during the Mutiny, and then in China, where he quelled the Red River rebellion without losing one of his men, had been High Commissioner in Cyprus, and held supreme civil and military command in Natal and the Transvaal. The Ouida who wrote *A Village Commune*, was passionately against conscription, and agreed with Eleanor Marx that people ought to disregard the mythical next world and insist on having what makes this world pleasant, was still now and again betrayed by a feeling strikingly like that of Queen Victoria for Dear Zouaves and Noble Fellows.

But her determined preoccupation with what was going on in the world beyond Florence did not prevent Ouida from writing as if for dear life—and work, which had always kept her from starving, now helped her retain her sanity. Her next novel, *In Maremma*, is the most visually evocative of all her books, and still likely to fascinate those who have seen the mysterious Etruscan tombs in their natural setting. Musa, the heroine, is a young girl whose mother is dead and whose father, Saturnino Mastarna, is condemned to the galleys for banditry. Particularly interesting are Ouida's references to the status of bandits in Italy, such as:

For many and many a year to come, the imagination of the Italian people will always be captivated and blinded by the bastard heroism of the brigand; he is born of the soil and fast rooted in it; he has the hearts of the populace with him; and his most precious stronghold is in their sympathy, from which no laws and no logic of their rulers can dislodge him yet.

This opinion was echoed, seven years after Ouida's death, by Norman Douglas in his account of the bandit Musolino in "Old Calabria"; and that it is still valid is proved by a booklet published in Milan in 1948 and entitled "Giuliano Vita del Re di Montelepre". The garishly-coloured paper cover carries a picture of the young Sicilian bandit who required an army to kill him in 1950; and thirty-two pages of close-printed text tell what purports to be the "intimate life-story of the King of Montelepre"—a story considerably nearer to Robin Hood than to Mickey Spillane. While the hunt for Giuliano was on, many small Italians used to end their evening prayers with "God bless mamma and papa and save Giuliano".

Musa is brought up by a peasant called Jocanda and once, when this kindly old woman is unwell, the child says:

"I will die if you do."
Jocanda looked at her, amazed and keenly touched.
"Do you love me so much then?" she cried suddenly.
"Is that love?" said the child. "I should not like to live if you were not here; I do not know if you call that love."

Which, incidentally, tells us something not only about Musa's feeling for Jocanda, but about Ouida's for Madame Ramé. As Ouida and her mother were only twice separated, and then only for short periods, they seldom wrote to each other and therefore this relationship, like happy countries, has no history—but it was certainly the most rewarding one of Ouida's life.

After Jocanda's death Musa makes a lair rather than a home for herself in one of the overgrown Etruscan tombs, still undisturbed by modern archæologists. Here she lives alone, enjoying the wild country around her:

She would watch the roseate cloud of the returning flamingoes winging their way from Sardinia, and the martins busy at their masonry in the cliffs, and the Arctic longipennes going away north-ward as the weather opened, and the stream swallows hunting early gnats and frogs on the water, and the kingfisher digging his tortuous underground home in the sand. . . . Behind the cliffs stretched moorland, marshes, woodland, intermingled, crossed by many streams,

holding many pools, blue-fringed in May with iris, and osier beds,
and vast fields of reeds, and breadths of forest with their dense thorny
underwood, where all wild birds came in their season, and where all
was quiet save for a bittern's cry, a boar's snort, a snipe's scream, on
the lands once crowded with the multitudes that gave the eagle of
Persia and the brazen trumpets of Lydia to the legions of Rome.
Under their thickets of the prickly sloe-tree and the sweet-smelling
bay lay the winding ways of buried cities; their runlets of water
rippled where kings and warriors slept beneath the soil, and the
yellow marsh lily, and the purple and rose of the wind flower and
the pasque flower, and the bright red of the Easter tulips, and the
white and gold of the asphodels . . . spread their innocent glory in
their turn to the sky and the breeze, above the sunken stones of
courts and gates and palaces and persons.

This odd semi-animal life is interrupted by the unexpected visit of
a distant relative of Jocanda's, and though the solicitude of this kind
young man merely puzzles and irritates Musa, it imperceptibly forces
her towards a more conventional way of life which, since she is not
suited to it, leads to tragedy.

Musa is one of Ouida's most attractive heroïnes, the odd combi-
nation of poetry, savagery, and literal-mindedness in her attitude
being not unlike that of some of Miss Rose Macaulay's least sociable
characters. In addition to containing Ouida's descriptions of a part of
Italy between Florence and Rome that was then completely wild,
and of the enthralling objects of art still buried in the Etruscans' under-
ground-house-like tombs, this book is full of the feeling for the poor,
whom Ouida had learnt in Italy to understand quite as well as she did
the rich. The fact that her own mind had a cutting edge did not prevent
her realizing that

the uneducated are perhaps unjustly judged sometimes. To the
ignorant both right and wrong are only instincts; when one remem-
bers their piteous and innocent confusion of ideas, the twilight of
dim comprehension in which they dwell, one feels that oftentimes
the laws of cultured men are too hard on them, and that, in a better
sense than that of justice and reproach, there ought indeed to be two
laws for rich and poor.

In Maremma was the last of Ouida's long novels set in Italy, the last
of the five books—the others being Pascarel, Signa, Ariadne, and A

Village Commune—that explain why Wilfrid Scawen Blunt thought that no other writer in English had provided so good a picture of "Italy in its romantic aspect of the Garibaldian age". The veracity of many of the more picturesque details of these novels was illustrated as recently as January 1956, in an article by Luigi Barzini, junior, published in Encounter. In this, after pointing out that before the first world war older Italians could remember "how Italy had been hastily put together, under exceptional circumstances, by a courageous minority", he describes some of the many picture-book aspects of Italy that still survive from that time. For example: "At Palermo, in the palazzo of the Duke Fulco dell Verdura, visitors are still announced by the ringing of the tower bell. The Duke, a New York and Paris dweller, is one of the most prominent men in International society. Yet in his house, still inhabited by his mother, the Duchess, the porter won't stop anyone from entering—as, indeed, was the custom in all the palazzi at Palermo. Anyone who wishes can walk in and go through the master's apartments. However, the bell is always sounded—one stroke for a woman, two for a man, three for the Duke, and a stroke and a half for a priest, who is considered half-way between a man and a woman. (At every stroke there is a great sticking-out of heads from the upper-floor windows and courtyard to see who has arrived.) Some years ago, the Duke's father came across a beggar in the ante-chamber doing an excellent business collecting alms." Luigi Barzini also describes present-day Italian aristocrats possessed of gallantry very like that of Ouida's heroes—such as the anti-fascist Count Paolo Caccia Dominioni of Sillavengo, who when his friends expressed surprise at his volunteering during the Second World War for combat duty at Tobruk, said "There's no doubt the war is lost, but let's lose it as well as we can, with dignity and honour."

Ouida had loved this world, as full of colour and heroism as her father's Napoleonic stories, and her love outlasted the man who has illuminated it for her; but she was suddenly very tired, and in her next book she returned to her pre-Italian manner.

To the average reader *Wanda* was too highly coloured to be credible and, for that reason, more attractive than the sober and moving *A Village Commune*. It begins with a vivid description of Russia, through which Prince Paul Ivanovitch Zabaroff is travelling. When he stops in a village near his estates, a boy is presented to him as Vassia, his own illegitimate son by Sacha, a peasant girl now dead. Prince Paul takes the boy to Paris and sends him to school there, but dies without making the will in which he intended to provide for his son. Determined to be

independent, Vassia runs away from school. A few years later the
beautiful Countess Wanda von Szalras, who is living with her aunt,
Princess Ottilie, at the Hohenszalrasburg Castle on Lake Szalrassee
comes across a poacher, obviously a man of her own class, who has just
been rescued from the lake—in which her beloved brother, Bela, was
recently drowned. She offers the poacher hospitality; he proves to be
the Marquis de Sabran, and before long he falls in love with her but,
having no money, decides to leave without revealing his feelings.
Thanks to Wanda's high-minded advice, he abandons wine, women,
and song for a political career, and in 1870 he fights gallantly against the
Prussians. Later, on going to help her tenants near Salzburg during dis-
astrous floods, Wanda finds Sabran there, also bent on rescue work. Ad-
mitting at last that they are in love with each other, they marry, despite
family opposition, particularly strong in the case of Wanda's cousin,
Prince Egon Vasarhely, a Colonel in the White Hussars who is in love
with her himself. Ideally happy, Wanda and Sabran have two sons and
a daughter. Then, as the result of a hunting accident, Sabran becomes
delirious and Prince Egon realizes from his ravings that Sabran is
really Prince Zabaroff's illegitimate son, Vassia. He refrains from making this public, for Wanda's sake; but Wanda's frivolous and malicious
sister-in-law, Madame Brancka, who has discovered this thanks to a
letter left lying about, has no such scruples. Class pride makes Wanda
send Vassia out of her life, but she realizes too late—they are reunited
when Vassia is dying—that mercy is preferable to justice. This dramatic
and popular story was dedicated

To
"A perfect woman, nobly plann'd"
Walpurga, Lady Paget
née
Countess von Hohenthal
This book is inscribed
With admiration and affection

The castle in which Wanda lives is a mixture of Puechau, where Lady
Paget was brought up, and the castle of Sommerschenburg in the
Hartz mountains, where Lady Paget's mother, Loida Eilie Neidhardt
von Guelsenau, was living with her brother when Count Hohenthal
came to court her; and Wanda is clearly another portrait of Lady Paget:

The Countess Wanda von Szalras was a beautiful woman; but she
had that supreme distinction which eclipses beauty, that subtle,

indescribable grace and dignity which are never seen apart from some great lineage with long traditions of culture, courtesy, and courage. She was very tall, and her movements had a great repose and harmony in them; her figure, richness and symmetry. . . . She was one of the most beautiful women of her country, and one of the most courted and the most flattered. Perhaps she is not precisely what we term amiable. She is rather too far from human emotions and human needs. The women of the house of Szalras have been mostly very proud, silent, brave, and resolute; great ladies rather than lovable wives.

Which corroborates Mabel Dodge's description of Lady Paget as an old lady, helping her young American friends give a reception: "She gave the gathering the sweeping examination of an old army officer who reviews his ranks with a faint personal disdain, well knowing the base and ignoble stuff of which they are compounded, well knowing, too, that they will win the battle for him, that indeed without them there can be no triumph. She wore the well-known doomed expression of a *femme du monde* whose wheel of life is society, whose position upon it she was born to, having inherited its imperative laws, and the specialized form of athletics that develop and sustain the individuals of that particular world. Yes, she looked down her nose at the party, but she also put a value upon it that I, not truly a member of her organization, was incapable of sharing or even of realizing."

It was because Ouida was capable of realizing, if not sharing, the values of that organization that she was once called the last representative of a class to which she did not belong. But at this moment she didn't feel as if she belonged to any world but the one she created when she sat down and picked up her quill pen. There was nothing left for her but writing and, steadily, she wrote on.

XXII

*F*RESCOES, WHICH WAS published the same year as *Wanda*, showed the development of Ouida's remarkable critical faculties. The bulk of the book consisted of four entertaining cosmopolitan sketches of no great value, but at the end came *Romance and Realism*, a remarkable essay on fiction, part of which had already been published in the Times. In this, with her usual fighting spirit, Ouida expressed her attitude towards her profession, and nothing about this is in the least out of date:

I do not object to realism in fiction; what I object to is the limitation of realism in fiction to what is commonplace, tedious, and bald—to the habit, in a word, of insisting that the potato is real and that the passion flower is not . . . the dome of St. Peter's is as real as the gasometer of East London. . . . I cannot suppose that my own experiences can be wholly exceptional ones, yet I have known very handsome people, I have known very fine characters, I have also known some very wicked ones, and I have also known many circumstances so romantic that were they described in fiction, they would be ridiculed as exaggerated and impossible.

The year this demand for the recognition in fiction of the highly coloured as well as the drab facts of life was published, the English circulating libraries refused to supply George Moore's "A Modern Lover" to subscribers other than those who specially asked for it— and this put them in a position similar to that of small-town Americans anxious to read the Daily Worker today. Around the same time died three men whose life-stories would certainly have been called exaggerated if presented just then by a novelist. Neither Karl Marx nor Richard Wagner had led lives that offered material suitable, by Mudie's standards, for family reading; and Turgeniev had undoubtedly led "an untrammelled life at Baden Baden"—although this did not strike Ouida, who wrote of him: "the quail to almost everybody is only a little juicy morsel to be wrapped in a vine-leaf and roasted; but Turgeniev had the vision to see in it the courage of devotion, the heroism of maternity, the loveliness of its life, the infinite pathos of its death."

Lacking the heart to write more, just then, of the country life she had hoped to share with della Stufa, Ouida embarked on *Princess Napraxine*, another society novel. Set on the French riviera, then an original setting and one which Ouida describes admirably, it tells the story of Princess Nadine Napraxine, a beauty with primarily cerebral passions, who is entirely indifferent to her good-natured husband, Platon, her equally good-natured would-be lover, Lord Geraldine, and the two small sons she has left in Russia. She is, however, unwillingly attracted by Count Othmar, a Croat nobleman, naturalized French, whose family fortunes resemble those of the Rothschilds: "Othmar had brought that dramatic element into her life without which, despite her really very high intelligence, ennui was apt to descend on her."

One of the ways in which the princess tries to elude boredom is by discussing politics, and the dialogue Ouida provides is particularly interesting in view of the fact that this was the period when the Russian Marxist party was formed:

the nobles have always dug their own graves before all revolutions everywhere. They call it "going with the times". They did it in France, they are now doing it in England, they are doing it (more secretly) in Russia. No one should forsake their order . . . that is why I like the party obedience in England . . . it is entirely unintelligent . . . but it is loyal. . . . In other years an ambassador had some pleasure in disentangling a delicate and intricate imbroglio, some chance of making a great name by his skill in negotiation. An able man was let alone . . . his knowledge of the country to which he was accredited was trusted. . . . Nowadays, telegrams rain in on him every hour; he is allowed no initiative . . . is dictated to and interfered with by his home government . . . what is the consequence? That there is scarcely a diplomat left in Europe—they are only delegates. . . . Meanwhile the world's only kind of peace is an armed truce. . . . Look at the Canal of Suez; it has only bred wars and pretexts for wars, and will probably embroil England and France for the next century—until, indeed, India shall have become Russian, or the African negro have avenged Abd-el-kadir.

Part of the material for this conversation was given Ouida by the Marchesa Incontri, formerly Princess Galitzine. In one of Ouida's letters to this friend she asks: "Are you writing any more Russian studies? There is no country more interesting, or qui a plus d'avenir." Incidentally, the present Marchese della Stufa is married to a member of the Incontri family who is herself a writer of distinction.

Before long Othmar's interest is aroused by a chance encounter with a Greuze-like local girl whom Melville, the good but worldly priest, not unlike the one in Paul Bonner's "S.P.Q.R.", identifies as Yseulte de Valogne, orphan survivor of an ancient family. Although the naïveté of this convent-bred child is unlikely to retain his interest, Othmar marries her, chiefly because she is so unlike the Princess Napraxine. Yseulte adores him, and they have every reason to be happy:

. . . great riches help one very nearly to happiness, simply because they remove so many material obstacles in the way of happiness . . .

one may say roughly that if his health be good, a very rich person is exempt from all other misfortunes than those which come to him from his affections or his friendships; his troubles are, in a word, entirely those of sentiment.

Though fond of his wife, Othmar still yearns for Nadine and as his longing grows, so does his boredom with his home. After Yseulte's child is born dead, she becomes increasingly subdued and incapable of satisfying Othmar. He tells the Princess of his feelings and, acting on a generous impulse, she writes to tell him they must give each other up. But her little coloured servant delivers the letter not to Othmar but to Yseulte, who kills herself, carefully making her death look like an accident. A year later Othmar marries Nadine who, though in love with him, agrees with the Prince de Ligne that "dans l'amour il n'y que les commencements qui sont charmants".

The publication of this opalescent study of seductive people devoid of emotional stamina, the first novel Ouida had written with a Russian heroine, coincided with the death in Paris of Marie Bashkirtseff, a twenty-four-year-old Russian girl fully as exorbitant in her demands on life as was the Princess Napraxine—and whose diary, which brought her posthumously the fame for which she had longed, caused Mr. Gladstone to remark cryptically that he was glad we were not constituted one another's judges. It also coincided with the arrival in Florence of Robert, first Earl of Lytton.

XXIII

THIS WAS NOT Ouida's first meeting with Lord Lytton. They had known each other in London during her Langham Hotel days. But at that time Robert Lytton had been overshadowed by his famous father, whose glitter and swagger, suggestive of both Byron and Disraeli, greatly impressed Louis Ramé's colour-hungry daughter. Since then, thanks partly to della Stufa, Ouida's taste had become subtler, and she was therefore more attracted by Robert now than she had been by Bulwer Lytton then. At fifty-three Robert Lytton still had a beautiful face, dreamy expression, and curly hair, and was widely considered one of the most charming men of his period.

Born in 1831, he had lived with his parents only until he was five.

They then parted, sending the child to a guardian in Ireland. After what he himself described as three idle years at Harrow, the boy studied with a tutor at Bonn before going, at nineteen, to be unpaid attaché to his uncle, Sir Henry Bulwer, then British Minister to the United States. In 1852 he was sent to Florence, where he made friends with the Brownings and published his first book of poems, "Clytemnestra", under the name of Owen Meredith—a pseudonym chosen because an ancestor of his named Ann Meredith had been connected with Owen Tudor, grandfather of Henry VII and founder of the Tudor dynasty. Since then Lytton had served in Paris, the Hague, Belgrade, and Vienna—where he met Wilfrid Scawen Blunt and Julian Fane, both, like himself, writers as well as diplomats. In 1864 he married the beautiful Edith Villiers, niece of his friend Lady Bloomfield and of the Earl of Clarendon. At the time of this marriage Lady Paget who, like her husband, was very fond of Robert Lytton, wrote: "it was indeed necessary for him to have a person who took charge of his well-being, as well as being a companion to him, for he himself had not the slightest idea of doing so. His household got into so unruly a state that I deprived myself of an excellent nursery maid, who had a great deal of character, and whom I installed as housekeeper. When later on she returned to me, she related how every morning quite early before the other servants were up, she used to go round and collect the money Mr. Lytton was in the habit of throwing down everywhere, in the wastepaper basket, on the floor or table, etc." Lady Paget also describes Lytton setting out for England from Copenhagen in a Norfolk jacket, wide knickerbockers of black velvet trimmed with astrachan, and a Polish cap, also trimmed with astrachan: "He was quite unconscious of doing anything out of the way in wearing this apparel for a sea voyage. He was at that time a Radical, and we were much amused when at dinner he addressed his servant, saying 'Mon cher Antonio, voudrez vous me donner encore un peu de sauce?' "

Black velvet, astrachan, and Radicalism were less evident in 1876, when Disraeli made Lytton Viceroy of India, where he dealt with the Afghan war, the famine relief, the salt duties, the new native civil-servant system, the vernacular press laws, and the proclamation of Queen Victoria as Empress of India. On returning to England, in 1880, he settled at Knebworth and wrote a biography of his father.

It was natural that such a man should impress Ouida. Della Stufa had broken her heart but, having few suicidal impulses, she had done her clumsy but courageous best to stick the pieces together again, with the result that, although her capacity for loving was irremediably

Crayon drawing of Ouida at thirty-nine.

I wd not have told Jane to
read the letters to Drummond
only there it seemed to
me wrong to ask anyone
to forward a letter of
theirs they did not know
the contents.

Once more thanks to
Meele a love me a
little dinner the 7th.

Monday   Ever yr aff   Ouida

Letter from Ouida to Lady Constance Leslie.

flawed, she had to imagine herself in love with someone. But just as her childish excitement over Mario had been a matter of fancy rather than fact, so now it was her imagination rather than her heart that was stirred by the prestige that prevented an attachment to Robert Lytton from seeming to her an anticlimax.

Soon after his arrival in Florence, Ouida invited twenty friends to an elaborate dinner-party for Lord Lytton. The occasion was a brilliant one, almost as exciting to the forty-five-year-old hostess as the prospect of seeing Boulogne had been to the dancing child. For a moment she was able to recreate in herself the exhilaration she had known when entertaining della Stufa. But the relationship that began now was to end in disappointment for her, and embarrassment for her guest of honour—and most of what became grotesque in it did so because to use a vividly precise American expression, she was acting strictly from hunger. From now on Ouida was increasingly often to behave as if her character were the result of a collaboration between Racine and Edward Lear, both working conscientiously at cross purposes.

Fortunately, Lord Lytton was not the only man to strike Ouida's fancy at this time. The former Viceroy of India appealed to the side of her nature that had made her gentle towards della Stufa whatever his behaviour to her; but an Englishman of twenty-six, who was to be Viceroy of India in the future, appealed to the side of her that liked heroes to appear to be of granite. When the future Lord Curzon came to visit Ouida he was not yet even a member of parliament, but his personality was already remarkable. Why he impressed Ouida is clear from a passage in Sir Harold Nicolson's "Curzon: the Last Phase": "His enamelled appearance, his statuesque presence, the alternation of his manner between lavish exuberance and icy reserve, his passion for the architectural in life and behaviour, his frequently salacious humour, his predilection for the less standardized forms of comfort, his abiding love of the rotund and balanced phrase, his frequent tears, the very quality of his classicism—all that suggested and confirmed the portrait of an English nobleman of 1779. Yet beneath this opulent exterior were other strains, deeper, less complacent and more essential. The pride of ancestry, the outspread magnificence of Kedleston, were counter-balanced for him by memories of ascetic penury in childhood and early life; of the petty brutalities of his governess, Miss Paraman; of the stark discipline imposed upon a clergyman's family in the later sixties."

Curzon accepted an invitation to luncheon on Easter Sunday and was as favourably impressed by Ouida's feeling for politics as she was to be by his grasp of them. The friendship that resulted was a solid one, based on mutual liking and respect and untroubled, probably owing to the difference between their ages, by any misplaced hopes on Ouida's side. They corresponded until the end of her life, and one of their most poignant exchanges occurred when Ouida telegraphed congratulations on his having resigned the viceroyalty. His answer was:

My dear Ouida,

How very good of you to have thought of me from your Italian retreat. My resignation, after much that I had experienced, was one of the happiest and proudest moments of my public life: and I leave India a happy man, my work for the most part done—and most of this harvest in the barn. How seldom we can feel this!

I deserve congratulation therefore rather than solace!

Yours sincerely,

Curzon.

But for once Ouida's admiration was as welcome to him as his to her; for, according to Sir Harold Nicolson, Curzon left India "after seven years of devoted service, convinced that he had been tricked by the Government, betrayed by his closest friends, and treated by public opinions with the grossest ingratitude".

Accompanying Curzon at this first meeting was the twenty-one-year-old Rennell Rodd, who was to prove a kind friend to Ouida during the saddest years of her life. Later, writing to Lady Constance Leslie, he observed: "Ouida feels that she has no longer any charm for men by her looks . . . and yet she can't think of anything else which can make a woman's life worth living, it is too sad—such a gifted mind—and yet so utterly ignorant of the secret of true happiness and of the faith which only can make people accept. . . . I always think you do her so much good—a femme du monde (as she calls it) who is 'also religious' is to her a sort of *blue rose*."

An echo of the political talk at the Villa Farinola which appealed to men as different from each other as these three, can be heard in the discussions about Russia that appeared in *Othmar*, the novel Ouida. published in 1885 as a sequel to *Princess Napraxine*:

at the present instant we are the oddest union of the most absolute barbarism and the most polished civilization that the world holds, society has nothing so perfectly cultured as the Russian patrician; Europe has nothing so barbarously ignorant and besotted as the Russian peasant. "Les extremes se touchent" more startlingly in

Russia than in any other country, and out of those conflicting elements will come the dominant race of the future.

Her English publisher having announced that she must write more in order to earn what she was accustomed to, Ouida quickly followed *Othmar* with *A Rainy June*, a short novel in letter-form describing an aristocratic marriage ruined by a honeymoon in England during a rainy June, which induces such boredom in bride and bridegroom that they hurry to Trouville, and its opportunities for infidelity. After this came *Don Guesaldo*, a story of a young Italian priest in a remote village called Marca. This book conjures up the atmosphere of rural Italy as surely as does Carlo Levi's "Christ Stopped At Eboli":

Everybody in Marca thought a great deal of their religion, that is, they trusted to it in a helpless but confident kind of way as a fetish, which, being duly and carefully propitiated, would make things all right for them after death. They would not have missed a mass to save their lives; that they dozed through it, and cracked nuts, or took a suck at their pipe stems when they woke, did not affect their awed and unchangeable belief in its miraculous and saving powers. If they had been asked what they believed, or why they believed, they would have scratched their heads and felt puzzled. Their minds dwelt in a twilight in which nothing had any distinct form. The clearest idea ever presented to them was that of the Madonna: they thought of her as of some universal mother who wanted to do them good in the present and future if only they observed her ceremonials: just as in the ages gone by, upon the same hill-sides, the Latin peasant had thought of the great Demeter.

After this, wanting a change, Ouida went to Hamburg for the summer, living the life that seems so poetic in Turgeniev's watering-place novels. It was while she was there that Harriet Waters Preston's study of her appeared in the Atlantic Monthly. In addition to the section on *Friendship* quoted earlier, this article contained a remarkably shrewd analysis of Ouida's intellectual background: "She was born, like all the restless and imaginative souls of our day who remember the 'forties', to the ardent and confident belief in a cause: and that was the cause of civil freedom, the propagation of the American idea, the emancipation of Europe's oppressed peoples from the supposed tyranny of their effete kings,—the cause of which Kossuth and Mazzini were the prophets, Lamartine the poet-laureate, and Garibaldi the doughty champion. That cause was by no means lost, still less was it admitted by its adherents to be lost, at the time when Ouida began to write."

Harriet Waters Preston had never met Ouida, and knew nothing of her childhood, but she was the first critic to sense the effects on her of having had a father in whose conversation such men as Kossuth, Mazzini, Lamartine, and Garibaldi played as prominent a part as the Three Bears in that of more conventional papas. Summing up, Miss Preston concluded: "It is no light thing to be a popular writer; and when one has been a popular writer for twenty-five years, more or less, and, under whatever variety and severity of protest, is quite as much read as ever at the end of that time, the phenomenon is undoubtedly worthy of attention."

This article brought Ouida new admirers and, together with the friendships formed that summer, increased her resilience. That winter she decided to visit London. It was fifteen years since she had lived at the Langham Hotel, and she was determined to return there in triumph. But in view of the cost of the journey, her mother decided to stay in Florence. This was to be Ouida's last attempt at social grandeur. Her flags were still flying, but they were also beginning to show signs of wear.

XXIV

DESPITE LOOMING FINANCIAL troubles, Ouida faced London at forty-seven as excitedly as she had done at eighteen. And, at first, her expectations were surpassed.

The management of the Langham received her as a great personage. Her rooms were full of flowers and invitations. A party was given for her at the French embassy, and another at Stafford House; and W. H. Mallock reports that no one could have been more agreeable and less affected than Ouida at the luncheon he gave for her at the Bachelors' Club, the other guests being Philip Stanhope, the Countess Tolstoy, Lord and Lady Blythswood, and Julia Lady Jersey. A nephew of J. A. Fronde, W. H. Mallock had won the Newdigate prize at Balliol in 1871, and six years later became known for his novel, "The New Republic, or Culture, Faith, and Philosophy in an English Country House", in which Ruskin, Jowett, Matthew Arnold, Walter Pater, and Violet Fane were shown discussing these topics.

Mr. Walter of the Times took Ouida over the offices in Printing House Square; and she was invited to dine at the House of Commons— where she met the Home Secretary, Henry Matthews, later Lord Llandaff, an interesting man who had been born in Ceylon, where his father was a judge, and who had studied in Paris before being called to the bar; the Chief Secretary for Ireland, Sir Michael Hicks-Beach, an anti-Home Rule Conservative; and the Lord Advocate, the Right Honourable John Hay Athol Macdonald who, in addition to having a distinguished legal career, had obtained many medals for inventions, including life-saving ones, had introduced postcards to Britain, and was an arbiter in disputes over international football matches. Her regular guests at the Langham included Browning, Oscar Wilde, Sir John Millais, the Lyttons, the Pagets, the Duke and Duchess of Abercorn, Lady Boo Lennox, Lord Orford's sister Lady Dorothy Nevill, the fashionable pianist Isidore de Lara (who is so admirably described in Sir Osbert Sitwell's "Noble Essences"), Violet Fane, the writer, who eight years later married Baron Currie, British Ambassador in Rome, Algernon Borthwick of the Morning Post, Mr. Walter of the Times, Lord Ronald Gower, sculptor, writer, and trustee of the National Portrait Gallery and of the Birthplace of Shakespeare Memorial building at Stratford-on-Avon, and two Americans with whom she became particularly friendly—Mrs. Ronalds, a beauty on whom Sir Winston Churchill's grandfather spent considerable sums, and Mrs. Bloomfield Moore, who had a passion for writers and motor cars.

The extent to which it had become fashionable to admire Ouida is indicated by the passage in George Moore's "A Drama in Muslin", in which the heroine reflects at a dance that "having read only one book of Ouida's it would be vain for her to hope to interest her partner in literature". So assured did Ouida's position seem just then that she was genuinely amused when Sir John Millais, to whose studio she was often invited, read her a parody of her novel *Strathmore* by Sir Francis Burnard, which had been published in Punch in 1878, a time when pre-occupation with della Stufa had prevented her noticing it.

But the truest friend Ouida made around this time was Lady Constance Leslie, a delightful woman, three years older than herself, who was the daughter of Mrs. Fitzherbert's beautiful adopted daughter, Minnie Seymour, and descended from Lady Mary Wortley Montagu. Her husband, Captain John Leslie, lived to be the oldest Life Guards officer, and their son, Jack, married Leonie Jerome, sister of Sir Winston Churchill's mother, Jenny Jerome. Lady Constance was witty as well as tender-hearted. Her great-granddaughter, Anita Leslie, says that she invented an enormous centre-piece of flowers for the dinner-table and called it a *cache-mari*, on the grounds that after thirty years of marriage one simply cannot see the same face chewing every day. When a particularly beloved son-in-law died, she said, "This is the first thing he has done to pain me." Although deeply religious, she did not allow her beliefs to interfere with her friendships, probably because, as she wrote to Ouida: "I don't care one fig for good people who are uncharitable. The whole beginning, middle and end of Religion is mercy and love." Ouida nicknamed her Madame de Sevigné because of the quality of her letters and, six years later, told her gratefully: "You send me echoes of a world which will never probably be mine again."

For us, too, Lady Constance's letters are full of echoes from the past: ". . . I am in travail of a Xmas tree! Cursed be the otherwise excellent Prince Albert for bringing over the German custom . . . Mrs. Perugini, a great friend of mine (Kate Dickens) was with Mrs. George Lewis during the riot and they sat *quite still* whilst the carriage was nearly wrecked and they robbed of everything—she said it was like her father's 'Tale of Two Cities'. . . . My husband gets happier every day as he seems to see every hour stronger indications of the *crashing fall* Gladstone is going to have. He really seems to expect to see him carried off in flames—like Don Giovanni and I hope he may! . . . I am going to meet Henry James and Bret Harte at dinner on Monday which I shall enjoy. . . . Parnell has a flirtation with Mrs. O'Shea—since the Galway Election last month '*Cherchez la Shea*'." She continued writing to Ouida until the end of the latter's life, and one of the most touching features of these letters is the way in which they convey, without a touch of either patronage or pity, gossip about the social life Ouida could no longer enjoy. Ouida wrote to her from her deathbed, and Lady Constance's delicate kindness certainly helped her not to feel entirely unwanted when she was old, poor, and lonely.

But, much as Ouida enjoyed making new friends, she was not prepared to neglect her chief reason for visiting England, which was in order to accept the invitation to Knebworth given her by Lord Lytton when he visited her in Florence. As he had accepted her hospitality, it was natural he should have said that if ever Ouida came to London she must be sure to visit him; but he certainly had not wished her to make the journey expressly for that purpose—and, by this time, her incipient possessiveness, encouraged by her success in London, alarmed him. So the stay to which Ouida had so eagerly looked forward—ordering an entirely new wardrobe from Worth complete with furs—was a failure from the start. An eyewitness account is provided by Lady Paget:

". . . In the evening I came here to Knebworth. I had promised dear Lytton to chaperon him in the train, for Ouida had insisted on his coming to London to fetch her and he fears her love much more than her hate. Lord Salisbury, the Prime Minister, described by Disraeli as 'a great master of gibes and flouts and jeers' as the result of his attitude to the Public Worship Regulation Act, got into the carriage where I was sitting with Sir Ashley Eden and said he did not wish to know Ouida. At that moment she appeared, be-furred and be-velveted, on Lytton's arm. Nobody volunteered an introduction and I felt she must never know she had missed this long-coveted opportunity of making Lord Salisbury's acquaintance." (That Ouida didn't recognize him proves that photography was still in its infancy.) ". . . I therefore tried to prevent her overhearing his conversation with Lytton as much as possible . . . when Lord Salisbury got out at Hatfield he shook hands with us and Ouida asked, 'And who was that?' Lord Lytton turned to me in the most disgracefully comic way and said, opening his green eyes very wide: 'yes, who was that?' I said: 'Yes, I know his face' and Sir Ashley Eden added: 'I think some local man.' "

Ouida frequently behaved extravagantly, but since on this occasion she was a guest, the behaviour of these clever and well-bred people seems to have been more appropriate to St. Trinian's than to St. Stephen's. Despite this inauspicious start, Ouida was determined to admire everything, including Knebworth itself, which Augustus Hare describes as a sham old house, with a sham lake, sham heraldic monsters, sham ancient portraits, etc. He mentions Lady Lytton as being beautiful, charming and courteous—but adds, in a tone that puts one in mind of a cat carefully washing its face, "I wish one did not know that the real name of the Lyttons is Wiggett."

It was preoccupation with the social value of names that provoked one of the most unfortunate episodes of this visit. The Lyttons' governess was a woman of Ouida's age, and came from Bury St. Edmunds. She therefore addressed Ouida as Miss Ramé, without the *de la*, and referred pointedly to parties they had both attended in Union Terrace. Irritated, Ouida said she did not remember such parties, after which the guests kept asking the governess what Ouida had been like as a child. It was foolish of Ouida to react in this way but, considering the importance attached by the Pagets and Lyttons to birth, not surprising. At that time no writer would have announced that he had once washed dishes for a living—because to do so would have been to put a considerable obstacle in the way of his earning a living by his books.

The guest with whom Ouida had the most in common was Alfred Austin, the future Poet Laureate, with whom she subsequently corresponded, and who was one of those responsible for getting her a Civil List pension at the end of her life. In his autobiography he mentions her having invariably treated him with kindness, and adds: "Poor Ouida! She had a touch of genius, and its supposed accompaniment, fecklessness and recklessness."

Recklessness certainly marked her attitude towards Lord Lytton, who now began behaving like Walter Mitty—even locking himself into his room on Sunday morning so as to make clear to the lady that he was not for burning. He incidentally made it clear that Lady Paget had done well to lend him a nursery maid, particularly one of unusual character. But his obvious recalcitrance did not prevent Ouida from subsequently calling on the Prime Minister's wife, Lady Salisbury, whom she had never met, and announcing, "I have come to tell you that the one man for Paris is Robert", to which Lady Salisbury replied, "And pray, if you please, who is Robert?" This anecdote of Ouida at her most eccentric is given a typical twist by the fact that Robert Lytton was indeed made ambassador in Paris the following year.

After this Ouida could no longer enjoy London—and the guests who flocked to the Langham began to impress her less than the fact that she was spending two hundred pounds a week on flowers. In her "Memories of Fifty Years", Lady St. Helier says: "Ouida was exceedingly extravagant, not so much from the gratification of her own personal wishes, as from carelessness and want of method in her pecuniary arrangements; also she was extremely generous. She had made large sums of money by her writings, and yet was supposed to be always in debt. So many unkind accounts of her were given on this particular point that I think there is no indiscretion in my mentioning an incident which came to my own personal knowledge. On the occasion when I first met her she also made the acquaintance of a well-known man, not a *litterateur*, but one who was interested in literature. Next day he received a letter from her saying that she had to meet a bill of £1,500, and had no means of doing so until a certain sum of money was sent her, which was not to be paid until ten days later. He came to see me, to consult me as to what he had better do. I felt incompetent to give him any advice, and left him to judge for himself. He decided to send her the money, and on the afternoon of the day on which she said she would be in a position to pay him he received a cheque from her. This, and one or two other incidents of a similar nature which came under my personal knowledge, should be known,

I think, in justice to her, because she was always being accused of appealing to her friends in her difficulties."

Ouida's last weeks in London were not easy ones. Politically, the atmosphere was hysterical. Lady Paget noted: "every country is arming, though everybody wants peace. Poor Castelli (a German poet) once said to me about pictures: 'It is not the things you see that make the pictures, it is the things you do not see.' I feel the same about this war which everybody talks about; it is not the things we foresee and fear and which all the stupid papers do their best to envenom. It is not Prince Bismarck's iron and brutal will, not Katkoff's fury, not Boulanger's *prepotenza*, which will make war break out, but the tiny spark which lurks hidden in some unobserved corner. . . ."

As sensitive to the chaotic atmosphere outside as she was to the incoherence within herself, Ouida began to think of going home. She knew, as she told her mother in a letter in which she thanked the latter lovingly for her "unselfish pleasure" in her daughter's success, that people made a fuss of her only because it was fashionable to do so—but she had not realized that entertaining the fashionable flocks would leave her without the money for her hotel bill. Lady Dorothy Nevill came to the rescue, and Ouida took help as naturally as she gave it.

But her spirits were even lower now than they had been immediately after the loss of della Stufa. Between him and herself genuine feeling had been wrecked, but genuine feeling is never entirely devoid of dignity; in the case of Lord Lytton she had allowed herself to imagine a most unsuitable attachment, and made a fool of herself in the process. She was middle-aged, and knew that she would never marry now, nor have children. Nevertheless, she was determined to convince her mother that her visit had been a triumph. Just so, ten years later, was the young Colette to try to convince her beloved mother, Sido, that being married to the ambiguous Monsieur Willy made her happy.

On the eve of leaving London, Ouida talked confidently of her next visit there. But more than half her life was spent out of England, and she never saw it again.

XXV

BACK HOME, OUIDA was rapturously received by her mother and her dogs. Her new novel, *The House Party*, a trivial but enjoyable story, was the result of a play she had failed to finish satisfactorily for the

Bancrofts—a surprising failure, since her dialogue was always good
and the plot should have proved agreeable to the public that in a few
years' time would be flocking to "Lady Windermere's Fan" and "The
Second Mrs. Tanqueray". But, for the first time in her life, her power
to write flagged.

The Jubilee provided her with an excellent opportunity for venting
her spleen; but the vehemence with which she attacked the Queen—
saying that she had appeared in a picture of Landseer's with gralloched
stags at her feet, that she allowed her children to play with wild ducks
that had just been shot, that she replaced the royal dogs when they were
old or ill, and above all that she did not immediately stop wars—sometimes blinded readers to what deserved attention in Ouida's opinion
that Queen Victoria's reign had been a long succession of wars, few
if any of them either necessary or inevitable. Disagreeing with most of
her friends, including Lady Paget, who celebrated the occasion with a
dress of *satin merveilleux gorge-de-pigeon* over embroidered cream
muslin, and a bonnet made entirely of green oats with a bunch of
guelder roses at the top, Ouida sent Lady Dorothy Nevill a postcard
saying:

> "Full half a century of measures small,
> Weak wits, weak words, weak wars, and that is all."

Weak-witted is what she would probably have called Augustus
Hare's description of the Queen on this occasion: "—alone—serene—
pale (not red)—beautifully dressed in something between a cap and
bonnet of white lace and diamonds, but *most* becoming to her—perfectly self-possessed, full of the most gracious sweetness, lovely and
lovable." But as for weak words, recent publications included Rim-
baud's "Illuminations", Bernard Shaw's "Cashel Byron's Profession",
de Amicis' "Cuore", Kipling's "Plain Tales from the Hills", Barrès'
"Les Deracinés", Henry James' "The Bostonians", Loti's "Pêcheur
d'Islande", Jules Valle's "L'insurgé", Lafcadio Hearn's "Some Chinese
Ghosts", and Conan Doyle's "Sherlock Holmes"—the famous detec-
tive making his first appearance in "A Study in Scarlet" in Beetons'
Christmas Annual. Nor were wars to be weak much longer, Alfred
Nobel having discovered how to make that "safe and manageable
explosive" dynamite.

For Ouida one of the most agreeable events of the Jubilee year was
a visit from Samuel Smiles, seventy-five thousand copies of whose
"Self Help" had already been sold in Italian under the less succinct
title "Chi si Aiuta Dio l'aiuta". This genial, handsome old gentleman,

who had been born in the reign of George III and could just remember rejoicings after Waterloo, was a welcome visitor. Among the many subjects on which they agreed was the iniquitousness of state lotteries. Writing home, he said "We went to church in the morning and devoted the afternoon to Ouida! Her villa is exquisite, beautifully furnished, and commanding lovely prospects. In front of the house, seen from the hall door, is a view across the valley to a Monte something or other, with a monastery on top. Such a view! Then, on the north, the other side of the Arno, you see the spurs of the Apennines dropping down towards Pisa. We found Ouida herself a charming person. She received us most graciously and was kindness itself. She lives with her mother. We had a cup of tea, and then she invited us to lunch on Thursday. We at once accepted."

But Ouida no longer felt that she commanded lovely prospects. In October the Italian premier, Crispi, had gone to Friedrichsruhe to confer with Bismarck, and as Ouida disliked Crispi as much as she did Joseph Chamberlain, and dreaded the results for Italy of the Triple Alliance, this frightened her. In an article for W. H. Stead, a fine journalist later drowned on the Titanic, she wrote with extraordinary prescience:

> Germany has always been fatal to Italy, and always will be. The costly armaments which have made her penniless are due to Germany. Her army and navy receive annual and insulting inspection by Prussian princes. The time will probably come when German troops will be asked to preserve "social order" in the cities and provinces of Italy. So long as the German alliance continues in its present form, so long will this danger for Italy always exist. . . . And if the House of Savoy be driven from the Quirinal, it will owe this loss of power entirely to its own policy.

Nor was she happier in the personal sphere. Money troubles were beginning to form a cloud considerably bigger than a man's hand on her horizon; and she had quarrelled with the Tassinaris for having obeyed the order—due to the presence in the district of a mad dog—that all dogs were to be shut up or muzzled on pain of a fine of forty francs per dog. Outraged by what she considered the Cavaliere's subservience, Ouida wrote to his daughter:

> it is horrible to put two great dogs together, and their blood boils until they become unsafe. If he does not let the dogs be free I will

cease all friendship for him and consign him to the disgust of posterity as second to the Cenci father in cruelty.

The Cavaliere Tassinari apparently shared Noel Coward's views on the claims of posterity, so before long it was not only the dogs whose blood was boiling. On top of which came tree trouble. Ouida's feeling for plants was second only to her feeling for animals, and when the owner of her villa required her to clip the tall laurel hedges of her garden, she merely replied: "How would the Marchese like to have his own arms and legs lopped off?"

Choleric old Walter Savage Landor, who had died in Florence twenty-four years earlier, would have understood Ouida's attitude, since he considered trees in their living state to be the only things money cannot command. So would the seductive Chevalier de Boufflers, who in 1779 wrote to his mistress, "You cut off trees' arms and legs without thinking. You will see things differently when you know, as I do, that trees have feelings. . . ." The Marchese Farinola, however, could not be made to see differently. Determined to get Ouida out of his villa, he consulted Sir Dominic Ellis Colnaghi, the British Consul in Florence, who turned to the Cavaliere Tassinari's son-in-law, Captain Danyell. "It appears," wrote Sir Dominic, "if I understand correctly, that there is some difficulty with regard to the cessation of the tenancy, and before taking any final legal measure the Marchese is anxious that an opportunity of a friendly settlement should not be lost. I said the question was one in which for various reasons I did not see that I could interfere officially, but that I knew a friend of Madame de la Ramé. . . ."

Disregarding the fact that Ouida considered his father-in-law second only to the Cenci's father in cruelty, Captain Danyell came to the rescue, and went to Senator Gadda, the Prefect of Florence. Whereupon Ouida announced that, though she was grateful to Captain Danyell, she must wait for her lawyer as she was a French subject, and had been presented at the Quirinal by the French Ambassadress. It was true that the French Embassy had shown her a great deal of attention both in London and in Rome, and it was true that her father was French; but neither of these truths provided her with the papers the Consul needed as proof of her nationality. This infuriated her into asking, "What does the Consul mean by establishing facts? They are established. Unhappily I have no papers of any kind; my father disappeared after the Commune and his papers with him."

When, after more quarrelling, the Marchese sent a handful of his peasants, supported by carabinieri, to evict Ouida, they found the gates barred, the doors locked and the windows shuttered. They then broke into the house, shouting abuse as they did so.

The scene was as far-fetched as any in Ouida's novels and, like so much that concerns her, combined tragic with grotesque elements: the beautiful garden, the fine old villa with its doors battered down and its shutters broken, the nobleman's peasants, pitchforks in their hands, like a crowd of supers in a play about the French Revolution, and the carabinieri with their picturesque uniforms and modern arms, all shouting at the incoherent servants, the barking dogs, and the two foreign women, the pretty old one frightened, the plain middle-aged one defiant. So, fighting to the last, Ouida was driven from the home in which she had spent the happiest years of her life.

This disaster confirmed Madame Ramé's worst fears. Like Madame Bonaparte, she had for years been anxiously praying "If only it'll last". But she still had her child and, as that child said, so long as one has the person one loves anything is bearable.

XXVI

During the period when Ouida was banished from the Villa Farinola and embarked on a life as obsessed by memories as that of the lost ladies in Henry James' "Aspern Papers", several events occurred which seem in retrospect to mark a watershed between periods of history.

In 1888 Edward Lear, melancholy king of exquisite Victorian non-sense, died in the company of Georgio Kokali, his Albanian servant, and Foss, his cat, at San Remo. Fifteen months later Adolf Schicklgruber, who was to make his pseudonym, Hitler, stand for a very different kind of nonsense, was born across the mountains in upper Austria. During the months that separated this regretted death from this regrettable birth, Queen Victoria's overbearing and hysterical grandson, William, succeeded his father as third German Emperor and ninth king of Prussia, his accession to the throne just preceding the inauguration in Paris of the Pasteur Institute, on which occasion the great Frenchman said: "Two opposing laws seem to me to be now in contest. The one, a law of blood and death, opening out each day new modes of destruction, forces nations to be always ready for battle. The other, a law of peace, work and health, whose only aim is to deliver man from the calamities that beset him."

Another Prussian, Nietzsche, whose ideal of the superman was to cause so much suffering, became mentally unhinged around this time, but this attracted less general attention than did the appearance of Mrs. Humphrey Ward's "Robert Elsmere", a novel that owed much of its success to the fact that Mr. Gladstone, thunderously reviewing it in the Nineteenth Century, accused the serious-minded author of trying to undermine religion. For the first time, Ouida began to worry about the change in popular taste. Stories featuring religious doubt were as remote from her range as they were to be from Colette's—and, also for the first time, where to write presented her with a problem.

At last, thanks to friends, she found an apartment in the Palazzo Magnani Ferroni (now Palazzo Amerighi) in the Via dei Serragli, a street that runs up from the Arno, between the Torrigiani and the Boboli gardens, to the Porta Romana and the road to Siena. Today trams and Vespas make the Via dei Serragli very noisy, and even in 1888 the change from a villa in the Tuscan countryside to an apartment in a narrow Florentine street must have been a considerable one. Not that the apartment itself was cramping: it had thirty rooms, large, dark, chilly rooms for which Ouida lacked furniture. But she chose it on account of its fine terrace, on which her mother and dogs could enjoy the sun and, with the same kind of grandiose folly as caused Mrs. Patrick Campbell to be described as a sinking ship firing on its rescuers, Ouida began by giving a party for Baron von Tauchnitz's eldest son, Christian Carl Bernhard, who was on holiday in Florence with his wife. Hired servants and sumptuous food and drink may have prevented the young Tauchnitzes from noticing the discomfort of the apartment and the faded condition of Ouida's once fashionable Worth frock.

After this she finished *Guilderoy*, for which she had already received and spent an advance of nine hundred pounds. Its hero, Evelyn, Lord Guilderoy, is obviously, if distantly, connected with the families of Maxim de Winter and Fabrice de Sauveterre. He marries the gently nurtured but disastrously unsophisticated country-bred Gladys Vernon merely because she looks like a Romney and has saved a fox cub from some yokels. Her scholarly father, John Vernon, is against the marriage, saying that Guilderoy will soon tire of so young a girl. But Guilderoy has his way, and Vernon soon proves to be right. Bored by Gladys, Guilderoy renews his connection with his brilliant Italian mistress, the Duchess Soria. Meanwhile Guilderoy's high-minded cousin, Lord Aubrey, has fallen in love with Gladys and, at last, realizing his worth she falls in love with him. But their behaviour is all rectitude and self-sacrifice. At last the Duchess tires of Guilderoy and he returns, as he thinks, to England, home, and beauty. But he finds Gladys very changed, and now that she can offer him only duty he begins, in vain, to love her.

Some readers thought Lord Guilderoy a portrait of Lord Lytton, but it is very unlike Lady Paget's descriptions of the latter. Though Lord Guilderoy might scatter money, he would certainly do so in the form of gratuities, not of absent-minded donations to waste-paper baskets; and though he might cross the North Sea in black velvet knickerbockers, even in ones trimmed with astrachan, he would certainly never hide from importunate ladies. Ouida herself told Lady Dorothy Nevill that it was "a very harmless novel, very Conservative, and containing a eulogy of Lord Salisbury". Harmless, it was, but not her best work. The conditions in which she was now living were not conducive to work of any kind. The fact that this was largely her own fault did not console her. There is no record of this fact having ever consoled anyone.

But though Ouida struggled vigorously to meet her debts with stories of rich people whose troubles were entirely a matter of sentiment, she did not succeed. Despite the efforts of friends, she had to leave the thirty dark rooms and the sunlit terrace. Her furniture was seized by creditors, her manuscripts were auctioned. Carefully kept letters and cherished souvenirs vanished in the disorder that, like a tornado, swept the Ramés, Ouida's maid Gori, and the dogs, out of the Via dei Serragli, and from hotel to hotel, from villa to villa, misery and pride developing unreason in Ouida as sunlight makes a plant grow.

To Madame Ramé's anxiety over her daughter was now added the grief of losing her youngest sister, Mary Anne. It was years since the Lockwoods had played any active part in the Ramé's life, but this death saddened them, reminding them of the happy aspects of the quiet but jolly life in Bury St. Edmunds that had been so deliciously interrupted from time to time by the arrival of dear dear papa, and making Ouida think of what she had written in *Ariadne*: "youth is supreme happiness in itself, because all possibilities lie in it, and nothing in it is yet irrevocable."

At last they settled in the Villa della Corona, Bellosguardo, which she described to Baron von Tauchnitz as "a beautiful old place . . . for seven centuries a monastary, until it was secularized by the Great Napoleon". The adjective great was no doubt intended to keep the dead Napoleon III in his place, and although the Villa della Corona (now the Burns Murdoch Villa) is a delightful place with its cypresses and limes, its lemon-trees in tubs, its great blue lilies and view of Michelangelo's house, Ouida's reference to its glorious past seems to have been made in the spirit that prompted Barrie's spinster charwoman in "The Old Lady Shows Her Medals" to call herself *Mrs.* merely to keep her end up. The same sturdy spirit enabled Ouida to maintain her interest in world affairs despite the shrinking of her own world. When a mining company at Kimberley expressed admiration for her by calling itself "the Ouida Prospecting Syndicate", she replied: "I consider the use of my name the greatest impertinence. . . . I abhor the greedy and shameless parcelling out of Africa by a mob of European speculators."

Around this time she made two new friends, Mr. and Mrs. Henry Huntington, a charming American couple who owned a handsome villa at Bellosguardo. Outside their entrance was a small obelisk bearing the names of famous writers who had lived on this beautiful hill. This now reads:

Qui dove la grazia del colle e del cielo
Esalta la qualita del pensiero e dell'arte
Soggiornarono ed operarono

Galileo Galilei   Ugo Foscolo

e queste eminente figli di patrie diversi

James Fenimore Cooper
Nathaniel Hawthorne
Elizabeth & Robert Browning
Henry James
Robert Lytton
Alfred Austin
Hans von Bülow
Hans von Marees
Adolf Hildebrand
Franz Brentano
Isa Blagden
Clara Schumann
Ouida
Jessie White Mario
Walburga Paget

Both the Huntingtons enjoyed Ouida's company and showed her kindness, and when Henry Huntington's book "Memories" was published in 1911 it contained a portion of the diary Ouida had written as a child, from 1850 to 1853, which Mr. W. Campbell Spence of Florence had inherited from his father. Judging by this book, the Huntingtons were charming, gentle, cultured people who must have been at ease in the company of the Wetmore Storys and Henry James; and Ouida was clearly ahead of her period in her grasp of the effect Europe had on Americans and vice versa. Her American friendships were partly responsible for *The Massarenes*, the one first-rate book that she wrote near the end of her life, on a theme later to be made familiar by Henry James.

Letter-writing and visiting enabled Ouida to keep up her spirits, but her visits were not always as welcome as they had been before her troubles began. Lady Paget continued to be astringently kind, but was hampered by the attitude of her husband, since Sir Augustus "could never appreciate an ugly woman, no matter what her gifts". Sitting, clean and cool, in a linen suit, he strongly objected to Ouida's looking hot and dishevelled, and even more strongly to her maintaining "that the usual morning dress of an English gentleman was a violet velvet morning coat and knickerbockers, a lace collar and a feathered wide awake"—an opinion for which Lord Lytton's sartorial idiosyncrasies were doubtless responsible.

Apart from this she was occupied by two more books. *Ruffino* was a collection of four long short stories: *Ruffino*, an account of the loves of a Roman prince and a young Russian aristocrat who has accompanied her Nihilist brother into exile (it is worth noting that whereas now Russia is said to be the country where it's U to be non-U, at this time what are now called White Russians were often Pink if not Red ones); *The Orchard*, a Verga-like story of peasant suffering; *Trottolino*, another peasant story, against conscription; and *The Bullfinch*, the story of a bird's fidelity. It was not the kind of book likely to sell well.

But the novel, *Syrlin*, which Ouida published the same year, was one of her best society novels, and full of acuity. Freda, the heroine (Wilfreda, Lady Avillion) is married but, like most of those in her circle, indifferent to her husband: "he had married her for her beauty, and had tired of it, and he disliked her intelligence, which had developed since their marriage." Her admirers include her cousin, Lord Beaufort, and a naive boy, Lord Flodden, whom she is anxious to form politically. But the only man who interests her, against her will, is Syrlin, a great actor of aristocratic birth. This does not prevent her from trying to stop Lord Beaufort from marrying his charming and devoted Creole mistress, Consuelo Laurence:

She was suspected of having such incredibly disgraceful intrigues, and of managing them all so exquisitely, that no one could do otherwise than envy and respect her. A very fair woman, with a colourless skin, a perfect figure, a manner of admirable finish, ease and sweetness, and eyes which had the candour of a child's, with a strange pathos in them which went to the heart of all men, Consuelo Laurence, with her great pearls about her throat, the only jewels she ever wore, looked such an incarnation of purity, ethereality and perfect womanhood, that it was delicious and delightful to everyone to know that she had sold flowers in Broadway, sung at cafés chantants, married a Cuban painter and shot him, been wrecked off Valparaiso, and picked up by a wealthy Mexican whose millions she had annexed and finished, migrated to Brazil, where she had ruined ministers and millionaires, and finally drifted to Paris, where she had been rescued just as she was springing off the parapet of the Pont Neuf to drown herself for want of five francs, whence, none knew how, she had suddenly appeared in London, and become the idol of society . . . to her other people were kind because she was popular, attractive, and extremely the fashion, and although the quality of the kindness did not deceive her, although she knew that if she became poor, or blind, or ill, on the morrow very few of them would ever ask where she had gone or what had become of her, she allowed herself to be etherised by that soporific yet stimulating atmosphere; it was so pleasant while it lasted!

Lord Avillion has an eighteen-year-old ward, Lady Ina d'Esterre who during a house party becomes friendly with Syrlin, partly because of their common interest in music, partly because Lady Ina is in love with Syrlin's best friend, Ernest Auriol, a gentle and gifted musician. Freda Avillion resents this relationship, just as she resents her own feeling for Syrlin, but after the latter has rescued her from a rioting crowd in Hyde Park, where she had driven from pure recklessness, she goes out of her way to treat him with friendliness. Lord Avillion watches this, at first, with cynicism:

"Never let yourself love a femme du monde," he said once to a young man whose welfare he desired, "they are exacting and uncompromising. They fleece you like Cabotines, but they never let you forget their position. You can never get away from them either, because you are eternally coming across them in society. Dido would inevitably have got hold of Eneas again, if on the evening of the day

that he broke with her, he had found himself obliged to take her in
to dinner in Arlington Street, or to give her his arm to her carriage
as she left the crush at Wharncliffe House.

But presently he comes to resent it. He himself is in love with a
French woman, Claire de Charolais, and he would like to be able to
prove something against Freda. Nor is Lord Beaufort pleased. He
thinks it in bad taste, just as he thinks the social life of the court in bad
taste: ' "The battue is German,' said Beaufort. 'The country is Ger-
manised by the Crown, and is very much the worse for it; we have got
the pickelhaube, we shall have the conscription.' " Unaware of what
is happening to her, Freda lets herself drift into love:

> clever as she was, Lady Avillion did not know that there is only one
> thing of which the interest can outlast both time and habit, and that is
> what for want of a clearer definition we call sympathy, which may
> exist without either love or passion being united to it, but without
> which neither love nor passion can have any durability. She did not
> know it because she had never felt it herself. She heard people talk
> about it, and she had no doubt that it was very nice, but it was only a
> word to her, and a word which conveyed no idea. Some people were
> miserable if they did not have lemon in their tea, or a doctor always
> travelling about with them; the need for sympathy seemed to her
> the same sort of faddishness . . . she wanted freedom, and yet free-
> dom would have been unendurable to her. She wanted simplicity,
> and yet simplicity would have been odious to her. She wanted solitude,
> and yet solitude would have been to her still more unsupportable
> than was the crowd in which she perpetually moved and had her
> being.

But for all her dissatisfaction she doesn't like hearing her circle decried
in this way:

> ". . . That the premier doesn't digest his dinner, that the Russian
> ambassador's gout is only sulks, that Tommy Goodchild is going to
> be thrown over to save the party, and the enfant terrible has turned
> head over heels into all the choicest principles of the Cabinet; that
> a letter did go to Hatfield in the middle of the night, though they all
> deny it, and that a private secretary did come up from Hawarden to
> Devonshire House, though they all declare he didn't—is that sort of
> thing interesting?"

"It is at least the best we have," said Lady Avillion, a little angered, "and it will all seem intensely interesting to our grandchildren when they read it fifty years hence in memoirs."

An entirely chance meeting between Freda and Syrlin at a skating party increases Lord Avillion's ill-tempered suspicions; and when Syrlin writes a play in which he portrays Lord Avillion as a contemptible character, the latter challenges him to a duel. Freda, outraged at what she chooses to regard as an insult, treats Syrlin so overbearingly that, before the duel can take place, he shoots himself. Grief rouses in her some recognition of the idiocy of her standards, and makes her urge Beaufort to marry Consuelo, and allow Ina to marry Auriol.

Syrlin was dedicated to "the beloved memory of Laurence Oliphant", the writer and traveller who had died in 1888; and to this loss Ouida had two years later to add that of Pierre Tchiatcheff, who died in Florence, and of Sir Richard Burton, who died in Trieste. Ouida had loved and understood both the Burtons, writing of them: "to women Burton had an unpardonable fault: he loved his wife . . . their marriage was romantic and clandestine; a love marriage in the most absolute sense of the words, not wise on either side, but on each impassioned."

One of Ouida's last pleasures at the Villa della Corona, at this moment when the past seemed to be slipping from her fast as water between fingers, was a visit from Lord Lytton, now ambassador in Paris. Either Lady Paget had noticed only the ludicrous aspects of Ouida's visit to Knebworth, or Lord Lytton felt remorseful—otherwise there is no accounting for his spending two days with her now, and coming to the breakfast she gave for Lady Paget's daughter, Gay, and her husband, Lord Windsor. This visit renewed Ouida's vitality, and therefore helped her work.

In 1891 she followed *Syrlin* by *Santa Barbara and Other Tales*, a collection of six short stories, one of which, *The Stable Boy*, describes a boy's search for a dog as moving as the old man's search for his dog in de Sica's beautiful film "Umberto D". Nor was there anything unlikely about the dog's prowess as Ouida described it—as recently as September, 1956, an Alsatian dog who had been adopted by a small French boy walked six hundred kilometres in two months to find the child, who had been sent away for a holiday. After this Ouida published *The Tower of Taddeo*, a short novel about an old bookseller and his daughter who are ejected from the ancient tower near the Ponte Vecchio in which they have always lived. It contains good descriptions of Florence, and this heartfelt one of a petty official: "The world was divided into two races, in his opinion. There were the people who seized goods, and there were the people whose goods were seized."

But before this book was published she knew more grief. While sitting at his desk in Paris, Lord Lytton collapsed and died of a heart attack. He was just sixty, and had been particularly full of energy during his last visit to Florence. In writing to Baron von Tauchnitz "that the death of my beloved friend Lord Lytton makes it impossible for me to attend to anything", Ouida was sincere; but the shock was a cumulative one: Mario was dead, della Stufa was dead, Lord Lytton was dead —and she herself now had to face old age without either familiar surroundings or financial security.

XXVII

By 1893 Ouida's situation was tragic. This is how Lady Paget describes a visit to her: "Ouida now inhabits the Villa della Corona, which is very large and dilapidated. Her only furniture seemed to be a plaster cast of Gay's bust, for which she asked me years ago. There were only two or three chairs in the many rooms I traversed, a pink-and-gold paper hung in rags from the wall, there were no fires, no carpets. A troupe of fluffy and rather dirty white dogs barked at me and then rolled themselves under Ouida's feet, amongst the folds of a draggled black-lace skirt. She wore a mantelet of some once bright but now faded colour, out of which her arms and tiny but ugly hands protruded. Her legs were encased in very bright blue stockings, and her feet in very thin white slippers. She insisted on walking through the lanes with me in this costume, with a whitey-browney hat with many feathers superadded, and a spotty veil."

That spring Madame Ramé had a fall, suffering internal injuries that kept her in bed for four months. Her spine, womb, and finally her brain were attacked. Ouida had had to move from the Villa della Corona to a smaller villa, la Campora, but even there doctor's bills left her with no money for the rent. She appealed to Baron von Tauchnitz for an advance, which this tender-hearted and appreciative man—it is surprising but delightful to know that his business prospered despite his generosity—sent her by return. But on September 10th, Ouida wrote to him: "she is dead."

The scene that followed was as dreadful as any by the great Elizabethan dramatists. There was no money in the house and, desperate with grief at losing her mother, frantic at the thought of having to bury her in a pauper's grave, and distracted by Madame Ramé's little dog, Rex, who refused to eat and kept begging beside her bed, Ouida refused to part with the body. As distraught as Rex, she wandered through the cold dark rooms of the unfamiliar villa, always coming back to the body from which, for the first time in her life, she could get no reply.

Her great capacity for love, the capacity to which her work owed its vitality and her life its tragedies, made her feel grateful, even when sick with crying, that it was she rather than her mother who had to bear the anguish of survival. Few of her friends understood the intensity of her grief. They had seen Ouida on the stage, as it were, not in the far longer, far more revealing periods she had spent in the dressing-room being helped and wished luck by her mother. No matter how fond they might be of their own mothers, they had husbands, wives, lovers, children. But Madame Ramé was all Ouida had—and she was the one person who had always loved and admired her passionately, whilst seeing her exactly as she was. Their relationship had been rooted in reliability, deepened by daily companionship, sweetened by the politeness members of the same family often reserve for strangers. As a writer Ouida glorified the more dramatic and romantic emotions of lovers; in her private life she showed an unusual capacity for domesticity.

It is not, therefore, surprising that with her mother's body in the house, Ouida should have been crazy as King Lear's fool. But it seems to have surprised Lady Paget, who describes being received by Ouida "in a draggled white nightgown, trimmed with lace, and a black cape. Eight dogs kept up an infernal noise, and went on mistaking the lace frill of her nightdress for a lamppost. She never attempted to put a stop to either of these habits. Mrs. Spencer Stanhope, whom I saw later, told me that Ouida firmly resists burying her mother and keeps her in a room upstairs in her villa. Ouida is now by her own folly denuded of everything."

This last statement was correct, if generosity be included under the label folly.

Ten days after her mother's death, Ouida wrote to Baron von Tauchnitz: "I thank you infinitely for your kind sympathy, and for the practical aid which you gave me during a period of unspeakable suffering, both physical and mental. I shall never forget the goodness of you and of your son. You are a real friend; the world holds but few."

By this time various Florentine friends were anxious to help her, but the fact that her mother was buried in the paupers' section of the Allori cemetery added bitterness to her grief, and made her reactions both arbitrary and inconsistent. Like most unhappy people of active temperament she wanted to hit out at something, at someone, at the amorphous and omnipresent *They* whom we all find so necessary when we want to complain. She began by scolding Lady Paget for having taken the Torre di Bellosguardo, since this would "undoubtedly drive the owls from the roof"—it was characteristic of Ouida to start worrying about displaced owls at a time when she herself seemed to have no place anywhere. It was also characteristic of her, when she particularly needed friends, to antagonise Lady Paget by suddenly declaring that her daughter was responsible for Madame Ramé's having only a pauper's grave.

Another friend arranged for hot cooked meals to be sent to her from a restaurant, but she gave this food to her animals, and kept herself alive on tea and biscuits. Madame Ramé's dog, Rex, had to be fed artificially; but although he was fond of Ouida, and she did everything she could for him, he continued to pine and, presently, died of cardiac paralysis.

Letters accumulated; some of them containing cheques. But, despite her need, she tore these up and returned the fragments to the donors. In November she wrote to Baron von Tauchnitz: "I cannot tell you how I miss my mother, nor how I am haunted by the remembrance of all her great sufferings after her fall. Her eyes were so beautiful to the last, and like those of a woman of twenty."

A few months later she was evicted by the carabinieri for being unable to pay her rent. At this point five Florentine banks failed. In the spring of 1894, weary of everything except her dogs, Ouida moved to Lucca. She had spent twenty-three out of her fifty-four years in Florence, and was not to see it again. To Alfred Austin she wrote: "I shall miss her as long as I live, and if the knowledge that all who cared for me are dead be bracing, I have that tonic."

PART V

1894–1908

"I have indeed lost such a friend as I never had or am again in the least likelihood to have, in this *stranger* world."
        Carlyle on the death of Harriet, Lady Ashburton

"If he were a horse, nobody would buy him."
        Bagehot of Henry Brougham

XXVIII

LUCCA IS A small town of great beauty, between Florence and the Mediterranean. Surrounded by great sixteenth-to-seventeenth-century ramparts planted with trees, full of palaces of pale-greenish marble striped with black, so that it seems a city for small zebras rather than mules, Lucca kept its independence until the start of the nineteenth century, when Napoleon turned it into a principality ruled by his sister, Marie-Anne-Elisa, who had married Felice Bacciochi, and was Grand Duchess of Tuscany until succeeded, in 1815, by Marie-Louise de Bourbon. The Duomo contains the beautiful tomb of a young bride, Ilaria del Carretto, made by della Quercia in 1406.

But, for the first time, Ouida was in no mood for sightseeing. As alarmed by unfamiliar surroundings as was young Proust, she wrote to Mrs. Huntington: "I don't like Lucca . . . I don't think I shall ever like anything ever again. . . . I should not like to live and die here; it does not seem Italy at all, and one never sees a flower."

Her capacity for feeling violently was not however exhausted. This year Captain Dreyfus was falsely accused of having delivered military secrets to a foreign government and it is odd, in view of her passionate and spontaneous feelings for the downtrodden, that Ouida believed him guilty. But it was not so easy then, as it now appears to have been, to form a correct opinion, and her views were influenced by the admiration for the regular army that coexisted in her with a detestation of conscription.

In England a different type of soldier was attracting public attention. The licence of the Empire Theatre had just been cancelled, and renewal made conditional on the abolition of the lounge. When it was reopened the bars were cut off from the promenade by canvas barriers. These were at once torn down by a group of young men headed by a twenty-year-old Sandhurst cadet, Winston Churchill, who climbed on to the debris and told the crowd, "You have seen us tear down these barricades tonight. See that you tear down those who are responsible for them at the coming election." This exciting occasion reminded the cadet of the death of Julius Caesar and the taking of the Bastille, and since Ouida was all for breaking down barriers, even canvas ones, she was on his side.

Despite the difficulty of procuring books in Lucca, she did read some of those that appeared this year—George du Maurier's "Trilby", of which she said, "I think Trilby was made by the press partly, and partly by its brio and freshness. The first volume is charming. The second I think is rubbish. I liked his Peter Ibbetson, which most found tiresome"; Antony Hope's "Dolly Dialogues", which contained the much-quoted remark, "bourgeois is an epithet which the riff-raff apply to what is respectable, and the aristocracy to what is decent"; and Anatole France's "Le Lys Rouge", which caused a stir among Ouida's friends because, apart from the impropriety of the love scenes—which showed no consideration whatever for prospective readers' unmarried sisters—it was set in Florence and one of the characters, Miss Bell, was said to represent Vernon Lee, while the central love affair was that of the author with Madame de Caillavet, a well-known Paris hostess.

Ouida forced herself to produce two books this year. *Two Offenders and Other Tales* was dedicated to Maupassant and contained *The Ingrate*, a story about an old Breton painter who loses his right hand in the Commune: "So many disappeared during the Commune, of whom there is no record. Their death is taken for granted. So was his in the Breton Village of his birth as in the streets of Paris." The other book, *The Silver Christ and the Lemon Tree*, consisted of three stories, two about Italian peasants: "the peasant does not look back; he only sees the road to gain his daily meal of bread or chestnuts. The past has no meaning to him, and to the future he never looks. That is the reason why those who want to cultivate or convince him fail utterly. If a man cannot see the horizon itself it is of no use to point out to him spires or trees or towers which stand out against it."

This was not what her publishers wanted from her and in her next book she tried to write as she had done when young. *Toxin* begins in somewhat the same manner as Louise de Vilmorin's charming "Madame de..." A young Italian countess loses her opals, an heirloom given her by her dead husband, midway between Venice and the Lido. The jewels lodge in a woodpile and are found by a young Sicilian prince—but instead of finishing as it begins, the story is bogged down by the prince's companion, a Svengali-like English surgeon through whom Ouida expresses her views on vaccination and vivisection: "the time is at hand when there will be no priests and no kings but those of science, and beneath their feet the nations will grovel in terror and writhe in death."

In January, 1895, Ouida, Gori, and the dogs—whose presence made it difficult for her to get hotel accommodation—moved to the Villa

Massoni in Sant' Allessio. Writing to Baron Tauchnitz, she said: "this place is very lovely; it is three miles from Lucca, with very fine trees, and gets the sea scent, and sea breeze. But it is quite out of the world—my world. Perhaps so much the better."

XXIX

Lᴵᴷᴱ ᴵᵀˢ ᴾᴿᴱᴰᴱᶜᴱˢˢᴼᴿˢ, this villa was too big for Ouida's needs—or furniture. It had four storeys and twenty-seven rooms. But small villas are rare around here, and even now a huge villa, with considerable land attached, can be bought outright for under six thousand pounds. Today the Villa Massoni is empty, with dust on its rosy tiles and spiders' webs lacing the faded Pompeian patterns on its walls. But its proportions are admirable, as is the garden, which reminded Ouida of her home in Florence; and the view of Lucca, beyond the woods, is dazzlingly beautiful. The present caretaker, a kindly man, told me he had heard that since the time of "the foreign writer" it had belonged to a German poet and a German sculptor, "nice gentlemen who received the visits of many nephews".

No nephew came to cheer Ouida, and her first year at the Villa Massoni was saddened by the death of Baron von Tauchnitz. None of her other publishers, several of whom made as much, if not more, money out of her, befriended her as did this remarkable man who had known her as a girl in London, in the days when Madame Ramé still looked young, and had the support of old Mrs. Sutton, the days when Louis Ramé's visits were still his daughter's greatest treats.

Oscar Wilde's trial occurred this year and in many homes gentlemen concealed newspapers lest ladies, particularly unmarried ladies, read disgraceful dialogue of this kind:

MR. CARSON: Were you on familiar terms with Granger? Did you have him to dine with you?

OSCAR WILDE: No, he waited at the table.

MR. CARSON: Did you ever kiss him?

OSCAR WILDE: He was a peculiarly plain boy. He was, unfortunately, very ugly. I pitied him for it.

MR. CARSON: Do you say that in support of your statement that you never kissed him?

After which piece of ill-considered flippancy, it was all up with poor Wilde. Commenting on this to Mrs. Huntington, Ouida wrote: "I am most grieved for his mother, a talented and devoted woman who has had nothing but sorrow all her life. It may be very immoral of me, but I do not think the law should meddle with these offences. The publicity caused does much more harm than the offence itself."

But Oscar Wilde's trial puzzled Ouida far less than did an interview with Mrs. Langtry, otherwise known as the Jersey Lily, published in "Galignani's Daily Messenger" at this time. This was one of the first newspaper interviews written up in the twentieth-century style, and although Mrs. Langtry had many of the attributes of an Ouida heroine, her attitude came through as expansive rather than dignified:

"I suppose you want me to tell you something about my early life, don't you? I was a young girl in my Jersey home, when a beautiful yacht sailed into the bay one fine morning. The owner on board was not so beautiful, but he made my acquaintance and then proposed to me. I thought that yachting on so fine a craft must be no end of fun, and I married him." None of Ouida's heroines, not even naughty Lady Dolly or the wicked Trefusis, had ever approached marriage in so blandly materialistic a spirit as that. This is one of those places where one is aware of Queen Victoria's reign drawing to a close and that of Edward VII beginning. Divorce would soon be possible even in the *right society*, and contraceptives would allow women some of the forms of choice hitherto restricted to men. "Sounds a bit matter-of-fact, doesn't it?" continued the Jersey Lily. "He took me away on the yacht for four months, and did not introduce me to a soul, which was not right. Then we went to London, where I knew only Lord Dudley and his daughters. I went out a little, and presently found myself quite in demand, which astonished me as I was very young. But I had a fair share of good looks then." After which she admitted to having been nicknamed Lalee, an Indian word meaning flirt, but "it is absurd, of course". She also declared herself interested by Theosophy and bicycles.

Always eager to plunge in, Ouida commented: "it would be wholly impossible, in an age which was not vulgar, for those journals which live on personalities to find a public. They are created by the greed of the multitude which calls for them. It is useless to blame the proprietors and editors who live on them; the true culprits are the readers."

More and more, she felt that she no longer understood the world in which she lived, and to Alfred Austin she admitted "I don't know what to do about publishers, I don't like offering myself". She liked very little of what was happening now. The discovery of X-rays, which was followed by that of the radio-activity of uranium, stirred her far less than did Dr. Jameson's raid into the Transvaal, or the emancipation of motor cars, which were no longer obliged to have men with red flags walking in front of them. To both of these developments Ouida strenuously objected; and the Distance Ride of German officers from Berlin to Vienna and back, in 1895, provoked her to write a furious letter, entitled "Decorated Butchers", to the secretary of the Peace Society: "If the riders had desired to prove their own endurance, they could have done so equally well with relays of horses ... To summon and fine, or imprison, a carter, for overworking his horse, whilst an officer who has ridden his charger to death is feasted and decorated by Emperors is one of those examples of 'one measure for the rich and another for the poor' which are the justification of the Anarchist." She also fought for the preservation of birds, and one of her articles on this subject was reproduced by the Italian Gazette five years after her death.

But out of this attitude of constant protestation came one of her most interesting books. A collection of nineteen essays, all but two of which had appeared in either the Fortnightly Review or the North American Review, *Views and Impressions* astonished many of those who had thought after reading *Toxin* that Ouida had no more to say. Not only had she plenty more to say, but she said it incisively, in a way that makes it possible for us to understand why clever men sought her company. These are her own opinions, not her own opinions adapted to the needs of fictitious characters.

Of conscription:

All the finest freedoms of mankind have been obtained, not by obedient, but by utterly disobedient persons; persons who, if they had failed, would have been thrown into prison or sent to scaffolds ... but were obedience the first of virtues, conscription does not teach it: it enforces it, which is a very different thing.

Of the state:

We have gained little by the emancipation of human society from the tyranny of the churches if in its stead we substitute the tyranny of the state.

Of a pro-German speech made by Lord Playfair to members of the British Association in 1885:

Are we not then justified in objecting to accept, whilst the chief issue of German culture is Militarism and anti-Semitism, such praises of Germany? . . . Playfair traces the defeat of France in 1870 to the inferiority of her university teaching, and gives the opinion of the Institut de France as his authority. It seems a singularly illogical and unphilosophical decision for such an august body to have given forth publicly. The causes of the defeat of France stretch farther back and have deeper roots than can be accounted for by the omission of the state to create more professors and laboratories. The whole teachings of history show that all states, after reaching their perihelion, gradually decline and sink into an inferior place amongst the nations. The day of France, as of England, is already past its noon.

Of Christianity:

"Rock of Ages cleft for ME," sighs the Christian; and this "immense ME" is, as Emerson has said of it, the centre of the universe in the belief of the unconscious egotist.

Of Disraeli:

No spectacle is more extraordinary than the power which Disraeli acquired after being laughed down by everyone; acquires and wields still, so many years after his death. I think that his most potent philtre lay in his flattery. He flattered his Sovereign, his party, and the nation itself, with all the florid eloquence and subtle suggestion of which he was so admirable a master. His famous "Peace with Honour" was an exact sample of his style: the peace was brittle and the honour was dubious, but his manner of presenting them was so magnificent that they were received as though they were gifts from heaven.

Particularly surprising is her Koestler-like observation: "there are no seismographic instruments in the political world."

This book showed an aspect of Ouida very unlike the one evoked by Lady Horner when writing about her invalid mother to Sir Edward Burne Jones: "When she is ill the only comfort she has is in a book—but, dear, it's not the Book as we were brought up to expect it should be—no—no—it is the words of a writer called Ouida, for which she craves, and nothing drier will satisfy her . . . and I have to read it aloud

70 Via Zanardelli, Viareggio, where Ouida died.

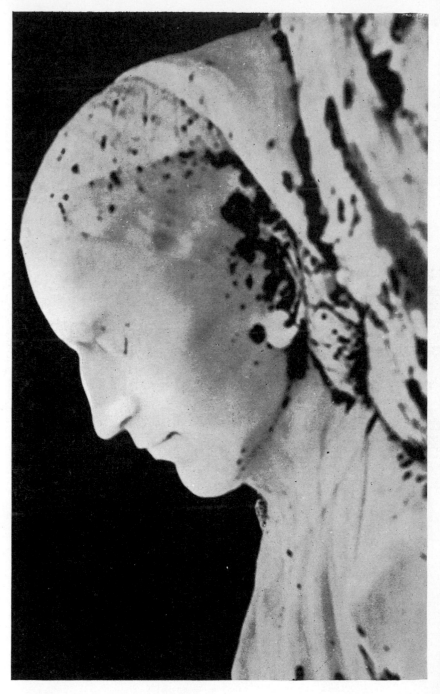

Ouida at sixty-eight. Her death mask

to her. . . . And I look up and see dear Mama's eyes wet with tears and she says . . . 'What I admire in Ouida is that Vice is Vice and Virtue is Virtue.' "

After *Views and Opinions* Ouida published *Le Selve*, the story of a Red-White Russian who acts as steward on an Italian estate near Rome, and attempts to deal fairly with the peasants, thereby provoking them to try to murder him. Although plausible, and embellished by good descriptions of the countryside between Rome and Viterbo, this book was not popular. Her publishers began to think that it was less her power to write than her power to write fiction that was failing—and at this point she wrote one of her finest novels.

XXX

THE MASSARENES, WHO give Ouida's next novel its title, are an elderly and vulgar husband and wife just returned to England from America, where William Massarene has made a fortune through energy and unscrupulousness. Now he is determined to get into smart society. Massarene is an excellently drawn character, based partly upon George Hudson, a York draper who became very powerful in England thanks to his shrewd exploitation of the current mania for railways. Queen Victoria and Prince Albert received Hudson, and although he told a board meeting that dividends might be paid out of capital, as this made people happy, no one seems to have suspected his unreliability until he was ruined, whereupon Punch published a parody:

> Toll for the Knave
> A Knave whose day is o'er!
> All sunk—with those who gave
> Their cash, till they'd no more.

The Massarenes' daughter, Katherine, who has been sent to England to be educated at an expensive school, is extremely unlike her parents. She is therefore shocked when her schoolfriend's father, Lord Framlingham, expresses what is the theme of the book:

> "My dear young lady, money is power. It is nothing new that it should be so; but in other ages it was subordinate to many greater

powers than itself. Now it is practically supreme; it is practically alone. Aristocracy in its true sense exists no longer. War in its modern form is wholly a question of supply. The victory will go to who can pay most and longest. The religious orders, once so absolute, are now timid anachronisms quaking before secular governments. Science, which cannot move a step without funds, goes cap in hand to the rich. Art has perished nearly. What is left of it does the same thing as science. The Pope, who ought to be a purely spiritual power, is mendicant and begs like Belisarius. What remains? Nothing except trade, and trade cannot oppose wealth, because it lives solely through it. For this reason, money, mere money, with no other qualities or attractions behind it, is omnipotent now as it never was before in the history of the world. It is not one person or set of persons who is responsible for this . . . in politics, as in war and in science, there is no moving a step without money. . . . Royalty recognising that money is stronger than itself, courts men of money, borrows from them, and puts out in foreign stocks what it borrows as a reserve fund against exile."

Thanks to his money, Massarene is able to persuade Lady Kenilworth (Mouse) to force society to accept his hospitality:

She had brought a "rattling good lot" with her; smart women and cheery men who could ride to hounds all day and play "bac" all night, or run twenty miles to see an otter-worry and be "fresh as paint" next morning; people with blue blood in their veins, and good old names, and much personal beauty and strength, much natural health and intelligence; but who by choice led a kind of life beside which that of an ape is intellectual and that of an amoeba is useful . . . people who could no more live without excitement than without cigarettes, who were never still unless their doctor gave them morphia, who went to Iceland for a fortnight and to Africa for a month; who never dined in their own homes except when they gave a dinner party, who could not endure solitude for ten minutes, who went anywhere to be amused, who read nothing except telegrams, and who had only two cares in life—money, and their livers.

Katherine Massarene is wretchedly aware that her father is making a fool of himself, but when she tries to tell her nice homely mother this:

"My dear," said Mrs. Massarene with solemnity, "a man never thinks he is ridiculous. He says to himself, 'I'm a man', and he gets a queer sort of comfort out of that, as a baby does out of sucking its thumb."

Nor is "Billy" Massarene as ridiculous as his daughter thinks—though even more odious. By dint of lending Mouse Kenilworth money he forces her to become his mistress, and enjoys making her pay for the many snubs he has endured from her. When Mouse's brother, Lord Hurstmonceau, who is very different from his sister, finds himself falling in love with Katherine, he is horrified—but Katherine is quite as determined as Hurstmonceau that he shan't disgrace his family by marrying "Billy's daughter". And after her father's murder, Katherine gives his money away in an attempt to make restitution for the way in which he obtained it. Now that she is no longer an heiress, those who previously admired her indubitable but severe beauty say "fine eyes, fine figure, but plain—and she was always so rude to the prince".

The Massarenes was said to have offended the Marlborough House Set. Judging by Miss Sackville West's admirable novel, "The Edwardians", it was certainly truthful enough to have done so. As obstinate over this as she had been over Friendship, Ouida told young Baron Tauchnitz: "there is not an iota of exaggeration in my book. . . . I would not say the whole of English society is thus, but the whole of what we call 'smart' society (which used to be called 'high society') is so."

The way in which The Massarenes was received prompted the twenty-five-year-old Max Beerbohm to make some suavely lethal references to incompetent critics—and to devote one of his most superb essays to Ouida. Since it is by far the finest piece of writing about her, it deserves lengthy quotation:

"Simpler, more striking, and more important, as an instance of reviewers' emptiness, is the position of Ouida, the latest of whose long novels, The Massarenes, had what is technically termed 'a cordial reception'—a reception strangely different from that accorded to her novels hitherto. Ouida's novels have always, I believe, sold well. Probably this is why, for so many years, no good critic took the trouble to praise them. . . . At length it occurred to a critic of distinction, Mr. G. S. Street, to write an 'Appreciation of Ouida', which appeared in the 'Yellow Book'. It was a shy, self-conscious essay, written somewhat in the tone of a young man defending the moral character of a barmaid who has bewitched him, but, for all its blushing diffidence, it was a very gentlemanly piece of work, and it was full of true and delicate criticism. I, myself, wrote later in praise of Ouida, and I believe that, at about the same time, Mr. Stephen Crane wrote an appreciation of his own in an American magazine. In a word, three intelligent persons had cracked their whips—enough to have called the hounds off. Nay more, the furious pack had been turned suddenly into a flock of nice sheep. It was pretty to see them gambolling and frisking and bleating around *The Massarenes*. . . . Ouida is essentially feminine, as much une femme des femmes as Jane Austen or 'John Oliver Hobbes', and it is indeed remarkable that she should be endowed with force and energy so exuberant and indefatigable. All her books are amazing in their sustained vitality. Vitality is, indeed, the most patent, potent factor in her work. Her pen is more inexhaustibly prolific than the pen of any other writer. . . . Ouida need not, and could not, husband her unique endowments, and a man might as well shake his head over the daily rising of the indefatigable sun, or preach Malthusianism in a rabbit-warren, as counsel Ouida to write less. Her every page is a riot of un-polished epigrams and unpolished poetry of vision. . . . Her style is a veritable cascade, in comparison with which the waters come down at Lodore as tamely as they come down at Shanklin. . . . Ouida grips me with her every plot, and—since she herself so strenuously believes in them—I can believe even in her characters. She cares for the romance and beauty and terror of life; not for its delicate shades and inner secrets. Her books are, in the true sense of the word, romances, though they are not written in Wardour Street. . . . She ranges hither and thither over all countries, snatching at all languages, realizing all scenes. Her information is as wide as Macaulay's and her slips in local colour are but the result of a careless omniscience. . . . Her delight in beautiful things has been accounted to her for vulgarity by those who think that a writer should take material luxury for granted. But such people forget, or are unable to appreciate, the difference between the perfunctory faking of description, as practised by the average novelist—as who should say 'soft carpets', 'choice wines', 'priceless Tintorettos'—and description which is the result of true vision. No writer was ever more finely endowed than Ouida with the love and knowledge of all kinds of beauty in art and nature. There is nothing vulgar in having a sense of beauty. . . . Ouida's descriptions of boudoirs and palaces are no more vulgar nor less beautiful than her descriptions of lakes and mountains." Sir Max then describes the guardsman so dear to Ouida in her Langham Hotel days: "Familiar with Cairene Bazaars as with the matchless deer-forests of Dunrobin, with the brown fens round Melton Mowbray as with the incomparable grace and brilliance of the court of Hapsburg; *bienvenu* in the Vatican as in the Quirinal; deferred to by Dips and

Decorés in all the *salons* of Europe, and before whom even Queens turned to coquettes and kings to comrades . . . passing from the bow windows of St. James' to the faded and fetid alleys of Stamboul, from the Quartier Breda to the Newski Prospect . . . Philip, nineteenth Marquis of Vauleris, as the world knew him—'Fifi of the First Life.'

"I am glad that in her later books Ouida has not deserted 'the First Life'. She is still the same Ouida, has lost none of her romance, none of her wit and poetry, her ebullitions of pity and indignation. The old 'naughtiness' and irresponsibility which were so strange a portent in the Medio-Victorian days, and kept her books away from the drawing-room table, seem to have almost disappeared. But, though she has become a mentor, she is still Ouida, still that unique, flamboyant lady, one of the miracles of modern literature. After all these years, she is still young and swift and strong, towering head and shoulders over all the other women (and all but one or two of the men) who are writing English novels. That the reviewers have tardily trumpeted her is amusing, but no cause for congratulation. I have watched their attitude rather closely. They have the idiot's cunning and seek to explain their behaviour by saying that Ouida has entirely changed. Save in the slight respect I have noted, Ouida has not changed at all. She is still Ouida. That is the high compliment I would pay her."

But when this essay appeared in his collection "More" in 1899, Max Beerbohm paid Ouida an even higher compliment. He dedicated the book:

To
Mlle de la Ramée
with the author's compliments
and to
Ouida
with his love

—thus assuring her a place in literary history, apart from her intrinsic merits.

XXXI

THE MASSARENES WAS not the only writing Ouida produced the year she was fifty-eight. *An Altruist*, a short novel satirizing a young aristocrat with a taste for socialism and vegetarianism, appeared during the same period and, of more importance, she wrote two excellent articles for the Fortnightly Review.

Ouida's article on Gabriele d'Annunzio, the Condottiere-like Italian poet, playwright, novelist—and, during the First World War, airman—was the first one devoted to him in English, and is appreciative and subtle:

> His morality is of the most primitive kind; or rather, he has none whatever, no more than has a South-Sea islander lying in the sun under a cocoa-nut tree whilst the surf bathes his naked limbs. It would be absurd to accuse him of immorality because the indulgence of the senses is as natural and as legitimate in his estimation, as Favetta's song among the golden furse, or the reaper's welcome of the purple wine. Yet by a not rare anomaly, this demand for perfect freedom of the passions is accompanied by a tendency to desire tyranny in political matters. He is disposed to deify force. In one or two expressions there is an echo of Carlyle.

It is interesting to compare this essay with the account of d'Annunzio in Sir Osbert Sitwell's "Noble Essences".

The second essay, on the French novelist, Georges Darien, was even more perspicacious, because whereas d'Annunzio was famous both as a writer and as a fashionable man of many love affairs, Georges Darien was known to few people even in France. No Irishman· was more violently against the government, no anarchist more violent in the expression of his feelings. He never attempted to disguise his opinion that soldiers were fools, priests unhealthy, policemen corrupt, and the bourgeoisie disgusting—and he threatened to murder one of his publishers. But Léon Blum, Léon Daudet, Jarry, and Alphonse Allais recognised his talent, and a young French publishing house has just recently discovered and started republishing him. Ouida's essay begins:

> Of all countries, France remains the land in which it is possible to tell the most truth. . . . In Italy, as in Germany and Austria, it [Darien's

anti-war novel, "Biribi"] would have been stopped by fine, exile, and seizure. In Russia it could never have been issued at all. In England it would have been as costly to the publisher as were his issues of Zola to the unhappy and martyrised Vizetelly. [A London-born printer's son, who had been Berlin and Paris correspondent of the Illustrated London News, Henry Vizetelly had started publishing translations of French and Russian authors, and had been prosecuted, fined, and imprisoned for publishing Zola's "La Terre". After analysing Darien's work with great care and feeling, Ouida comments:] To represent war as it is done in the terrible pages of "La Débâcle", or in the heartrending sketch of the "attaque du Moulin", is not difficult to the novelist who has power and knowledge. To represent the effects of war on entirely uninteresting and commonplace persons, and yet keep the attention riveted to what is passing in one ordinary household during a frightful national calamity, is a far more difficult feat.

Ouida's essays were in demand now, and during the next three years twenty-eight of them were published in the Fortnightly Review, the North American Review, the Nineteenth Century, and the Nuova Antologia. One of them, written at W. H. Stead's request, about the state of modern Italy, aroused governmental disapproval. Telling Baron Tauchnitz about this, Ouida commented: "I hear Crawford is banished from Court in Rome because the Queen is so angry at what he said about the Quirinal, etc. She would be wiser to reflect that when two persons so unlike each other as Crawford and I both condemn a regime, there must be grave faults in it. But Royal people put their heads in a sack and never see daylight."

The Crawford in question was Marion Crawford, the American novelist. Fifteen years younger than Ouida, he was the son of an American sculptor, Thomas Crawford, who had settled in Italy in order to study under Thorwaldsen, and also a nephew of Julia Ward Howe, the distinguished prison reformer and suffragette whose Battle Hymn of the Republic was published in the Atlantic Monthly in 1862. Born in Bagni di Lucca, then a very fashionable watering place, Marion Crawford had had an excellent and varied education, and edited the Allahabad Indian Herald before writing his first novel, "Mr. Isaacs", and returning to Italy, where he settled to novel-writing.

There were many reasons why Ouida might not have cared for Crawford's work—his point of view was intensely devout and conservative, and since he was a foreigner writing about Italy she might, illogically but comprehensively, have felt that he was poaching on her preserves. But in fact she did not. She reviewed his novel, "Don Orsino", in a way that made people want to read it:

> There are many pathetic touches in Crawford's portrait of Spicca and little incidents entirely true to the life of an Italian gentleman of aristocratic race and straitened means, as when in his distress of mind his servant persuades him to eat "a little mixed fry" with fresh salad, "the salad is very good today"; and Spicca, touched and refreshed, examines his meagre purse and takes out a ten-franc note which he gives to the man, remarking that it will buy him a pair of boots, and this ten-franc note is, when his purse lies on the table at night, slipped back into it by the servant, who knows that his master "never counts".

The fact that such types as Spicca still exist is, incidentally, shown by de Sica's portrayal of the aristocratic old gambler in the film "The Gold of Naples".

Of Crawford's work as a whole, Ouida comments that "it is surprising that he does not write for the stage, since his command of incident and of intricacies of circumstance would raise him high above many playwrights of the London theatre". And she ends by urging him to write a novel set in modern Rome: "But he must realize that the 'unbelievers' and revolutionists, who at present horrify him, constitute the keenest intellectual element in Italy, indeed, the only healthy one, and contain the only hope there is . . . of any attainment by the nation in the future to any true liberty."

Another contemporary writer whom Ouida admired at this time was Wilfrid Scawen Blunt. This strikingly handsome man had distinguished himself as poet, traveller, diplomat, rebel, and eccentric. In his youth he had been the lover of Skittles, one of the most famous courtesans of the period; he had bred Arab horses and taken part in bullfights; and his wife was Byron's granddaughter. No wonder Ouida wrote:

> There are few men of our time more interesting than the man who bears this name. Fresh with English air, and dark with desert suns, passionately liberal in thought and nobly independent in opinion, spending his winters on the shores of the Nile, on the edge of the desert, and his summers between the vale of Shoreham . . . he touches life at its most different facets. . . . His private life is equally of interest

... since he is the husband of Byron's granddaughter, the father-in-law of Neville Lytton, the companion in youth of Owen Meredith, the friend of the Arab, the champion of the dumb, and the standard-bearer of all lost causes.

Some remarks by Henley irritated her into adding:

> I do not think it was necessary for Mr. Henley to say that Mr. Blunt is not John Milton. It would not occur to anyone that he was. ... We can none of us judge what posterity may do or say. I fear it will be too engrossed with itself to take much heed of anything which went before it. Or, possibly, there will be no posterity at all, but only a shattered earth; scattered into space by some exploit of that boastful learning called science.

This article brought her into correspondence with Blunt, who had recently been imprisoned for two months for taking part in a forbidden meeting in Ireland, and the violence of his views encouraged her disgust at the Boer War. "Words," she wrote to him in November, 1899, "however powerful, utterly fail to turn the tide of the sort of brutal insanity which is now possessing the English. ... I fear that for many thousands of years Africa will be a field of battle. The powers who hate each other are there cheek by jowl, like live snakes shut up in a basket. ... The war party sends lecturers to rouse even remote little provincial towns with the most horrible stories of the 'atrocities' of the Boers. It makes one think of the Bulgarian atrocities, when 'the impaled Christians' turned out to be posts of wood to mark the height of the river." (These views were shared by David Lloyd George, the member for Carnarvon Boroughs, with the result that on one occasion a mob outside the Birmingham Town Hall called for his blood.)

Next spring Blunt paid Ouida a visit, accompanied by Sir Sydney Cockerell, then a young man of twenty-three. This occasion is described in Blunt's diary.

"We went, Cockerell and I, to call on Ouida at her Villa at S. Alessio. Our driver did not know the house or understand who it was that we wanted to visit, but at last suggested, in answer to our questions, 'the lady with the many dogs'. 'Oh yes,' we said, 'the lady with the dogs.' And so, sure enough, it was. Arrived there, we found it to be a nice old villa, with trees and a high garden wall and an eighteenth-century iron gate, towards which, from inside, seven or eight dogs, poodles and nondescripts, came at us open-mouthed. The noise was deafening, and it was some time before we could make our ringing heard. At last the bell was answered by a portly man-cook in cap and apron, who, after some delay consequent on my sending in my card, admitted us. At the end of ten minutes we were shown into a front hall, and there found the lady of the house, seated at a small table (as one finds in the opening scene of a play)—a little old lady," (Ouida was sixty-one at the time, one year older than Blunt himself) "dressed in white, who rose to meet us and to reprove her dogs, who were yelping at us still in chorus. A mild reproof it was, nor did it save us from their caresses. The largest poodle placed his paws upon my knees, and another took my hat in his mouth. 'They do not often bite,' she explained, 'except beggars.'

"We sat down and talked. I had been prepared, by the violence of some of her writings, to find her somewhat loud and masculine; but she proved the reverse of this. In face Ouida is much more French than English; her father, she told us, was French, Monsieur Ramé, and her mother an Englishwoman. She is small-featured, soft and distinguished, though she can never have been pretty, with a high forehead, rather prominent blue eyes, dulled and watery with age, almost white hair, and that milk-and-roses complexion which old people sometimes get, and which gives them a beatified look. . . . Her conversation is good, intellectual, but not affected or the talk of a blue stocking; it gives one the impression of a woman who has thought out her ideas and has the courage still of her opinions. . . . She was greatly taken with Cockerell, perhaps for his modesty, and was curious as to who he could be, for I had not introduced him. . . . When at the end of a couple of hours we moved to go, she would have detained us and made us both promise to come again. She cannot go now to England on her dogs' account: altogether she is a somewhat pathetic figure, condemned to solitude, not by choice but by necessity. . . . We both left her with feelings of respect, almost of affection, certainly of sympathy."

Neither ever saw her again, but Sydney Cockerell, always responsive to talent, wrote to her regularly. At first she hesitated to respond to his kindness, telling him: "I should have written, but you are young, and must have so much to interest and occupy you, that I hesitated to take up your time." In addition to letters he sent her books, including ones by William Morris and Samuel Butler that she found true and interesting, by Kipling, whom she considered all vitriol and blood, and by Tolstoy, whose opinions excited her as a bone does a dog and drove her to expostulate:

If you do not believe in the divinity of Christ what remains? What of course was always there, a poor man of fine instincts sore troubled by the suffering and the injustice which torment Tolstoy today. He drew the poor after him, naturally, by his assurances that the future would compensate them for their painful labour. . . . 'One must believe in something', I am told. Why? Why should one need a belief? The whole of existence is a mystery; and science does not explain it more than ignorance. . . . The mere sentimental 'do unto others' etc. cannot restrain the passions, or rein in the appetites, or solve the problems of life. Tolstoy is dangerous because he is misleading. He is an educated Christ. If he had been born in France he would have been a very great man, but the frightful life of Russia has disturbed his brain.

She also thought that "his morality and monogamy are against nature and common sense".

But although Sydney Cockerell kept her in touch with current events, he could not make these agreeable to her. She was neither a stupid nor a reactionary woman, but the extent of the changes to which people of her generation were required to adapt themselves can be gauged by the fact that the world into which she was born contained no bicycles, bombs, cash registers, combustion engines, electric light, fountain pens, gramophones, radios, motion pictures, machine-guns, telephones, tanks, barbed-wire, anaesthetics, or typewriters. Now the first aeroplane had left the ground; the Curies had discovered radium; Planck had formulated the Quantum theory; and Freud had founded psychoanalysis. Yet at the opening of the twentieth century England was again at war. Like many liberals at this time, Ouida was so disgusted by the Boer War as to be inclined to blame it on the technical progress that had preceded it.

XXXII

BY TODAY'S STANDARDS the Boer War was a small one. Nevertheless it aroused feelings as violent as any recently stirred by the Suez Canal. In 1836 some South African Dutch farmers, outraged by the British having abolished slavery without giving them the financial compensation they wanted, moved away and formed two republics

north and south of the river Vaal. Here they maintained their own way
of living until the discovery of gold and diamonds, around 1868,
brought a rush of fortune-hunters to the Rand, which had been
annexed by Disraeli in 1877 and restored by Gladstone four years later.
Before long Kruger, the Dutch leader, became convinced that these
foreigners, known as Uitlanders, were plotting, with British help, to
grab his state. Meanwhile the British became convinced that Kruger
was using part of the country's recently discovered wealth to plot
against themselves with the support of Germany—and when the Kaiser
congratulated Kruger on the defeat of Jameson's raid into the Transvaal, public opinion in England became bellicose. There were, however, private opinions, and many English liberals were as pro-Boer as
was feeling on the Continent, where the Boers were considered a
handful of Davids bravely facing a regiment of Goliaths. Opinion was
deeply shocked by the deaths of Boer women and children in concentration camps. Over 20,000 perished, far more than died on the battle-
field; and Ouida reflects the liberal attitude at its most violent.

To Baron Tauchnitz she wrote: "It is a frightful thing that this war
should be carried on solely to suit the manœuvres of Chamberlain,
Rhodes, and the Stock Exchange. Europe should have intervened last
August"; to George de Sarmento: "Just now I can think of nothing
but of the disasters of the brave Boers and the disgusting drunken
vileness of the English"; and to Frederic Harrison, editor of the
Positivist Review, she sent a poem addressed to Queen Victoria
beginning

> "Before your failing sight, the hot-red glare
>   Of burning homesteads must inflame the night"

and proceeding

> "Could you not, even in the chills of age,
>   Have found some strength to rise and to refuse?"

Although she knew Frederic Harrison to be a professor of Jurisprudence and International Law, Ouida was amazed by his refusal to
allow the Queen to be insulted in the pages of his magazine. "I am
sure Byron would have said what I say," she told him—a reply in
which logic and the lack of it are characteristically mixed, since Byron
very probably would have shared her views, but to an editor with
laws of libel to consider this was not a relevant point.

Among the wartime stories carried by newspapers, one of the most colourful was that of twenty-six-year-old Winston Churchill. His behaviour was so like that of a character in one of Ouida's books that it was difficult for her to withhold admiration. Already he had taken part, sabre in hand, in the last cavalry charge in India, and fought as a volunteer with the Spaniards against the Americans in Cuba. Now he was in South Africa as correspondent for the Morning Post and, before long, was taken prisoner. Scarcely had the press announced in Boys' Own Paper tones that, beyond a slight bullet wound in his left hand, Mr. Churchill was "well and hearty, though naturally chafing at his enforced idleness", than Mr. Churchill had made a sensational escape and returned home to take his seat as a conservative M.P.

The war was still on when Queen Victoria died, in her eighty-second year. The shock to England was comparable with that sustained when the Duke of Wellington died. The great majority of her subjects could remember no other ruler and, as in the case of Wellington, an awed uneasiness increased their grief. Many of them felt that in losing her they were losing some unspecified but valuable form of protection, and the fact that her death occurred in wartime, and at the turn of the century, seemed to increase its significance. Ouida was less affected. "At least," wrote she of Edward VII, "he is a man of the world, and he won't publish silly books in bad English."

When at last the Boer War drew to a close many of those who shared Ouida's feelings about it thought its end as depressing as its beginning. The Treaty of Vereeniging made the Boers part of the British Empire, but gave them three million pounds with which to start rebuilding their farms; and when their General Botha came to London, he was astonished to hear crowds cheering him. Ouida's comment to Sydney Cockerell was:

> I thought the Boers, at least, knew how to die, and would show the old Thermopylean spirit to the end. Whereas everything collapses, and finishes in a grotesque and pantomime-like manner, and one does not see why or for what they have been resisting two years and eight months . . . the whole thing is sickening and more like a Christmas burlesque than a chapter in the history of Great Britain.

Ouida's own existence was about to collapse in a way that was grotesque, pantomime-like, and tragic. Her taxes, as she told Norman Douglas, had been increased by one-third, and the tax collector had threatened sequestration. Her immediate, and typical, reaction was to ask Wilfrid Scawen Blunt if he knew of revolvers small and light enough for her to fire, yet "sternly effective".

XXXIII

Ouida had paid the rent of the Villa Massoni for eight years, but doing so had left her little money over and her maid, Gori, had formed the habit of feeding her mistress with leftovers collected from the kitchen of Madame Grosfils, the neighbour who owned the Villa Massoni and was married to the Belgian Consul at Lucca. Gori had done this with the best intentions—but without Ouida's knowledge, and it encouraged Madame Grosfils in her determination to make Ouida relinquish the villa. As Madame Grosfils had no legal justification for asking Ouida to break the existing agreement, she consulted Mr. Montgomery Carmichael, the British Consul at Leghorn. He tried to explain Madame Grosfils' point of view to Ouida, who at last agreed to leave on November 17th, 1903.

But Madame Grosfils was among those who given an inch take several ells. Not content with a victory she had had no right to expect, she sent her sons to take possession of the villa on November 16th. Accompanied by a number of louts, they broke into the grounds, pillaged the villa, and seized personal belongings such as a dispatch-box containing Ouida's letters from Lord Lytton. So isolated was the villa that this repulsive behaviour caused them no immediate inconvenience. On the contrary. They were able to keep all they could grab of Ouida's paintings, china, books, manuscripts, and personal letters. After a happy looting session they settled down to drinking and brawling until two o'clock, when they fell asleep. Next morning, Ouida told Baron Tauchnitz: "At 7 a.m. they came up and insisted on me and my maid getting into a vehicle they had sent for and going to Viareggio (where I intended to go), eighteen miles, without bath or breakfast. I was foolish not to send for the carabiniers, but I was not sure what rights I had, as it was the last day, and I was very ill from fasting and sleeplessness." (The Grosfils and their accomplices could easily have prevented her or Gori leaving.) "I took the dogs, of course; they would not let me take anything else except some linen."

The next seven months were spent by Ouida, in great distress, at the Hotel de Russie, Viareggio. Full of misplaced zeal—misplaced in

the sense that it was of no material benefit to herself—she determined
to bring a case against the Grosfils. Mr. Carmichael tried to dissuade
her, not because he sympathized with the Grosfils, which he did not,
but because he thought Ouida had neither the strength nor the money
to fight the case. He under-estimated her strength so far as character
was concerned, but it would have been better for her had she followed
his advice.

While preparing to attack the Grosfils, Ouida visited d'Annunzio,
who was temporarily living in the neighbourhood. He was then forty-
one, and had just brought his famous love affair with the great actress,
Eleanora Duse, to an end by putting her into his novel "Il Fuoco",
which caused her great pain. In it he gave the impression that his
mistress was considerably older than himself. In fact, she was only four
years older. Ouida describes his villa as a mere cotton-box with a
dreary waste around it, the pines having been cut down. He had taken
the house for six months, but only stayed two, and the peasants told
Ouida that he cried a great deal. This small village, with its six miles of
sand, and its pine woods associated in both their minds with Byron
and Shelley, was an oddly appropriate place for the meeting of this
vigorously emotional pair.

Nor did Ouida ignore more, conventionally speaking, ordinary
companions. Two months after her villa was sacked, this lonely
woman of sixty-five was writing to Sir Sydney Cockerell: "In Lucca
a cook and an ostler quarrelled about frying; the latter ripped open the
former's abdomen. In front of my villa at S. Alessio a girl sat on a wall,
plaiting; she chaffed a peasant passing by; he shot at her with a revolver.
The bullet entered her brother's thigh; he was three months in hospital.
These are everyday occurrences. No one blames them; and unless the
offender is a socialist or an anarchist, they are seldom punished." She
also wrote deploring his sympathy with the Japanese in the Russo-
Japanese war: "If Russia and Japan could eat each other up like Kil-
kenny cats it would be well for the world. They are both cruel savages
with a veneer of civilization. I remember my father saying when I was
a child that the yellow race would overrun the European countries. . . .
War, as we know it, may end, because armies will mutually blow each
other into space. . . . Patriotism is not what we want in Europe and
America. It is a much wider, finer, more impersonal feeling." But
her loneliness showed in a postscript to a letter to Sarmento: "tell me
all the people you see."

Once sure that she was going to attack them, the Grosfils parents
prudently went to Belgium; but the two sons appeared in court at

Bagni di Lucca on December 19th, 1904. Ouida wore a black dress, a black cloak lined with grey plush, and a black hat with ostrich feathers. She curtseyed to the judge, and meant to be on her best behaviour: but, when false evidence was given, could not resist exclaiming "What a lie!", which distressed her lawyer. Fortunately she was admirably supported by Gori, whose evidence, as Ouida informed Sarmento, won the case. The judge told Henri Grosfils that every word he uttered was a lie, and both he and his mother were sentenced to ten months in prison, while Ouida was awarded costs. The Grosfils parents then took the case to the Lucca Court of Appeal, where they lost again. After which they tried the Court of Cassation at Rome, where they also lost. Justice was done, but it was of no material use to Ouida. Writing to Baron von Tauchnitz, she said: "You were quite right that it was a terrible risk to run, to embark on this litigation; but I had no choice. I was forced either to prosecute or meekly have my throat cut. As yet I have not been reimbursed a farthing, although they are legally condemned to pay all costs and damages."

Ouida never received a farthing of the payment awarded her. Perhaps because of Monsieur Grosfils' position, which should have enabled him to teach his sons civility, the prison sentence was commuted by a Royal Act of Clemency to a fine, and the boys were allowed to leave the country. The civil action for damages and recovery was still going on six years after Ouida's death.

After the case Ouida returned to Viareggio, and presently took a small villa at Camaiore, a village ten miles inland. Even now, two world wars later, it has not greatly changed, with its narrow streets, seventeenth-century houses with handsome doors topped by carved escutcheons, its cathedral with black-and-white marble floor, its tawny and grey Jesuit *trompe l'oeil* and, outside, a delightful fountain dominated by marble dolphins and seashells given by Robert, last Duke of Parma-Bourbon to reign.

Here she tried to work on *Helianthus*, a long-planned novel satirizing royalty. She had already signed a contract for it with Macmillan, whose kindness, she told Baron von Tauchnitz, was "constant and beyond praise". But she found it very difficult to work. She was sixty-seven and her health was failing. Yet even this book, dragged out of her by will power, contained flashes of talent.

Helianthus is an imaginary country, very like Greece, and its ruler a portrait of the Kaiser—the appalling results of whose behaviour Ouida clearly foresaw. The king's second son, Prince Elim, a character based in part on Rudolf of Hapsburg, goes to visit an old revolutionary and falls in love with his granddaughter, Ilia. This leads to several political incidents. The death of the Crown Prince makes Elim the heir, but the old king is determined to prevent his reigning—and here the manuscript breaks off.

Ouida's attempts to keep at this—she had never yet failed to fulfil a contract—were interrupted by the temporary enforcement in Camaiore of a muzzling order. More concerned for her animals' comfort than for her own, she hired a carriage and took Gori and the dogs to Viareggio where the muzzling order, which was seasonal and varied from place to place, was no longer in effect. On arrival she sent Gori to stay with her mother, who lived nearby, and took the dogs and herself to the Hotel de Russie. But the hotel was full, as were all the other places to which she applied. At last, in despair, she hired a cab which the driver consented to leave in the station piazza while he and his horse went home. In this Ouida and her dogs spent the night. The semi-detached house in Bury St. Edmunds had been a poor place compared with the Villa Farinola, but paradise beside this dark cab, surrounded by white mists blowing in from the sea.

In the morning Ouida's right eye was inflamed. The inflamation became glaucoma. A month later that eye was blind. Writing to Sir Sydney she said: "It is no disfigurement, but the sight is gone. And my sight has been so wonderful. Last autumn I could see the satellites of Jove without a glass." Perhaps her lingering vitality reminded her now of what she had written in *Syrlin*:

> Other people were kind because she was popular, attractive, and extremely the fashion, and although the quality of the kindness did not deceive her, although she knew that if she became poor, or blind, or ill, on the morrow very few of them would ever ask where she had gone to or what had become of her, she allowed herself to be etherized by that soporific of stimulating atmosphere; it was so pleasant while it lasted.

In addition to the sight of one eye, she partially lost the use of one ear. But her dogs had not been muzzled. And she still had the courage of her convictions.

Thanks to Gori's mother, summer accommodation was found for the old woman and her four dogs in Mazzarosa, a mountain village half-way between Viareggio and Lucca. It consisted of three small rooms looking out over a drab kitchen garden containing a well upon which the entire village depended for water. When, later, Mrs.

Whipple, American Red Cross worker and writer, visited this village and asked the local people if they had liked the English writer, they said, "Si, Signora, La Signora Inglese era sempre molto gentile verso di noi ed anche, era la mama dei cani." (The English lady was always very nice to us, and also she was the dogs' mother.)

From here reports of her distress spread, all admirably illustrative of the fable of the cricket and the ant, except that in this case the cricket had not only danced but also worked harder than a regiment of ants. To Ouida's horror, Marie Corelli made an appeal on her behalf in the Daily Mail; and Lady Paget—but Ouida didn't know this was who it was—asked the Prime Minister, Sir Henry Campbell-Bannerman, to grant her a Civil List Pension of a hundred and fifty pounds a year.

Most feeling of all, since it contained more admiration than pity, was the behaviour of Vernon Lee, as shown by an article in the Westminster Gazette of July 27th, 1907. Passing through Lucca railway station, Vernon Lee had been shocked to see an English newspaper placard headed "Ouida in Want". The article's exaggeration—"Ouida's carriage and pair of her Florence days turned into forty horses"—made Miss Lee dismiss the whole report as untrue, until she found it confirmed by the Italian papers. She then telegraphed to an old friend, an English trained nurse who lived in Lucca, asking her to go to Mazzarosa. The friend went and reported that Ouida was weak, and had been made ill by reading the article in question.

This was true. Ouida wrote to Lady Dorothy Nevill: "What an extraordinary thing that publication by the Daily Mirror of a portrait of an old peasant as me!—because they could not see me, they gave an old woman on a neighbouring farm five francs to sit to them, and actually published her photograph as mine. The Italian papers meanwhile got a photograph of my mother (who died in '94) and issued it as a recent one of me." And she told the British Consul at Leghorn: "Meanwhile it is enormously painful and injurious to me. For the saying of Voltaire is so true: calomniez, calomniez, calomniez! Toujours quelque chose restera. There will always be many who will believe I was starving on the seashore, though I was seven months at the Hotel Gran Bretagna [a cheaper one than the Hotel de Russie] and left there ten days ago; they are not people to have let me depart had I not paid them the uttermost farthing."

Although weak, Ouida was not bedridden, and still exercised her unmuzzled dogs in the kitchen garden. Gori looked after her devotedly, going into Viareggio to get her fish and fetch her mail, of which she still received plenty. Her rent was paid regularly, and both the Prefect of Lucca's secretary and the British Consul visited her, as did others whom she was not always well enough to receive. She was obliged to stay where she was not only by lack of money, but because hotels would not accept her dogs, and the muzzling order made towns inacceptable to her.

Although Ouida had known Vernon Lee in Florence she had not been particularly interested in her—perhaps because this scholarly woman, born in France of English parents, was not at all the kind of person who set her imagination working—but she knew her value well enough to be touched by Vernon Lee's generous article:

"I have applied to Ouida the epithet *illustrious* and, in order to show that I have done so deliberately, I must enter upon some remarks for the benefit of critics in particular and superfine people in general. In calling Ouida *illustrious* I do not imply that her novels will be published in ornamental editions all through the ages. Still less that their every particular . . . would meet the taste of my juniors. . . . I do not hold that the chief function of literature is to suit the future . . . the real business of a book is to serve and satisfy its own day. . . . Twenty-five or thirty years ago she gave us critical elderly people who forget or despise her some of the most fruitful pleasure of our youth. Bred in the reign of Bulwer Lytton and Disraeli, with Byronian and Sandesque romanticism still in the air, before Flaubert was heard of, or Mr. George Moore, and when the earliest style of Mr. Henry James was still in the lap of his nurse; moreover, when Italy, barely freed of Austrian garrisons and Calabrian brigands, was not yet the playground of excursions . . . Ouida gave her readers . . . one of the many successive, constantly renewed revelations of the Land of Lands. . . . Those too young to recognize the influence of Ouida's Italian novels in their thoughts, can find an objective proof of my assertion by comparing her books with those of her juniors, whenever they have dealt well with things Italian. There is Ouida in the finest recent historical romance on an Italian subject, Mrs. Wharton's "Valley of Decision"; there is Ouida, come through heaven knows what unnoticed channels, in the admirable pages about Italy by M. Barres and Madame de Noailles; I venture to say that there is Ouida even in the medieval fantasies of Anatole France . . . there is Ouida at every step in D'Annunzio's prose. . . . All this—this power of seeing and feeling and creating in a particular way—is what Ouida has given us . . . and this being so, what does it matter if the shapes, the symbols, the tricks of invention and expression . . . are not of the sort which we today happen to consider immortal?"

But for one article of this kind there were dozens pandering to their readers' silliest instincts, and Ouida was so humiliated that she ceased to be able to distinguish kindness from officiousness. Feeling "no one cares. It does not matter to anyone", she even resented the obligation to state her age if she was to receive the Civil List Pension and, refusing the Mayor of Lucca's offer of a free apartment, she returned to Viareggio, this time to 70, Via Zanardelli. The Via Zanardelli is a small street running straight from the beach to the pine woods behind Viareggio. Number seventy, unchanged since then, except for one ceiling damaged by bombs during the second world war, is a small two-storey house, slightly humbler than the one in which she was born. It has black-and-white-marble floors, white-washed walls, heavy wooden doors and shutters, and a well in the small back courtyard. There are two windows, one on either side of the front door, and three above; the shutters are grey, and the façade distempered a faded tawny-orange colour. At the corner of the street is the market-place, with great plane trees. Architecturally, the circle of her life was complete.

While Ouida was here she received a big offer, transmitted by Mr. Carmichael, to write her autobiography. But consistently—she was as consistent in important matters as she was arbitrary over trivial ones— she refused, saying that memoirs, even the delicious French ones, cannot but betray the dead. In many respects she was as loyal as her guardsmen and her dogs. And although convinced that, as she told Sir Rennell Rodd, the end of her life "was destined to be like that of an old horse, all misery", she had not lost her grasp intellectually. In reply to a letter from Lady Constance Leslie, she wrote:

All religions are interesting as testifying the need and hope of the mind for something it has not. .... Christianity is only a reproduction of great Oriental myths; and myself I am much more satisfied by a pure deism which hopes someday to have the mystery of life solved, and hopes for a great Spirit to which it can commend its beloved. The Psalms are beautiful for they are the eternal cry of the human heart 'Why has Thou created me if I must perish in darkness?' But I protest against Christianity arrogating to itself the title of one only, or even of the best religion. In the history of the world it is a thing of yesterday. Were it logically followed society would go to pieces tomorrow and if its professors really carried out its precepts there would be sheer Socialism over all the world. It is the Socialism in it which makes it so acceptable to the democracy of the day

There were great and beautiful lives thousands of years before Christianity was known. There will be thousands of such lives long after it has passed away.

At last Ouida's body, which had always been inferior to her mind and, being unsuited to her temperament, had often served her ill, came to her rescue by proving unequal to pneumonia. So at one o'clock on the morning of Saturday, January 25th, 1908, *Maria Louise Ramé*, so long known as *Mademoiselle de la Ramée*, acquired a death certificate as *Louisa della Ramee, detta Ouida, Letterata.*

XXXIV

THE DEATH CERTIFICATE was witnessed by Mr. Carmichael, who told Lady Constance Leslie that if he could recover a hundred pounds due to Ouida, he would be able to pay her few debts and funeral expenses. Lady Paget found the dogs good homes, and Ouida's body was taken to the Protestant Cemetery at Bagni di Lucca and given— by an admirer who preferred to remain anonymous—a marble tomb, based on that of young Ilaria del Caretto in Lucca Cathedral, showing her in effigy lying with a little dog at her feet. On it is written:

IN MEMORY

OF

LOUISE DE LA RAMÉE
OUIDA

WRITER OF INCOMPARABLE NOVELS

This cemetery is one of the loveliest in the world, even lovelier than the Protestant Cemetery in Rome. Mrs. Whipple, who was buried there herself twenty-two years later, describes it as follows:

"Looking across the river, another cypress-guarded enclosure is seen, the little English cemetery on a forest slope above the quiet road, the silence only broken by the murmur of trees and river. In autumn the grey walls burn with blood-red diaperies of woodbine, bringing into relief the white effigy of Ouida, for here the once popular story-teller rests. Perhaps there is nothing more pathetic in the whole valley to those familiar with Ouida's declining years than the recumbent figure with a little dog at her feet. The memory comes of those later days of poverty and pride, of her seclusion with a bevy of half-fed dogs, in the humble *contadino* house at Mazzarosa; of her long illness, and then the silent journey from Viareggio, where she died, to her resting-place by the Lima River. Gazing upon that sad face, her eccentricities and vanities fade away in the light of her untiring efforts for the welfare of little children and animals, and especially for the Italian peasants."

Where untiring efforts for others were concerned, Mrs. Whipple, wife of the Bishop of Minnesota, knew what she was talking about. When she died in London, in 1930, she left instructions that she should be buried in Bagni di Lucca where she had nursed cases of Spanish 'flu in 1918. Beside her lies Elizabeth Cleveland of New York, another nurse, who died of the Spanish 'flu in 1918. They are near Ouida's tomb, with its rambler roses, violets, and primroses, and it is as if the Catherine of "Farewell to Arms" had wandered into Princess Napraxine's country. For the majority of the hundred and thirty-six graves in that now deserted riverside, mountain-surrounded garden shelter people belonging to the world of Ouida's books: Frederick Charles Philips, Esq., Late of the 13th King's Hussars, in which regiment he served in the Peninsular War and at the battle of Waterloo; Baron Julius de Sass, privy-counsellor to H.I.M. the Empress of Russia; Colonel Henry Sisted of the Royal Dragoons, a Gallant Gentleman and Accomplished Soldier; Mario Caccia, Colonello dei Bersaglieri, 1879, who lost an arm in the Italian War of Independence; Charles Isidore Hemans, youngest son of Felicia Hemans, author of "Casabianca" ("The boy stood on the burning deck"); Martha Sabina, daughter of Thomas Philips Lamb, Baron of the Cinque Ports. Ouida would have liked her new neighbours.

She had come a long way from Bury St. Edmunds, but she was not forgotten in her birthplace. The Daily Mirror started a memorial fund; a performance of *Under Two Flags* was given at the Lyceum; and a year later, the year Louis Blériot flew the English channel, a drinking fountain for dogs and horses was unveiled in Bury St. Edmunds. The inscription, composed by Lord Curzon, was:

"Born at Bury St. Edmunds, January 1st, 1839. Died in Viareggio, Italy, January 25th, 1908. Her friends have erected this fountain in the place of her birth. Here may God's creatures whom she loved assuage her tender soul as they drink."

When I reached Bagni di Lucca in the summer of 1956, the grass-grown, flower-starred cemetery was padlocked. But a labourer in a neighbouring field said he was going into the village for lunch and would tell the gardener I was there. Delighted that Ouida should have found so wild and lovely a resting place, I sat down beside the river. It was so quiet that the noise of water, birds, and insects seemed loud yet each sound distinct. Presently a man in faded blue overalls bicycled into sight and produced a big rusty key. When I apologised for bothering him, he said it was no trouble, no trouble at all; "She has many visitoirs".

At first I thought his proprietary interest due merely to his having vaguely heard of her. But it soon became apparent that he was considerably older than he seemed. When he was a child, English residents had often asked him to take Ouida "cakes and other delicacies—but she was a very proud old lady, and she gave the cakes to the dogs". Beside the tomb he picked a rose and gave it to me; then, after showing me the Baron, "a very important gentleman", and the American nurses, "very good ladies", he took me to the village.

Judging by photographs, Bagni di Lucca has not changed much since the days when the Brownings and the Storys summered here. A municipal councillor, hailed by the gardener, gave me a photograph of Bagni di Lucca. He too could remember her—not only her pride and her retinue of dogs but her bonnets: "like those of Queen Victoria". Now he wanted to take me to the house where Shelley lived, "because if you are interested in her you must be interested in him too". Assenting, I remembered that one of the reasons for Ouida's loving this part of the river Lima was because it meant so much to Shelley in the days when he was generally considered no more than an odd young man who was causing his father, Sir Timothy, a lot of trouble, don't you know.

Standing there with the councillor and the gardener gazing proudly and possessively from the rose in my hand to Shelley's house and back again, I suddenly seemed to hear Ouida telling Baron Tauchnitz not to add Louise de la Ramé to Ouida in his catalogues because "I love 'Ouida'. It is my very own as children say. I don't care for any of the other names I bear". As suddenly, I saw in my mind a series of pictures:

a child in Bury St. Edmunds cutting out cardboard knights and painting them in bright colours because she wanted to make past history live again; a little girl in Boulogne dancing to look a flesh-and-blood Bonaparte in the face; a crinolined adolescent walking in the grounds of Hardwick House and listening to her exotic father's stories of recent history; a young girl in London beginning to write her own history on paper; a nineteenth-century woman exploring the continent and finding Garibaldi's Italy; a successful writer pursuing love through the labyrinths of Florentine history; a middle-aged eccentric in retreat from the present—yet always at hand to fight for oppressed minorities, stray dogs, tortured birds, and lopped-off trees; a crazy old woman, in a bonnet like Queen Victoria's, giving her cakes to the dogs (and to mother them was her only reason for survival); and, last, but not least, a formidable marble death mask, very ugly from some angles, almost beautiful from others, but from every angle faintly smiling, as if belatedly appreciating the irony of the fact that, though all her life she consciously pursued love, it was her unconscious pursuit of the coloured facets of history that made her into an historical figure, minor perhaps but certainly authentic: "a unique flamboyant lady". Passionate and ludicrous, prejudiced and brave, this talented woman may not have been what she herself called a thoro'bred—but she had the royal touch.

BIBLIOGRAPHY

Books by Ouida

Held in Bondage. Tinsley, 1863.
Strathmore. Chapman and Hall, 1865.
Chandos. Chapman and Hall, 1866.
Under Two Flags. Chapman and Hall, 1867
Cecil Castlemaine's Gage and other Novelettes. Chapman and Hall, 1867.
Idalia. Chapman and Hall, 1867.
Tricotrin. Chapman and Hall, 1869.
Puck. Chapman and Hall, 1870.
Folle-Farine. Chapman and Hall, 1871.
A Dog of Flanders and Other Stories. Chapman and Hall, 1872.
Pascarel. Chapman and Hall, 1873.
Two Little Wooden Shoes. Chapman and Hall, 1874.
Signa. Chapman and Hall, 1875.
In a Winter City. Chapman and Hall, 1876.
Ariadne. Chapman and Hall, 1877.
Friendship. Chatto and Windus, 1878.
Moths. Chatto and Windus, 1880.
Pipistrello and Other Stories. Chatto and Windus, 1880.
A Village Commune and Other Stories. Chatto and Windus, 1881.
Bimbi: Stories for Children. Chatto and Windus, 1882.
In Maremma. Chatto and Windus, 1882.
Wanda. Chatto and Windus, 1883.
Frescoes: Dramatic Sketches. Chatto and Windus, 1883
Princess Napraxine. Chatto and Windus, 1884.
Othmar. Chatto and Windus, 1885.
A Rainy June. Maxwell, 1885.
Don Guesaldo. Tillotson's Shilling Fiction. Routledge, 1886.
A House Party. Hurst and Blackett, 1887.
Guilderoy. Chatto and Windus, 1889.
Ruffino and Other Stories. Chatto and Windus, 1890.
Santa Barbara and Other Tales. Chatto and Windus, 1891.
The Tower of Taddeo. Heinemann, 1892.
The New Priesthood: a Protest against Vivisection. Pamphlet published in 1893
    and republished by Unwin in 1901.
Two Offenders and Other Tales. Chatto and Windus, 1894.
The Silver Christ and a Lemon Tree. Unwin, 1894
Toxin. Unwin, 1895.
Views and Opinions. Methuen, 1895.
Le Selve and Other Tales. Unwin, 1896.

The Massarenes. Sampson Low, 1897.
Dogs. Simpkin, Marshall, 1897.
An Altruist. Unwin, 1897.
La Strega and Other Stories. Sampson Low, 1899.
The Waters of Edera. Unwin, 1900.
Critical Studies. Unwin, 1900.
Street Dust and Other Stories. White and Bell, 1900.
Helianthus. Macmillan. Published posthumously, unfinished, 1908.

Biographies of Ouida.

Ouida: a Memoir by Elizabeth Lee. Fisher Unwin, 1914.
Ouida: a study in ostentation, by Yvonne ffrench. Cobden-Sanderson, 1938.
Ouida the Passionate Victorian, by Eileen Bigland. Jarrolds, 1950.

Other books consulted.

Albini. "La Culture Italienne" by Maria Brandon-Albini. Editions André
    Bonne, 1950.
Allingham. "William Allingham: a Diary" ed. by H. Allingham and D.
    Radford, 1907.
Aubry. "Le Second Empire" by Octave Aubry.
Austin. Autobiography of Alfred Austin. 1911.
Barzini. "Italy and its Aristocracy" by Luigi Barzini, junior. Published in
    "Encounter", January, 1956.
Beerbohm. "Works and More" by Sir Max Beerbohm. John Murray, 1896.
Blanch. "The Wilder Shores of Love" by Lesley Blanch. John Murray, 1954.
Blunt. "My Diaries" by Wilfrid Scawen Blunt. Martin Secker, 1919-20.
Briggs. "Victorian People" by Asa Briggs. Odhams, 1954.
Chesterton. "The Victorian Age in Literature" by G. K. Chesterton.
Cockerell. "Friends of a Lifetime". Letters to S. C. L. Cockerell, edited by
    Viola Meynell.
Crawford. "Ave Roma Immortalis" by Marion Crawford.
Cruikshank. "Roaring Century" by R. J. Cruickshank. Hamish Hamilton,
    1946.
Cunard. "Grand Man, Memories of Norman Douglas" by Nancy Cunard.
    Secker and Warburg, 1954.
de Langle. "Alexandrine Lucien Bonaparte, Princesse de Canino" by Fleuriot
    de Langle. 1939.
Douglas. "Alone" by Norman Douglas. 1921.
Edel. Selected Letters of Henry James, edited by Leon Edel. Rupert Hart-
    Davis, 1956.
Evelyn. "A Diary of the Crimea" by George Palmer Evelyn. Duckworth,
    1957. Ed. by C. Falls.
Gernsheim. "L. J. M. Daguerre, the history of the Diorama and the Daguer-
    rotype" by Helmut and Alison Gernsheim. Secker & Warburg, 1956.
Greville. The Greville Memoirs. 1814-60.
Guedalla. "The Second Empire" by Philip Guedalla. Hodder & Stoughton,
    1922.

Guest. "Fanny Cerito, the life of a romantic ballerina" by Ivor Guest. Phoenix House. 1956.

Hare. Italian Guide Books and "My Life With Mother" and "My Solitary Life" by Angustus Hare, edited by Malcolm Barnes. Allen & Unwin, 1952 and '53.

Horner. "Time Remembered" by Lady Frances Horner. Heinemann, 1933.

Howells. "Italian Journeys" by W. D. Howells. Heinemann, 1901.

Huntington. "Memories" by Henry G. Huntington. 1911.

Hutton. "Florence" by Edward Hutton. Methuen, 1907.

James. "William Wetmore Story and His Friends" by Henry James. Blackwood, 1903.

Laffont. "Dictionnaire des Oeuvres" Laffont-Bompiani, 1955.

Luhan. "European Experiences" by Mabel Dodge Luhan. Harcourt, Brace & Co., 1935.

Lutyens. "The Birth of Rowland". Letters between Robert Lytton and his wife, edited by Lady Emily Lutyens.

Mallock. "Memoirs of Life and Literature" by W. H. Mallock. Chapman and Hall, 1920.

Maurois. "Miss Howard" by Simone André-Maurois. Gallimard, 1956.

Maxwell. "God Protect Me From My Friends" by Gavin Maxwell. Longmans, Green & Company, 1956.

Morris. "Grandfather's London" by I. J. Morris.

Nevill. "Under Five Reigns" by Lady Dorothy Nevill. Methuen, 1910.

Nicolson. "Small Talk" and "Curzon" by Sir Harold Nicolson. Constable.

Norris. "Fashions and Costume in the XIXth Century" by Herbert Norris and Oswald Curtis. J. M. Dent and Sons, 1933.

Paget. "Embassies of Other Days" (1923), "The Linings of Life" (1928) and "In My Tower" (1934) by Walpurga, Lady Paget.

Papashvily. "All the Happy Endings" by Helen Waite Papashvily. Harper Brothers, 1956.

Pearl. "The Girl with the Swansdown Seat" by Cyril Pearl. Muller, 1955.

Pope-Hennessy. "Monckton Milnes" by James Pope-Hennessy. Constable, 1949–51.

Rodd. "Rome of the Renaissance and Today" by Sir Rennell Rodd. Macmillan, 1932.

Rudman. "Italian Nationalism & English Letters" by Harry W. Rudman. Columbia University Press.

St. Helier. "Memories of Fifty Years" by Lady St. Helier. E. Arnold, 1910.

Saunders. "A Distant Summer" by Edith Saunders. Sampson Low, 1946. "The Age of Worth" by Edith Saunders. Longmans, Green & Co., 1954.

Sermonetta. "Things Past" and "Sparkle Distant Worlds" by Vittoria Colonna, Duchess of Sermonetta.

Sforza. "Contemporary Italy" by Count Carlo Sforza. Muller, 1946.

Sitwell. Autobiography of Sir Osbert Sitwell, Macmillan.

Smiles. "Samuel Smiles and His Surroundings" by Aileen Smiles. Robert Hale, 1956.

Story. "Roba di Roma" by W. W. Story.

Strachey. "Queen Victoria" and "Eminent Victorians" by Lytton Strachey.

Street. "An Appreciation of Ouida" by G. S. Street. Yellow Book, Volume VI, July 1895.

Thompson. "The Victorian Heroine" by Patricia Thompson. Oxford, 1956.

Tinsley. "Random Recollections of an Old Publisher" by William Tinsley. Simpkin, Marshall & Co., 1900.

Treves. "The Golden Ring, the Anglo-Florentines 1847–52" by Giuliana Artom Treves. Longmans, Green and Company, 1956.

Valynseele. "Le Sang des Bonapartes" by Joseph Valynseele, 1954.

Varé. "Ghosts of the Spanish Steps" by Daniele Varé. Murray, 1905.

Verga. "Little Novels of Sicily" by Giovanni Verga. Oxford, 1935.

Waterfield. "Lucie Duff Gordon" by Gordon Waterfield. John Murray, 1937.

Whipple. "A Famous Corner of Tuscany" by Evangeline E. Whipple. Jarrolds, 1928.

Woodham-Smith. "Florence Nightingale" and "The Reason Why" by Cecil Woodham-Smith. Constable, 1950.

Yates. "Celebrities at Home" by E. H. Yates. 1877.

Young. "Victorian England" by G. M. Young. Oxford, 1953.

INDEX